Outlines of Scepticism, by the Greek philosopher Sextus Empiricus, is a work of major importance for the history of Greek philosophy. Its first part contains an elaborate exposition of the Pyrrhonian variety of Scepticism; its second and third parts are critical and destructive, arguing against 'dogmatism' in logic, epistemology, science and ethics. The *Outlines* is the fullest extant account of ancient Scepticism, and it is also one of our most copious sources of information about the other Hellenistic philosophies. Moreover, the redis-covery of Sextus in the sixteenth century brought about a revolution in philosophy. Julia Annas and Jonathan Barnes provide an accurate and readable English translation, with a short introduction and brief annotation.

Anyone interested in the history of philosophy will gain from an acquaint-ance with Sextus; and for students of Hellenistic philosophy his writings are indispensable.

Sextus Empiricus: Outlines of Scepticism

Sextus Empiricus
Outlines of Scepticism

—

TRANSLATED BY

JULIA ANNAS

Professor of Philosophy, University of Arizona, Tucson

and

JONATHAN BARNES

Professor of Ancient Philosophy in the University of Oxford

CAMBRIDGE
UNIVERSITY PRESS

Published by the Press Syndicate of the University of Cambridge
The Pitt Building, Trumpington Street, Cambridge CB2 IRP
40 West 20th Street, New York, NY 10011–4211, USA
10 Stamford Road, Oakleigh, Melbourne 3166, Australia

© Cambridge University Press 1994

First published 1994

Printed in Great Britain at the University Press, Cambridge

A catalogue record for this book is available from the British Library

Library of Congress cataloguing in publication data

Sextus, Empiricus.
[Pyrrōneioi hypotypōseis. English]
Outlines of scepticism / Sextus Empiricus: translated by Julia Annas
and Jonathan Barnes.
p.   cm.
Includes bibliographical references and index.
ISBN 0 521 30950 6 – ISBN 0 521 31206 X (pbk.)
1. Skepticism – Early works to 1800.
I. Annas, Julia.   II. Barnes, Jonathan.   III Title.
B621.P972E5   1994
186'.1–dc20   93–6177   CIP

ISBN 0 521 30950 6 hardback
ISBN 0 521 31206 X paperback

Contents

Contents

Introduction

I

Scepticism is one of the high points of Greek philosophy, and Sextus Empiricus is one of the most important ancient philosophers.

Two decades ago this sentiment would have seemed eccentric; but it would have met with little disagreement in the period after the rediscovery of Sextus' works and their first modern edition in 1562. It is only recently, after a time in which Plato and Aristotle have dominated the study of ancient philosophy, that we have returned to the former perspective, a perspective both wider and more just, in which Scepticism and the other philosophical movements which flourished after Aristotle have regained their salience. And Sextus is the key figure for ancient Scepticism. Before the rediscovery of his works, something was known about the ancient Sceptics through the works of Cicero. But only Sextus provides us with the lifeblood of Sceptical practice – argument against the Dogmatists: argument, argument, argument.

Scepticism begins in ancient philosophy with the strange figure of Pyrrho of Elis (c. 360–c. 270 BC). Like Socrates, he wrote nothing, but became the symbolic figurehead for a new way of doing philosophy. But whereas Socrates sparked interest in a number of directions and inspired widely different types of philosophy, Pyrrho remained a symbol of limited and specific concern. He founded no school; he seems to have lacked interest in institutionalizing his ideas, or indeed in traditional philosophical inquiry in general. His pupil, Timon, defended him in the only appropriate way – by attacking other philosophers, in a mixture of prose and verse; and he also produced a telegraphic summary of his master's message:

> Pyrrho's pupil, Timon, says that anyone who is going to lead a happy life must take account of the following three things: first, what objects are like by nature; secondly, what our attitude to them should be; finally, what will result for those who take this attitude. Now he says that Pyrrho shows that objects are equally indifferent and unfathomable and undeterminable because neither our senses nor our judgements are true or false; so for that reason we should not trust in them but should be without judgement and without inclination and unmoved, saying about each thing that it no more is than is not or both is and is not or neither is nor is not. And Timon says that for those who take this attitude the result will be first non-assertion, then tranquillity.[1]

Pyrrho simply favours some general strategies for showing that current positive beliefs about the world are baseless, and he suggests that once we realize that we have no grounds for the claims that we make, we will cease to be bothered in the way that the Dogmatic believers are. The idea that things are 'equally' indifferent, etc. seems to imply a version of what Sextus will later characterize as equipollence: we come to appreciate that there is as much to be said against any claim as in its favour. And 'non-assertion' looks very like the notion of *epochē* or suspension of judgement. But Pyrrho, consistently with his anti-academic stance, has no worked-out account of his own position – at least, none that we have any knowledge of.

Scepticism next appears in, of all places, Plato's Academy. Arcesilaus of Pitane (*c.* 315–240 BC), the head of the school, returned to the practice of argument which we find in Plato's early dialogues, and also in a later dialogue which the Sceptical Academy were to stress, the *Theaetetus*. In this dialogue Socrates compares himself to a barren midwife: he does not himself come out with ideas, he insists, but merely enables others to produce and articulate their own, and to subject them to destructive criticism. Just as Socrates is portrayed as criticizing various contemporaries, particularly the sophists, so the Sceptical Academy saw their task as that of taking on the sophists of

---

[1] Aristocles, in Eusebius, *Preparation for the Gospel* XIV xvii 2–4. The translation is taken from ANNAS and BARNES [1985]. We accept Zeller's emendation of διὰ τοῦτο to διὰ τό.

their own day – predominantly the Stoics, the prime examples of philosophers with Dogmatic beliefs and a firm commitment to them.

Not much has survived from the Sceptical Academy; a pupil of one of its stars, Carneades (214–129/128 BC), wrote down 400 books of his arguments, but of all this we have only a few paraphrastic reports. But we do know enough to be sure of two points. One is that Academic arguments were typically *ad hominem*: they argued against their opponents very precisely and specifically, trying to understand the theories so as to counteract their every claim. Secondly, whatever the force of their appeal to their own heritage, the Sceptical Academics went beyond Socratic practice in one respect: Arcesilaus held that appreciation of the equal force of arguments for and against would leave one in a state of suspension of judgement (*epochē*), a Pyrrhonian kind of result.

The third movement of ancient Scepticism arises in reaction to the second. In the final phase of the Sceptical Academy, one of its members, Aenesidemus (first century BC), broke away, considering the Academy to have settled down to a weak form of scepticism which had lost the original impulse to inquiry. This more radical wing, harking back to the symbolic figurehead of Pyrrho, made little contemporary impact, but some kind of Pyrrhonian tradition developed, of which we find Sextus as the last and most prolific representative. It is tempting to see in Sextus' Pyrrhonism a synthesis of aspects of the two previous sceptical movements. He retains Pyrrho's insistence on tranquillity as the final goal of the Sceptic; but he retains the Academics' relentless pursuit of particular Dogmatic philosophical ideas, their sense that the sceptical battle can only be fought by paying close attention to the opponents' theories. Nevertheless, Sextus identifies his own position as Pyrrhonian, while sharply distinguishing it from the Sceptical Academy.

Why would argument lead anyone to tranquillity? If Sceptics are enquirers, why do they even expect considerations for a claim to be equally balanced by considerations against it? Can we suspend judgement without covertly presupposing some substantial beliefs (for example, about the value of suspending judgement)? Sextus was writing at the end of centuries of discussion of these matters. There is no better introduction to these problems than the opening chapters of the *Outlines*, and no better elaboration of sceptical arguments than the rest of the work.

About Sextus himself we know very little. He probably lived in the second century AD, and seems to have been a doctor of the Empirical school. It is perhaps fitting that he survives, for us, merely as a name attached to a sceptical position and a host of arguments. The *Outlines of Scepticism*, in three books, is, as Sextus keeps reminding us, a brief introductory account of Pyrrhonian Scepticism. Sextus produced other writings, and in particular he often refers to a longer treatment of Scepticism. Only two other works of his survive. One, which we call *Against the Mathematicians* VII–XI, corresponds to books II and III of the *Outlines*. However, it expands the arguments, sometimes following different strategies and tactics, and it includes long expository accounts of the positive views to be demolished. The other, which we call *Against the Mathematicians* I–VI, is a collection of short demolitions of bodies of academic knowledge, such as grammar, rhetoric and music.

Sceptics do not start from a position of their own – they do not have a set of beliefs, nor even a view as to how philosophy ought to be done. Rather, they follow the going practice of philosophy, and work from within to undermine it. So, when we read Sextus, we must be careful not to drift into assuming that, although he argues against specific beliefs of other philosophers, Sextus himself endorses the ancient assumptions that frame them – for example, that philosophy has three divisions, into logic, physics and ethics, or that any philosophy has its own final end, standard and method. Sextus takes over these assumptions because they are held by the philosophers against whom he will argue – the Dogmatists, the philosophers with positive beliefs. But in the end, as he reminds us, Scepticism purges itself along with what it opposes, like a drug that flushes itself out along with the harmful substances it counteracts. A Sceptical argument against a Dogmatic claim is not meant to convince us that the Dogmatic claim, about time, or value, for example, is wrong, and that the Sceptical argument establishes the truth of the counter-claim. Rather, we are meant to feel the force of *both* claims, and to end up in suspension of judgement because we are unable to come down on one side rather than the other. For the Sceptic, a claim that one argument is decisively better than the counter-argument is a sign that we have stopped too soon, and failed to investigate the counter-argument as vigorously as we might have done. The same goes for the assumptions and framework on which the arguments rest. We take over assumptions about the way in which philosophy is done – because we have to, if we want to engage with the subject. But at the same time we feel the force of considerations that can be pressed against them. The Sceptic is detached from his canons of argument as well as from the truth of his premises. That is why we can say, as Sextus memorably does at the end of the book, that his use of arguments is pragmatic; like a doctor with his medicines, he uses only what is needed, and is careful not to over-prescribe.

It is possible to read Sextus as a source for ancient Dogmatic philosophy, and as such he is very informative. But it is more interesting to observe his strategy and its radical nature, as he takes over the positive philosophers' framework with the intention, ultimately, of leading the reader to suspension of judgement not just about time, or matter, or value, but about argument itself and what it establishes. Modern forms of scepticism have typically been very limited, dealing merely with claims to knowledge, for example, or assuming that one type of philosophical claim is secure and criticizing others for failing to be like it. The radical nature of ancient Scepticism is beginning to be appreciated once more: we hope that this translation will help to further familiarity with Sextus' methods, and the conception of scepticism which they support.

II

The translation has been done with the interests of philosophical readers in mind. Our primary aim has always been to present as clearly and faithfully as possible the philosophical themes and arguments which Sextus expounds and discusses. Literary merit has been, at best, a secondary goal.

Sextus' Greek is usually simple and usually clear. He is restrained in vocabulary and style, rarely striving for rhetorical effect. (He does, however, have the occasional extended passage where the presentation of the material is spiced with irony or sarcasm.) His sentences are sometimes long, but their syntax and structure are remarkably lucid, a model of philosophical Greek. These features ease the translator's task.

Technical terms offer, of course, their usual intractable difficulties. We initially attempted a strict correspondence: each technical or semi-technical Greek word would be matched by a single English word. Subsequent revisions softened this puritanism in the interest of intelligibility; where this softening has occurred, it can be discerned in the Glossaries.

A further point should be made. Sextus himself divides the *Outlines* into three books; and most scholars believe that the chapter-divisions and their headings are also Sextus' own work. But further subdivisions are modern: the division of the books into numbered sections goes back only to Fabricius' edition of the text; and although we have incorporated his numerals into our translation (since references to Sextus are usually, and conveniently, made by book- and section-number) we have not felt constrained to divide the translation according to these sections. Readers should be aware that the para-graphing in our text is our own, and that it sometimes insinuates an interpretation of Sextus' train of thought which other scholars might wish to contest.

III

The translation is not equipped with a commentary, but there are two series of annotations, as well as an Index of names.

The Index offers a brief sentence of information on each of the people whom Sextus cites or mentions, and also on the major sources cited in the Notes.

The alphabetical series of notes is textual. It records, baldly and without explanation, each place at which we have chosen to depart from the standard Greek text of the *Outlines*, namely MUTSCHMANN–MAU [1958]. Many of the departures are trivial and make no discernible difference to the sense. Some, however, are substantial – and here the notes include a translation of the standard text.

The numerical series of notes serves four functions. (1) Occasionally we have made an exegetical remark or two. (2) There are references to the modern secondary literature.[2] These references do not constitute a bibliography of modern writings on Sextus; and – since our readers, we suppose, will be anglophone – they are largely limited to works in English. (3) We have provided a scattering of references to ancient texts other than Sextus, which parallel or illustrate or substantiate claims made in the *Outlines*. It need not be said that these references are less than comprehensive; but it should be confessed that they are also less than systematic. (4) Finally, there are many – perhaps too many – cross-references to passages in Sextus himself. We have tried to give all the main parallels to the *Outlines* which are to be found in Sextus' other works, and we have also added references to and fro in the *Outlines* itself, references which we hope may help readers new to Sextus to find their way about in his text.

---

[2] Author's name in small capitals, date in square brackets, chapter- or page-number where apposite: e.g., just above, 'MUTSCHMANN–MAU [1958]'. Full details in the Bibliography.

Abbreviations

When an ancient text is cited more than once, its title is given in an abbreviated form. The abbreviations shorten the standard Latin titles: the full versions in the following list are usually English.

ALEXANDER
an mant	*de anima mantissa*
fat	*On Fate*
in APr	*Commentary on Aristotle's Prior Analytics*
in Top	*Commentary on Aristotle's Topics*

AMMONIUS
in Int	*Commentary on Aristotle's de Interpretatione*

ANONYMUS
in Theaet	*Commentary on Plato's Theaetetus*

APULEIUS
dog Plat	*On the Doctrines of Plato*
int	*de interpretatione*

ARISTOTLE
EN	*Nicomachean Ethics*
Phys	*Physics*
Top	*Topics*

CICERO
fat	*On Fate*
fin	*de finibus*

Luc	*Lucullus*
nat deorum	*de natura deorum*

CLEMENT
| *strom* | *stromateis* |

EPICURUS
ad Hdt	*Letter to Herodotus*
ad Men	*Letter to Menoeceus*
KΔ	*Principal Doctrines*

EUSEBIUS
| *PE* | *Preparation for the Gospel* |

GALEN
an pecc dig	*Diagnosis and Cure of the Errors of the Soul*
inst log	*Introduction to Logic*
PHP	*On the Doctrines of Hippocrates and Plato*

[GALEN]
def med	*Medical Definitions*
hist phil	*History of Philosophy*
opt sect	*On the Best Sect*

ORIGEN
| *c Cels* | *Against Celsus* |

PHILO
| *ebr* | *On the Drunkenness of Noah* |

PHOTIUS
| *bibl* | *bibliotheca* |

PLATO
Parm	*Parmenides*
Theaet	*Theaetetus*
Tim	*Timaeus*

PLUTARCH
adv Col	*Against Colotes*
comm not	*Common Notions*
Stoic rep	*On Stoic Self-Contradictions*

PORPHYRY
  abstin   *On Abstinence*

SENECA
  ep   *Letters*

SEXTUS
  M   *Against the Mathematicians*
  PH   *Outlines of Scepticism*

SIMPLICIUS
  in Cat   *Commentary on Aristotle's Categories*

STOBAEUS
  ecl   *eclogae*

Outlines of Scepticism

BOOK I

These are the Contents of the First Book of the *Outlines of Scepticism*:

i The most fundamental difference among philosophies

[1] When people are investigating any subject, the likely result is either a discovery, or a denial of discovery and a confession of inapprehensibility, or else a continuation of the investigation. [2] This, no doubt, is why in the case of philosophical investigations, too, some have said that they have discovered the truth, some have asserted that it cannot be apprehended, and others are still investigating.

[3] Those who are called Dogmatists in the proper sense of the word think that they have discovered the truth – for example, the schools of Aristotle and Epicurus and the Stoics, and some others. The schools of Clitomachus and Carneades, and other Academics, have asserted that things cannot be apprehended.[1] And the Sceptics are still investigating. [4] Hence the most fundamental kinds of philosophy are reasonably thought to be three: the Dogmatic, the Academic, and the Sceptical. The former two it will be appropriate for others to describe: in the present work we shall discuss in outline[2] the Sceptical persuasion. By way of preface let us say that on none of the matters to be discussed do we affirm that things certainly are just as we say they are: rather, we report[3] descriptively on each item according to how it appears to us at the time.[4]

ii The accounts constitutive of Scepticism

[5] The Sceptical philosophy contains both a general and a specific account.[5] In the general account we set out the distinctive character of Scepticism, saying what the concept of it is, what are its principles and

---

[1] The same is said of the Cyrenaics at I 215. For the New Academy see I 220–31; and note that other sources expressly say that the Academics did *not* 'assert that things cannot be apprehended'.

[2] ὑποτυπωτικῶς: the work is an outline or ὑποτύπωσις, and Sextus frequently reminds us of the fact: I 206, 222, 239; II 1, 79, 185, 194; III 1, 114, 167, 279. Note also his assurances that he is only offering 'few out of many' examples (I 58, note) and that he is concerned to be brief (I 163, note); and see I 94; II 84, 212; III 56, 71, 135, 168.

[3] For this use of the term 'report' see I 15, 197, 203.

[4] Cf. e.g. I 191; II 187.

[5] Cf. *M* VII 1.

what its arguments, what is its standard and what its aim, what are the modes of suspension of judgement, how we understand sceptical assertions, and what distinguishes Scepticism from neighbouring philosophies.[6] [6] The specific account is the one in which we argue against each of the parts of what they call philosophy.

Let us first deal with the general account, beginning our sketch with the names given to the Sceptical persuasion.

iii The nomenclature of Scepticism

[7][7] The Sceptical persuasion, then, is also called Investigative, from its activity in investigating and inquiring;[8] Suspensive, from the feeling that comes about in the inquirer after the investigation; Aporetic, either (as some say) from the fact that it puzzles over[9] and investigates everything, or else from its being at a loss whether to assent or deny; and Pyrrhonian, from the fact that Pyrrho appears to us to have attached himself to Scepticism more systematically and conspicuously than anyone before him.[10]

iv What is Scepticism?

[8] Scepticism is an ability to set out oppositions among things which appear and are thought of in any way at all,[11] an ability by which, because of the equipollence in the opposed objects and accounts, we come first to suspension of judgement and afterwards to tranquillity.

[9] We call it an ability not in any fancy sense, but simply in the sense of 'to be able to'. Things which appear we take in the present context to be objects of perception, which is why we contrast them with objects of thought. 'In any way at all' can be taken either with 'an ability' (to show that we are to understand the word 'ability' in its straightforward sense, as we said), or else with 'to set out oppositions

---

6 The programme (with which compare the resumé at I 209) corresponds well to the contents of *PH* I – except that I 13–20 do not appear to be covered.
7 With I 7 cf. Diogenes Laertius IX 69–70.
8 The verb translated 'inquire' is σκέπτεσθαι, cognate with σκεπτικός ('sceptical').
9 'Puzzle over' renders ἀπορεῖν, from which 'aporetic' derives.
10 On this explanation of the name 'Pyrrhonism' see BARNES [1992], pp. 4284–6.
11 See Diogenes Laertius IX 78 (reporting Aenesidemus).

among the things which appear and are thought of': we say 'in any
way at all' because we set up oppositions in a variety of ways –
opposing what appears to what appears, what is thought of to what is
thought of, and crosswise, so as to include all the oppositions.[12] Or
else we take the phrase with[a] 'the things which appear and are thought
of', to show that we are not to investigate how what appears appears
or how what is thought of is thought of, but are simply to take them
for granted.[13]

[10] By 'opposed accounts' we do not necessarily have in mind
affirmation and negation, but take the phrase simply in the sense of
'conflicting accounts'.[14] By 'equipollence' we mean equality with
regard to being convincing or unconvincing: none of the conflicting
accounts takes precedence over any other as being more convincing.[15]
Suspension of judgement is a standstill of the intellect, owing to
which we neither reject nor posit anything.[16] Tranquillity[17] is
freedom from disturbance or calmness of soul. We shall suggest in the
chapter on the aim of scepticism how tranquillity accompanies
suspension of judgement.[18]

v The Sceptic

[11] The Pyrrhonian philosopher has been implicitly defined in our
account of the concept of the Sceptical persuasion: a Pyrrhonian is
someone who possesses this ability.

vi The principles of Scepticism

[12] The causal principle of scepticism we say is the hope of becoming
tranquil.[19] Men of talent, troubled by the anomaly in things and

---

[a] Reading ἢ τῷ in place of ἢ καθ᾽ οἱονδήποτε τρόπον, as Mau suggests. The
sense is not in doubt, and Mau's emendation makes it clear.

[12] See I 31–2; M VIII 46.
[13] Cf. I 19.
[14] Cf. I, 190, 198, 202.
[15] See I 190; cf. 196, 198, 202.
[16] See I 196 (and cf. I 192, on non-assertion); and note esp. COUISSIN [1929].
[17] ἀταραξία: 'untroubledness' – the word is formed from an alpha privative and
ταράττειν, 'to trouble'.
[18] I 25–32 (cf. 232).
[19] Cf. I 26; see STRIKER [1990a]; ANNAS [1993a], ch. 8.

puzzled as to which of them they should rather assent to, came to investigate what in things is true and what false, thinking that by deciding these issues they would become tranquil.

The chief constitutive principle of scepticism is the claim that to every account an equal account is opposed;[20] for it is from this, we think, that we come to hold no beliefs.

vii Do Sceptics hold beliefs?[21]

[13] When we say that Sceptics do not hold beliefs, we do not take 'belief' in the sense in which some say, quite generally, that belief is acquiescing in something; for Sceptics assent to the feelings forced upon them by appearances[22] – for example, they would not say, when heated or chilled, 'I think I am not heated (or: chilled)'. Rather, we say that they do not hold beliefs in the sense in which some say that belief is assent to some unclear object of investigation in the sciences;[23] for Pyrrhonists do not assent to anything unclear.

[14] Not even in uttering the Sceptical phrases about unclear matters – for example, 'In no way more', or 'I determine nothing', or one of the other phrases which we shall later discuss[24] – do they hold beliefs. For if you hold beliefs, then you posit as real the things you are said to hold beliefs about; but Sceptics posit these phrases not as necessarily being real. For they suppose that, just as the phrase 'Everything is false' says that it too, along with everything else, is false (and similarly for 'Nothing is true'), so also 'In no way more' says that it too, along with everything else, is no more so than not so, and hence it cancels itself along with everything else. And we say the same of the other Sceptical phrases. [15] Thus, if people who hold beliefs posit as real the things they hold beliefs about, while Sceptics utter their own phrases in such a way that they are implicitly cancelled by

---

20 See I 202–5 (cf. I 18).
21 The Dogmatists alleged that the Sceptics did in fact hold beliefs: see e.g. Aristocles, apud Eusebius, PE xiv xviii 9–12; Diogenes Laertius IX 102–4 (cf. IX 68). – On the controversy surrounding the issues raised by this chapter see FREDE [1979]; BURNYEAT [1980a], [1984]; BARNES [1988], [1990a], pp. 2617–49.
22 Cf. I 29, 193, 229–30; II 10.
23 Cf. I 16, 193, 197.
24 See I 187–208.

themselves, then they cannot be said to hold beliefs in uttering them.[25]

But the main point is this: in uttering these phrases they say what is apparent to themselves and report their own feelings without holding opinions, affirming nothing about external objects.[26]

viii Do Sceptics belong to a school?[27]

[16] We take the same attitude to the question: Do Sceptics belong to a school? If you say that a school involves adherence to a number of beliefs which cohere both with one another and with what is apparent,[28] and if you say that belief is assent to something unclear, then we shall say that Sceptics do not belong to any school. [17] But if you count as a school a persuasion which, to all appearances, coheres with some account, the account showing how it is possible to live[b] correctly (where 'correctly' is taken not only with reference to virtue, but more loosely, and extends to the ability to suspend judgement[c]) – in that case we say that Sceptics do belong to a school. For we coherently follow, to all appearances, an account which shows us a life in conformity with traditional customs and the law and persuasions and our own feelings.

ix Do Sceptics study natural science?

[18] We say something similar again when investigating the question of whether Sceptics should study natural science. We do not study

---

b   Deleting δοκεῖν, as Mutschmann suggested.
c   We close the parenthesis after διατείνοντος rather than after ἀφελέστερον: the clause καὶ ... διατείνοντος is part of the gloss on ὀρθῶς and not explanatory of τοῦ λόγου.

25 Cf. 1 206.
26 Cf. 1 208.
27 Some denied that Pyrrhonism constituted a school of philosophy: see Diogenes Laertius I 20; cf. Aristocles, apud Eusebius, PE XIV xviii 30; Clement, strom VIII iv 16.2. On the concept of a school see GLUCKER [1978].
28 'Cohere with' etc., here and in the section, translate ἀκολουθεῖν and its cognate noun. The verb literally means 'follow', and so we normally translate it (we also use 'follow' for the compounds κατακολουθεῖν and παρακολουθεῖν and for ἔπεσθαι); but, for the noun, 'implication' and 'validity' have sometimes been preferred, and the adjective ἀκόλουθος comes out as 'apposite'.

natural science in order to make assertions with firm conviction about any of the matters on which scientific beliefs are held. But we do touch on natural science in order to be able to oppose to every account an equal account,[29] and for the sake of tranquillity.[30]. This is also the spirit in which we approach the logical and ethical parts of what they call philosophy.[31]

x Do Sceptics reject what is apparent?[32]

[19] Those who say that the Sceptics reject what is apparent have not, I think, listened to what we say.[33] As we said before,[34] we do not overturn anything which leads us, without our willing it, to assent in accordance with a passive appearance – and these things are precisely what is apparent. When we investigate whether existing things are such as they appear, we grant that they appear, and what we investigate is not what is apparent but what is said about what is apparent – and this is different from investigating what is apparent itself. [20] For example,[d] it appears to us that honey sweetens (we concede this inasmuch as we are sweetened in a perceptual way); but whether (as far as the argument goes[35]) it is actually sweet is something we investigate – and this is not what is apparent but something said about what is apparent.[36]

And if we do propound arguments directly against what is apparent, it is not because we want to reject what is apparent that we set them out, but rather to display the rashness of the Dogmatists; for if reasoning is such a deceiver that it all but snatches even what is apparent from under our very eyes, surely we should keep watch on it in unclear matters, to avoid being led into rashness by following it?

---

d   Retaining the MSS text: Mutschmann–Mau follow Heintz in adding ⟨ὅτι μέν⟩.

29 See I 12.
30 See I 10, 25–30.
31 For the three parts of philosophy see II 12–13.
32 See Diogenes Laertius IX 103–4.
33 For other complaints of misrepresentation see I 200, 208.
34 See I 13, 17
35 The same Greek phrase occurs frequently elsewhere, and its meaning is usually plain; but here its import is obscure and different scholars have construed it in different ways: see BRUNSCHWIG [1990].
36 Cf. II 72 (and on honey see I 101).

xi The standard of Scepticism[37]

[21][38] That we attend to what is apparent is clear from what we say about the standard of the Sceptical persuasion. 'Standard' has two senses: there are standards adopted to provide conviction about the reality or unreality of something (we shall talk about these standards when we turn to attack them[39]); and there are standards of action, attending to which in everyday life we perform some actions and not others – and it is these standards which are our present subject.

[22] We say, then, that the standard of the Sceptical persuasion is what is apparent,[40] implicitly meaning by this the appearances; for they depend on passive and unwilled feelings and are not objects of investigation. (Hence no-one, presumably, will raise a controversy over whether an existing thing appears this way or that; rather, they investigate whether it is such as it appears.)

[23][41] Thus, attending to what is apparent, we live in accordance with everyday observances, without holding opinions – for we are not able to be utterly inactive.[42] These everyday observances seem to be fourfold, and to consist in guidance by nature, necessitation by feelings, handing down of laws and customs, and teaching of kinds of expertise. [24] By nature's guidance we are naturally capable of perceiving and thinking.[43] By the necessitation of feelings, hunger conducts us to food and thirst to drink. By the handing down of customs and laws, we accept, from an everyday point of view, that piety is good and impiety bad.[44] By teaching of kinds of expertise we are not inactive in those which we accept.[45]

And we say all this without holding any opinions.

---

37 On the notion of a standard or κριτήριον see STRIKER [1974], [1990b]; HUBY and NEAL [1989].
38 Cf. *M* VII 29–31.
39 See II 14–17.
40 See Diogenes Laertius IX 106, reporting the view of Aenesidemus.
41 With I 23–4 compare I 237–9 (cf. I 226, 231; II 102, 246, 254; III 2, 119, 151, 235); see e.g. BARNES [1990a], pp. 2641–9; ANNAS [1993a], ch. 8.
42 On the question, Can the Sceptic Live? see *M* XI 162–166; Diogenes Laertius IX 104–105; Aristocles, apud Eusebius, *PE* XIV xviii 25–6; see e.g. BURNYEAT [1980a]; BARNES [1988a], [1990b].
43 See e.g. *M* VIII 203.
44 Cf. III 2; *M* IX 49.
45 For types of expertise allegedly acceptable to Sceptics see *M* I 99; V 1–3.

xii What is the aim of Scepticism?

[25][46] It will be apposite to consider next the aim of the Sceptical persuasion. Now an aim is that for the sake of which everything is done or considered, while it is not itself done or considered for the sake of anything else.[47] Or: an aim is the final object of desire.[48] Up to now we say the aim of the Sceptic is tranquillity in matters of opinion and moderation of feeling in matters forced upon us. [26] For Sceptics began to do philosophy in order to decide among appearances and to apprehend which are true and which false, so as to become tranquil;[49] but they came upon equipollent dispute, and being unable to decide this they suspended judgement. And when they suspended judgement, tranquillity in matters of opinion followed fortuitously.

[27][50] For those who hold the opinion that things are good or bad by nature are perpetually troubled. When they lack what they believe to be good, they take themselves to be persecuted by natural evils and they pursue what (so they think) is good. And when they have acquired these things, they experience more troubles; for they are elated beyond reason and measure, and in fear of change they do anything so as not to lose what they believe to be good. [28] But those who make no determination about what is good and bad by nature neither avoid nor pursue anything with intensity; and hence they are tranquil.

A story told of the painter Apelles applies to the Sceptics.[51] They say that he was painting a horse and wanted to represent in his picture the lather on the horse's mouth; but he was so unsuccessful that he gave up, took the sponge on which he had been wiping off the colours from his brush, and flung it at the picture. And when it hit the

---

46 With I 25–30 cf. III 235–8, M XI 110–67; Timon, frag. 841 Lloyd-Jones and Parsons (see BURNYEAT [1980b]); Diogenes Laertius IX 107–8. See esp. STRIKER [1990a]; ANNAS [1993a], chh. 1, 17.

47 A standard definition: e.g. Cicero, *fin* I xii 42 (Epicureans); Arius ap. Stobaeus, *ecl* II 77.16–17 (Stoics), 131.2–4 (Peripatetics).

48 Again, a standard definition; see e.g. Arius ap. Stobaeus, *ecl* II 76.21–4 (Stoics), 131.4 (Peripatetics); Alexander, *an mant* 150.20–1, 162.34.

49 See I 12.

50 Cf. III 237–8; M XI 112–18, 145–6 (and below, I 215).

51 On this paragraph see ANNAS and BARNES [1985], pp. 167–171.

picture, it produced a representation of the horse's lather. [29] Now the Sceptics were hoping to acquire tranquillity by deciding the anomalies in what appears and is thought of, and being unable to do this they suspended judgement. But when they suspended judgement, tranquillity followed as it were fortuitously, as a shadow follows a body.[52]

We do not, however, take Sceptics to be undisturbed in every way[53] – we say that they are disturbed by things which are forced upon them; for we agree that at times they shiver and are thirsty and have other feelings of this kind.[54] [30] But in these cases ordinary people are afflicted by two sets of circumstances: by the feelings themselves, and no less by believing that these circumstances are bad by nature. Sceptics, who shed the additional opinion that each of these things is bad in its nature, come off more moderately even in these cases.

This, then, is why we say that the aim of Sceptics is tranquillity in matters of opinion and moderation of feeling in matters forced upon us. (Some eminent Sceptics have added as a further aim suspension of judgement in investigations.[55])

xiii The general modes of suspension of judgement

[31] Since we have been saying that tranquillity follows suspension of judgement about everything, it will be apposite here to say how suspension of judgement comes about for us.

It comes about – to put it rather generally – through the opposition of things. We oppose what appears to what appears, or what is thought of to what is thought of, or crosswise.[56] [32] For example, we oppose what appears to what appears when we say: 'The same tower appears round from a distance and square from nearby'.[57] We oppose

---

52 See Diogenes Laertius IX 107 (referring the image to Timon and Aenesidemus); below, I 205.
53 Cf III 235–6; *M* XI 141–60.
54 See I 13.
55 So Timon and Aenesidemus, according to Diogenes Laertius IX 107.
56 See I 8–9.
57 A standard example: e.g. I 118; II 55; *M* VII 208, 414; Lucretius IV 353–63; see ANNAS and BARNES [1985], pp. 104–6.

what is thought of to what is thought of when, against those who seek to establish that there is Providence from the orderliness of the heavenly bodies, we oppose the view that often the good do badly while the bad do well and conclude from this that there is no Providence.[58] [33] We oppose what is thought of to what appears, as Anaxagoras did when to the view that snow is white,[c] he opposed the thought that snow is frozen water and water is black and snow is therefore black.[59]

In another sense we sometimes oppose present things to present things (as in the above examples) and sometimes present to past or future things. For example, when someone propounds to us an argument we cannot refute, [34] we say to him: 'Before the founder of the school to which you adhere was born, the argument of the school, which is no doubt sound, was not yet apparent, although it was really there in nature. In the same way, it is possible that the argument opposing the one you have just propounded is really there in nature but is not yet apparent to us; so we should not yet assent to what is now thought to be a powerful argument'.[60]

xiv The Ten Modes[61]

[35] So that we may get a more accurate impression of these oppositions, I shall set down the modes through which we conclude to suspension of judgement. But I make no affirmation either about their number or about their power – they may be unsound, and there may be more than those I shall describe.

[36] The older sceptics[62] normally offer ten modes in number through which we are thought to conclude to suspension of judge-

---

[c] Like Mau, we reject Mutschmann's insertion of κατασκευάζοντι.

[58] Cf. I 151.
[59] Cf. II 244.
[60] With this compare the occasional appeal to merely possible examples: I 89, 96, 143; II 40; III 233–4.
[61] On this chapter see ANNAS and BARNES [1985]; and for the comparison between Sextus and Diogenes Laertius see BARNES [1992], pp. 4273–9 (with bibliography).
[62] They contrast with the more recent sceptics of I 164; at M VII 345 Sextus refers to Aenesidemus as author of the Ten Modes (but it is not clear how closely he is following Aenesidemus here in PH).

ment. (They use 'arguments' and 'schemata' as synonyms for 'modes'.) They are:[63] first, the mode depending on the variations among animals; second, that depending on the differences among humans; third, that depending on the differing constitutions of the sense-organs; fourth, that depending on circumstances; fifth, that depending on positions and intervals and places; sixth, that depending on admixtures; [37] seventh, that depending on the quantities and preparations of existing things; eighth, that deriving from relativity; ninth, that depending on frequent or rare encounters; tenth, that depending on persuasions and customs and laws and belief in myths and dogmatic suppositions. [38] (We use this order for the sake of argument.[64])

Superordinate to these are three modes: that deriving from the subject judging; that deriving from the object judged; that combined from both. For under the mode deriving from the subject judging are ranged the first four, since what judges is either an animal or a human or a sense, and[f] is in some circumstance. The seventh and tenth are referred to the mode deriving from the object judged. The fifth, sixth, eighth and ninth are referred to the mode combined from both. [39] These three are in turn referred to the relativity mode. So we have as most generic relativity, as specific the three, as subordinate the ten.[65]

So much by way of a plausible account of their number: now for their power.

[40][66] First, we said, is the argument according to which animals, depending on the differences among them, do not receive the same appearances from the same things. This we deduce both from the differences in the ways in which they are produced and from the variation in the composition of their bodies.[67]

[41] In the case of the ways in which they are produced, this is because some animals are produced without copulation and some as a

f   Reading καί with the MSS: Mutschmann–Mau emend to ἤ ('or').

63 Cf. Diogenes Laertius XI 78–9; Philo, *ebr* 169–70; Aristocles, *apud* Eusebius, PE, XIV xviii 11–12.
64 For alternative orderings of the modes see Diogenes Laertius IX 87: cf. ANNAS and BARNES [1985], pp. 26–30; BARNES [1992], pp. 4278–9.
65 Compare the taxonomy at I 136; cf. ANNAS and BARNES [1985], pp. 141–2.
66 With I 40–79 cf. Diogenes Laertius IX 79–80; Philo, *ebr* 171–5; see ANNAS and BARNES [1985], pp. 39–53.
67 On the structure of this argument see BARNES [1992], pp. 4276–7.

result of intercourse. Of those produced without copulation, some are produced from fire, like the little creatures which appear in ovens, some from stagnant water, like mosquitoes, some from wine turning sour, like gnats, some from earth, ⟨like . . .⟩,[68] some from slime, like frogs, some from mud, like maggots, some from donkeys,[g] like dung-beetles, some from fruit, like the gall-insects which come from wild figs, some from rotting animals, like bees which come from bulls and wasps which come from horses. [42] Of animals produced as a result of intercourse, some are bred from the same species, like the majority, some from different species, like mules. Again, in general, some animals are produced viviparously, like humans, some oviparously, like birds, and some carniparously, like bears.[69]

[43] It is likely, then, that the dissimilarities in the ways in which they are produced should lead to large differences in the ways in which they are affected, thence giving rise to imbalance, disharmony and conflict.

[44] But it is the differences among the most important parts of the body, especially those which are naturally fitted for deciding and perceiving, which can produce the greatest conflict of appearances. For instance, people with jaundice say that what appears white to us is yellow, and people with a blood-suffusion in the eye say that such things are blood-red.[70] Since, then, the eyes of some animals are yellow, of others blood-shot or white or some other colour, it is likely, I think, that their grasp of colours is different.

[45] Further, when we have stared for a long time at the sun and then bend over a book, we think that the letters are golden and moving around. Since, then, some animals have a natural brilliance in their eyes and give off a fine mobile light from them so that they can see even at night, we shall rightly deem that the external objects do not give us and them similar impressions.

[46] Further, magicians, by smearing lamp-wicks with bronze-rust

---

[g] Perhaps read ἐξ ὄνων ⟨κοπροῦ⟩ ('from the dung of donkeys'): see ANNAS and BARNES [1985], p. 184.

[68] A word has apparently dropped out of the text: earthworms, grasshoppers and mice have been suggested.

[69] A semi-jocular allusion to the vulgar belief that bears are born as lumps of flesh.

[70] Cf. I 101, 126; II 51. The remark about jaundice is repeated in modern texts; but it is apparently quite false.

or cuttlefish-ink, make the by-standers appear bronze-coloured or black, all through a slight sprinkling of the mixture. It is surely far more reasonable, given that animals' eyes contain mixtures of different humours,[71] that they should also get different appearances from existing objects.

[47] When we press one of our eyes from the side, the forms and shapes and sizes of the objects we see appear elongated and narrow. It is likely, then, that those animals (such as goats, cats and the like) which have slanting and elongated pupils, should view existing objects differently and not in the same way as animals with round pupils suppose them to be.

[48] Mirrors, depending on their differing constructions, sometimes show external objects as minute (e.g. concave mirrors), sometimes as elongated and narrow (convex mirrors); and some of them show the head of the person reflected at the bottom and their feet at the top. [49] Since, then, some of the vessels of sight protrude and project beyond the body because of their convexity, while others are more concave and others are set level, it is likely that the appearances are altered by this too, and that dogs, fish, lions, humans and locusts do not see the same things as equal in size or similar in shape; rather, what they see depends upon the kind of imprinting produced in each case by the eye which receives what is apparent.

[50] The same account holds for the other senses too. How could it be said that touch produces similar effects in animals with shells, animals with fleshy exteriors, animals with prickles, and animals with feathers or scales? How can there be a similar grasp of sound in animals with a very narrow auditory channel and those with a very broad one? or in animals with hairy ears and those with ears which are bare? After all, we too hear things differently when we stop up our ears and when we use them in the ordinary way.

[51] Smell too will differ depending on the variation among animals. For we too are affected in one way when we are chilled and

[71] Sextus alludes to the theory of the four 'humours' or juices – blood, phlegm, bile and black bile – which, according to normal medical theory, constitute the most important stuffs in the body and determine the physical and psychological state of its owner (see esp. Galen, *On Temperaments*). See also I 51, 52, 71, 80, 102, 128.

there is an excess of phlegm in us,[72] and in another way when the region of the head collects an excess of blood, rejecting what others think fragrant and deeming ourselves as it were battered by it. So, since some animals are naturally flabby and full of phlegm while others are extremely rich in blood and in others yellow or black bile is dominant, it is reasonable on this account that what they smell should appear different to each of them.

[52] Similarly with objects of taste, since the tongues of some animals are rough and dry while those of others are very moist. For we too, when in fevers our tongue is drier than usual, deem that what we are offered is earthy and unpalatable, or bitter – and we are also affected in one way or another depending on the different dominance in us of the so-called humours.[73] Since, then, animals have organs of taste which differ and in which different humours are excessive, they will receive different appearances of existing objects with regard to taste too.

[53] Just as the same nourishment when dispersed becomes in one place veins, in another arteries, in another bone, in another sinew, and so on, displaying different powers depending on the differences among the parts receiving it; and just as the same undifferentiated water when dispersed in trees becomes in one place bark, in another a branch, in another fruit – and hence figs and pomegranates and so on; [54] and just as the same pressure of the hand on a lyre produces in one place a low sound and in another a high one:[74] in the same way it is reasonable that external existing objects should be observed as different depending on the different constitutions of the animals receiving the appearances.

[55] One can learn this with greater evidence from the things which animals choose and avoid. For instance, perfume appears very pleasant to humans but intolerable to dung-beetles and bees. Olive oil benefits humans but when sprayed over wasps and bees it destroys them. Sea-water is unpleasant to humans when they drink it, and poisonous, but it is very pleasant and drinkable to fish. [56] Pigs find it more pleasant to wash in the most foul-smelling mud than in clear,

---

[72] A reference to the four humours: see I 46.
[73] See I 46.
[74] Cf. I 95.

pure water. Among animals, some feed on grass, some on shrubs, some in forests,[h] some on seeds, some on flesh, some on milk. Some enjoy their food rotten and others fresh, some enjoy it raw and others prepared by cooking. And in general, what is pleasant to some is to others unpleasant and to be avoided – or even[i] fatal. [57] For instance, hemlock fattens quails and henbane fattens pigs – which indeed enjoy eating salamanders, just as deer enjoy eating venomous animals and swallows enjoy eating blister-beetles. Ants and mosquitoes, if swallowed by humans, cause displeasure and griping; but if she-bears feel weak in some way they lick them up and so recover their strength. [58] Vipers are numbed by the mere touch of an oak-branch, just as bats are by the touch of a plane-leaf. Elephants avoid rams, lions avoid cocks, sea-beasts avoid the crackling of beans as they are pounded, tigers avoid the noise of drums.

More cases than these can be given;[75] but let us not be thought to waste time unnecessarily – if the same things are unpleasant to some animals and pleasant to others, and if the pleasant and unpleasant lie in appearances,[76] then appearances produced in animals from existing objects are different.

[59][77] But if the same objects appear dissimilar depending on the variation among animals, then we shall be able to say what the existing objects are like as observed by us, but as to what they are like in their nature we shall suspend judgement. For we shall not be able ourselves to decide between our own appearances and those of other animals, being ourselves a part of the dispute and for that reason more in need of someone to decide than ourselves able to judge.[78]

[60] And besides, we shall not be able to prefer our own appearances to those produced in the irrational animals either without giving a proof or by giving a proof. For quite apart from the fact that there is no doubt no such thing as proof, as we shall suggest,[79] the

---

h Perhaps read ὑληφάγα ('feeding on wood') for ὑληνόμα, to preserve the symmetry of the examples.

i Reading ἢ καί, after the Latin translation: Mutschmann–Mau follow the MSS and print καί.

75 For this refrain, 'a few out of many', see I 85; II 130; III 20, 245, 273; cf. I 4, note.

76 Cf. I 87: see ANNAS and BARNES [1985], pp. 59–60.

77 With I 59–61 compare II 34–6.

78 On this argument see BARNES [1990c].

79 See II 134–92.

so-called proof will itself be either apparent to us or not apparent. If it is not apparent, then we shall not bring it forward with confidence. But if it is apparent to us, then since what is being investigated is what is apparent to animals, and the proof is apparent to us, and we are animals, then the proof itself will be under investigation to see whether it is true as well as apparent. [61] But it is absurd to try to establish the matter under investigation through the matter under investigation, since the same thing will then be both convincing and unconvincing (convincing insofar as it aims to offer a proof, unconvincing insofar as it is being proved), which is impossible. We shall not, therefore, have a proof through which to prefer our own appearances to those produced in the so-called irrational animals. If, therefore, appearances are different depending on the variations among animals, and it is impossible to decide among them, then it is necessary to suspend judgement about external existing objects.

[62] But for good measure[80] we do compare the so-called irrational animals with humans in respect of appearances. For after the substantial arguments we do not rule out a little ridicule of the deluded and self-satisfied Dogmatists.[81] Now we Sceptics are accustomed straightforwardly to compare the irrational animals *en masse* with humans; [63] but since the Dogmatists with their subtleties say that the comparison is unequal, we – for extra good measure – will carry the ridicule further and rest the argument on one animal, for example, on the dog, if you like, which is thought to be the lowest animal of all. We shall find even so that the animals which the argument concerns do not fall short of us as regards the convincingness of what appears to them.

[64] That this animal excels us in its perception the Dogmatists agree. By its sense of smell it grasps more than we do, tracking down by its means wild beasts it cannot see – and with its eyes it sees them more quickly than we do; and with its sense of hearing it perceives more acutely.

[65] Let us turn to reasoning. Of this, one kind is internal and the

---

[80] Cf. I 63, 76; II 47, 96, 192, 193; III 273.
[81] Cf. II 211.

other expressed.[82] So let us first look at the internal kind. This (according to those Dogmatists who are our chief opponents here, namely the Stoics[83]) seems to be anchored in the following things: choice of what is appropriate[84] and avoidance of what is alien to you; knowledge of the kinds of expertise contributing towards this; grasping and relieving your own feelings; acquisition of the virtues relevant to your own nature.[j]

[66] Now the dog, on which we thought we would rest our argument for the sake of an example, does choose what is appropriate and avoid what is harmful to himself: he pursues food and retreats from a raised whip.

Further, he has an expertise which provides what is appropriate to him: hunting.

[67] Nor is he outside the scope of virtue. At least if justice is a matter of distributing to each according to his value, the dog, which fawns on and guards his friends and benefactors but frightens off enemies and offenders, will not be outside the scope of justice. [68] But if he has this, then, since the virtues follow from one another,[85] he has the other virtues too – which wise men deny to most humans. He is courageous, as we see when he frightens off enemies; he is clever, as Homer witnessed when he portrayed Odysseus as unknown by all the people in his household and recognized only by Argus[86] – the dog was not deceived by the alteration to the man's body and did not

---

[j] The text offered by the MSS is certainly corrupt; and the version suggested by the Latin translation and printed by Mutschmann–Mau is no good. We now opt, *pace* ANNAS and BARNES [1985], p. 185, for the drastic remedy proposed by HEINTZ [1932], pp. 11–13: ... τῇ ἀντιλήψει ⟨καὶ παραμυθίᾳ τῶν οἰκείων παθῶν, τῇ δὲ ἀναλήψει⟩ τῶν κατὰ τὴν οἰκείαν φύσιν ἀρετῶν [τῶν περὶ τὰ πάθη].

[82] I.e. there is thought ('internal reasoning') and speech ('external reasoning'); see e.g. *M* VIII 275.

[83] For specifically Stoic allusions in what follows see ANNAS and BARNES [1985], p. 47.

[84] 'Appropriate' renders οἰκεῖος: the word, which originally meant 'to do with one's household', was used by the Stoics to characterize what we naturally tend to in our rational and moral development. Sextus plays on the different uses of the word in this passage: 'friends' in I 67 is οἰκεῖοι (and 'enemies' is ἀνοίκειοι); similarly, 'people in his household' (68).

[85] A Stoic doctrine: e.g. Diogenes Laertius VII 125; Plutarch, *Stoic rep* 1046E.

[86] See Homer, *Odyssey* XVII 300.

abandon his apprehensive appearance,[87] which he appears to have kept better than the humans. [69] According to Chrysippus, who is particularly hostile[k] to the irrational animals,[88] the dog even shares in their celebrated dialectic.[89] Thus our author says that the dog focusses on the fifth unprovable with several disjuncts when he comes to a crossroads and, having tracked down the two roads along which the wild animal did not go, starts off at once along the third without tracking down it. For, our early author says, he is implicitly reasoning as follows: 'The animal went either this way or this or this; but neither this way nor this: therefore this way.'[90]

[70] Further, he can both grasp and relieve his own feelings. When a thorn has got stuck in him he tries to remove it by rubbing his paw along the ground and by using his teeth.[91] And if he has a wound anywhere, then, since dirty wounds heal with difficulty while clean ones are easily cured, he gently wipes away the pus which gathers. [71] Indeed, he keeps to Hippocratic practice extremely well. Since the way to cure a foot is to rest it, if he ever gets a wound in his foot he lifts it up and favours it as far as he can. And when he is disturbed by inappropriate humours,[92] he eats grass, with the help of which he vomits up what was inappropriate and gets well again.

[72] If, then, it has appeared that the animal on which we have rested our argument for the sake of an example chooses what is appropriate and avoids what is disturbing, has an expertise which provides what is appropriate, can grasp and relieve his own feelings, and is not outside the scope of virtue, then, since in these things lies

---

k   Reading πολεμοῦντα, with the MSS: Mutschmann–Mau print συμπολεμοῦντα, which gives exactly the opposite sense.

87 Cf. II 4, note.
88 Hostile both theoretically, in that he denied animals reason and virtue and other honourable attributes (e.g. Porphyry, *abstin* III xii 5), and also practically, in that he held that animals might be treated in any way conducive to human utility (see Cicero, *fin* III xx 67).
89 Dialectic is a virtue, according to the Stoics (see e.g. Diogenes Laertius VII 46): I 69 is thus continuous with I 67–8.
90 The doggy syllogism is often reported; see especially Philo, *On Animals* 45–6, 84; Plutarch, *de sollertia animalium* 968F–969B; Aelian, *On the Nature of Animals* VI 59; Porphyry, *abstin* III xxii 6. On the Stoic 'unprovables' see below, II 157–8.
91 Cf. I 238.
92 See I 46.

the perfection of internal reasoning, the dog will be, in this respect,[1] perfect. This is, I think the reason why some philosophers have glorified themselves with the name of this animal.[93]

[73] As for expressed reasoning, first it is not necessary to investigate it; for some of the Dogmatists themselves have deprecated it as working against the acquisition of virtue, which is why during their time of learning they practised silence.[94] And again, let us suppose that a man is mute: no-one will say that he is irrational.

But to pass over these matters, note in particular that we observe the animals which we are now discussing uttering sounds which are actually human – animals such as jays and some others.

[74] But to leave this aside too, even if we do not understand the sounds of the so-called irrational animals, it is nevertheless[m] not unlikely that they do converse and we do not understand them. For when we are listening to the sounds made by foreigners we do not understand them but believe that they are undifferentiated. [75] And we hear dogs producing one sound when frightening people off, another when howling, another when they are beaten, and a different one when fawning. Generally, if someone were to study this matter, he would find that there is much variation of sound (in the case of this animal and of others) in different circumstances; so for this reason it could be said with some likelihood that the so-called irrational animals share in expressed reasoning too.

[76] But if they fall short of humans neither in the accuracy of their senses nor in internal reasoning nor (saying this for good measure[95]) in expressed reasoning, they will be no less convincing in respect of the appearances than we are. [77] It is no doubt possible to rest the case on any one of the irrational animals and show[n] the same thing. For instance, who would deny that birds stand out in shrewdness and have the use of expressed reasoning? They have a knowledge not only

---

[1] Reading τοῦτο, with two MSS and the Latin translation: Mutschmann–Mau print τοῦτον (Heintz).
[m] Reading ὅμως (Wendland) for ὅλως (MSS, Mutschmann–Mau).
[n] Reading ὑποδεικνύειν with the MSS: Mutschmann–Mau print ἀποδεικνύειν, 'prove'.

93 I.e. the Cynics, οἱ κυνικοί, from κύων, 'dog' (see e.g. Diogenes Laertius VI 13).
94 Sextus alludes to the celebrated Pythagorean rule of silence, for which see e.g. Porphyry, *On the Pythagorean Way of Life* 19.
95 Cf. I 62.

of the present but also of the future, and they make this clear to those who can understand them, giving various signs and in particular foretelling things by their cries.

[78] I have made this comparison, as I noted before,[96] for good measure, having before° shown adequately, I think, that we are not able to prefer our own appearances to those produced in the irrational animals.

So, if the irrational animals are no more convincing than we are when it comes to judging appearances, and if different appearances are produced depending on the variations among animals, then I shall be able to say how each existing object appears to me, but for these reasons I shall be forced to suspend judgement on how it is by nature.

[79][97] Such is the first mode of suspension of judgement. The second, we said, was the mode deriving from the differences among humans. For even were one to concede by way of hypothesis that humans are more convincing than the irrational animals, we shall find that suspension of judgement is brought in insofar as our own differences go.

There are two things from which humans are said to be composed, soul and body, and in both these we differ from one another. For example, in body we differ in our shapes and our individual peculiarities.[98] [80] There is a difference in shape between the body of a Scythian and an Indian's body, and what produces the variation, so they say, is the different dominance of the humours. Depending on the different dominance of the humours, the appearances too become different, as we established in our first argument.[99] Further, in virtue of these humours there are many differences in our choice and avoidance of external things; for Indians enjoy different things from us, and enjoying different things shows that varying appearances come from existing objects.

° Retaining the second, inelegant ἔμπροσθεν, which Mutschmann–Mau excise.

[96] I.e. at I 62.

[97] With I 79–90 compare Diogenes Laertius IX 80–1; Philo, *ebr* 176–7; see ANNAS and BARNES [1985], pp. 57–65.

[98] Or idiosyncrasies, ἰδιοσυγκρασίαι ('individual commixtures ⟨of the humours⟩'): 'Most doctors, I think, name these things idiosyncrasies – and they all agree that they are inapprehensible' (Galen, *On the Therapeutic Method* X 209 Kühn).

[99] See I 52 (cf. I 46).

[81] In our individual peculiarities we differ in such a way that some people digest beef more easily than rock-fish, and get diarrhoea from weak Lesbian wine. There was (so they say) an old woman in Attica who consumed four ounces of hemlock without harm. Lysis actually took half an ounce of opium without distress. [82] Demophon, Alexander's waiter, used to shiver when he was in the sun or the baths and felt warm in the shade. When Athenagoras of Argos was stung by scorpions or poisonous spiders he was not hurt. The Psyllaeans, as they are called, are not harmed when bitten by snakes or asps, [83] and the Tentyritae in Egypt are not harmed by crocodiles. Further, the Ethiopians who live by the river Astapus on the other side of Meroe eat scorpions and snakes without harm. When Rufinus – the one from Chalcis – drank hellebore he neither vomited nor suffered any other purgative effects, but consumed and digested it as though it were something normal. [84] If Chrysermus the Herophilean doctor ever consumed pepper he suffered a heart attack. If Soterichus the surgeon ever smelt sheathfish cooking he was seized by diarrhoea. Andron of Argos was so free from thirst that he travelled through waterless Libya without seeking drink. The Emperor Tiberius could see in the dark. Aristotle describes a Thasian who thought that the image of a man was always preceding him.[100]

[85] Since there is such variation among humans in body (to be satisfied with a few examples out of the many[101] which the Dogmatists provide[P]), it is likely that humans differ from one another in their souls too; for, as the science of physiognomy shows, the body is a kind of picture of the soul.[102]

The chief indication of the great – indeed infinite – differences among humans with regard to their intellect is the dispute among the Dogmatists about various matters and in particular about what we should choose and what reject. [86] The poets have got it right here. Pindar says:

P Retaining τῶν παρὰ τοῖς δογματικοῖς κειμένων, which Mutschmann–Mau follow Heintz in deleting.

[100] See Aristotle, *Meteorology* 373a35–b10; cf. ANNAS and BARNES [1985], p. 61.
[101] Cf. I 58.
[102] Cf. II 101; *M* VIII 155, 173.

> One man is gladdened by the honours and garlands of his
>   storm-footed horses,
> another by life in gilded palaces;
> another rejoices as he crosses the swell of the sea in a swift ship.[103]

And Homer says:

> Different men rejoice in different deeds.[104]

Tragedy too is full of such things:

> If nature had made the same things fine and wise for all alike,
> there would be no disputatious strife among human kind.[105]

And again:

> Strange that the same thing should please some mortals
> but by others be hated.[106]

[87] Since, therefore, choice and avoidance are located in pleasure and displeasure, and pleasure and displeasure lie in perception and appearance, then when some choose and others avoid the same things, it is apposite for us to deduce that they are not similarly affected by the same things, since otherwise they would have chosen and rejected the same things in similar ways.[107] But if the same things affect humans differently depending on the differences among them, then it is likely that suspension of judgement will be introduced in this way too, since we are no doubt able to say how each existing thing appears, with reference to each difference, but are not able to assert what it is in its nature.

[88] For we shall be convinced either by all humans or by some. If by all, we shall be attempting the impossible and accepting opposed views. But if by some, then let them say to whom we should assent. The Platonist will say 'to Plato', the Epicurean 'to Epicurus', and the others analogously, and so by their undecidable dissensions[108] they will bring us round again to suspension of judgement.

---

103 frag. 221 Snell.
104 *Odyssey* XIV 228.
105 Euripides, *Phoenissae* 499–500.
106 Unknown, frag. 462 Kannicht/Snell.
107 See I 57.
108 'Undecidable' translates ἀνεπίκριτος – but see BARNES [1990d], pp. 17–19.

[89] Anyone who says that we should assent to the majority view is making a puerile suggestion. Nobody can canvass all mankind and work out what is the preference of the majority,[109] it being possible[110] that among some nations of which we have no knowledge what is rare with us is true of the majority and what is true of most of us is there rare – for example, that most people when bitten by poisonous spiders do not suffer though some occasionally do suffer, and analogously with the other individual peculiarities I mentioned earlier. So suspension of judgement is necessarily introduced by way of the differences among humans too.

[90] When the self-satisfied Dogmatists say that they themselves should be preferred to other humans in judging things, we know that their claim is absurd. For they are themselves a part of the dispute, and if it is by preferring themselves that they judge what is apparent, then by entrusting the judging to themselves they are taking for granted the matter being investigated before beginning the judging.

[91][111] Nonetheless, so as to arrive at suspension of judgement even when resting the argument on a single person, such as the Sage they dream up,[112] we bring out the mode which is third in order. This, we said, is the one deriving from the differences among the senses.

Now, that the senses disagree with one another is clear. [92] For instance, paintings seem to sight to have recesses and projections, but not to touch.[113] Honey appears pleasant to the tongue (for some people) but unpleasant to the eyes; it is impossible, therefore, to say whether it is purely pleasant or unpleasant. Similarly with perfume: it gratifies the sense of smell but displeases the sense of taste. [93] Again, since spurge-juice is painful to the eyes but painless to the rest of the body, we will not be able to say whether, so far as its own nature goes, it is purely painless to bodies or painful. Rainwater is beneficial to the

109 Cf. II 45 (and also e.g. Cicero, *nat deorum* I xxiii 62).
110 Cf. I 34.
111 With I 91–9 compare Diogenes Laertius IX 81; see ANNAS and BARNES [1985], pp. 68–77.
112 For the Dogmatic, and especially Stoic, notion of the Sage see II 38, 83; III 240. The Sage, who is also virtuous and embodies all human perfection, is an ideal, a logical construction put together for philosophical purposes. The numerous texts on the Stoic Sage are collected in VON ARNIM [1903–5] III 544–684.
113 Cf. I 120 (and note Plato, *Republic* 602C–603B).

eyes, but is rough on the windpipe and lungs – so too is olive oil, though it comforts the skin. The sea-ray, when applied to the extremities, paralyses them, but can be put on the rest of the body harmlessly. Hence we will not be able to say what each of these things is like in its nature, although it is possible to say what they appear to be like on any given occasion.

[94] More cases than these can be given; but so as not to waste time, given the purpose^q of our essay,[114] we should say this. Each of the objects of perception which appears to us seems to impress us in a variety of ways – for example, an apple is smooth, fragrant, sweet, and yellow.[115] It is unclear, then, whether in reality it has these qualities alone, or has only one quality but appears different depending on the different constitution of the sense-organs, or actually has more qualities than those which are apparent, some of them not making an impression on us.

[95] That it has only one quality can be argued from what we said before[116] about the nourishment dispersed in our bodies and the water dispersed in trees and the breath in^r flutes and pipes and similar instruments; for the apple can be undifferentiated but observed as different depending on the differences among the sense-organs by which it is grasped.

[96] That the apple may have more qualities than those apparent to us we deduce as follows. Let us conceive of[117] someone who from birth has touch, smell and taste, but who hears and sees nothing. He will suppose that there is absolutely nothing visible or audible, and that there exist only those three kinds of quality which he is able to grasp. [97] So it is possible that we too, having only the five senses, grasp from among the qualities of the apple^s only those we are capable of grasping, although other qualities can exist, impressing other

---

^q Deleting τοῦ τρόπου (Mutschmann).

^r We follow the MSS text: Mutschmann–Mau excise ἐν before αὐλοῖς and add ἐμπνεομένου after ὀργάνοις.

^s Retaining ἐκ τῶν περὶ τὸ μῆλον ποιοτήτων, deleted by Mutschmann–Mau after Heintz.

¹¹⁴ See I 4, note.
¹¹⁵ Cf. *M* VII 103.
¹¹⁶ I 53–4.
¹¹⁷ Cf. I 34, note.

sense-organs in which we have no share, so that we do not grasp the objects perceptible by them.[t]

[98] But nature, someone will say, has made the senses commensurate with their objects.[118] What nature? – given that there is so much undecidable dispute among the Dogmatists about the reality of what is according to nature. For if someone decides this question (namely, whether there is such a thing as nature), then if he is a layman he will not be convincing according to them, while if he is a philosopher he will be part of the dispute and under judgement himself rather than a judge.

[99] So if it is possible[u] that only those qualities exist in the apple which we think we grasp, and that there are more than them, and again that there are not even those which make an impression on us, then it will be unclear to us what the apple is like.

The same argument applies to the other objects of perception too. But if the senses do not apprehend external objects, the intellect is not able to apprehend them either (since its guides fail it[119]), so by means of this argument too we shall be thought to conclude to suspension of judgement about external existing objects.

[100][120] In order to end up with suspension of judgement even if we rest the argument on any single sense or actually leave the senses aside, we also adopt the fourth mode of suspension. This is the mode which gets its name from circumstances, where by 'circumstances' we mean conditions. It is observed, we say, in natural or unnatural states, in waking or sleeping, depending on age, on moving or being at rest, on hating or loving, on being in need or sated, on being drunk or sober, on anterior conditions, on being confident or fearful, on being in distress or in a state of enjoyment.[121]

---

[t]　Reading κατ' αὐτά for κατ' αὐτάς (MSS, Mutschmann–Mau). See ANNAS and BARNES [1985], p. 185.
[u]　Reading εἰ ἐγχωρεῖ (Heintz): ἐνεχώρει (MSS ungrammatically), ⟨εἰ⟩ ἐνεχώρει (Mutschmann–Mau).

[118]　Cf. M IX 94, citing Xenophon, Memorabilia I iv 2; and see e.g. Apuleius, dog Plat I xiv 209.
[119]　See I 128 (cf. II 63); and compare Democritus, frag. 125 Diels–Kranz.
[120]　With I 100–17 compare Diogenes Laertius IX 82; Philo, ebr 178–80; see ANNAS and BARNES [1985], pp. 82–98.
[121]　Cf. II 51–6 for a reprise, and I 218–19 (with M VII 61–4) where the same material is used in Sextus' account of Protagoreanism.

[101] For example, objects produce dissimilar impressions on us depending on our being in a natural or an unnatural state, since people who are delirious or divinely possessed believe that they hear spirits, while we do not; and similarly they often say that they grasp an exhalation of storax or frankincense or the like, and many other things, while we do not perceive them. The same water seems to be boiling when poured on to inflamed places, but to us to be lukewarm. The same cloak appears orange to people with a blood-suffusion in the eye, but not to me; and the same honey appears sweet to me, but bitter to people with jaundice.[122]

[102] If anyone says that it is the mixing of certain humours[123] which produces inappropriate appearances from existing objects in people who are in an unnatural state,[124] we should say that, since healthy people too have mixed humours, it is possible that these humours make the external existing objects appear different to the healthy, while they are by nature the way they appear to those who are said to be in an unnatural state. [103] For to grant one lot of humours but not the other the power of changing external objects has an air of fiction. Again, just as healthy people are in a state natural for the healthy but unnatural for the sick, so the sick are in a state unnatural for the healthy but natural for the sick, so that they too are in a state which is, relatively speaking, natural, and they too should be found convincing.

[104] Different appearances come about depending on sleeping or waking. When we are awake we view things differently from the way we do when we are asleep, and when asleep differently from the way we do when awake; so the existence or non-existence of the objects[v] becomes not absolute but relative – relative to being asleep or awake. It is likely, then, that when asleep we will see things which are unreal in waking life, not unreal once and for all.[w] For they exist in sleep, just as the contents of waking life exist even though they do not exist in sleep.

---

v Retaining αὐτοῖς with the MSS: Mutschmann–Mau print αὐταῖς (Apelt).
w Retaining, after Heintz, the words ἐν τῷ which Mutschmann–Mau delete.

122 Cf. I 44, 211, 213; II 51–2, 63.
123 See I 46.
124 For the idea that something is F if it appears F to those in a natural state see II 54–6; *M* VII 62–3.

[105] Appearances differ depending on age. The same air seems cold to old men but mild to the young, the same colour appears faint to the elderly but intense to the young, and similarly the same sound seems to the former dim but to the latter clearly audible. [106] Those who differ in age are also affected dissimilarly depending on their choices and avoidances. Children, for example, are serious about balls and hoops, while the young choose other things, and old men yet others. From this it is concluded that different appearances come about from the same existing objects depending on differences in age too.

[107] Objects appear dissimilar depending on moving or being at rest. Things which we see as still when we are stationary seem to us to move when we sail past them. [108] Depending on loving and hating: some people have an excessive revulsion against pork, while others consume it with great pleasure. Menander said:

> How foul he appears even in his looks
> since he has become like this! What an animal!
> Doing no wrong actually makes us beautiful.[125]

And many men who have ugly girl-friends think them most attractive. [109] Depending on being hungry or sated: the same food seems most pleasant to people who are hungry but unpleasant to the sated. Depending on being drunk or sober: things which we think shameful when sober do not appear shameful to us when we are drunk. [110] Depending on anterior conditions: the same wine appears sour to people who have just eaten dates or figs, but it seems to be sweet to people who have consumed nuts or chickpeas. And the bathhouse vestibule warms people entering from outside but chills people leaving if they spend any time there. [111] Depending on being afraid or confident: the same object seems fearful and dreadful to the coward but not so at all to someone bolder. Depending on being in distress or in a state of enjoyment: the same objects are annoying to people in distress and pleasant to people who are enjoying themselves.

[112] Since, therefore, there are so many anomalies depending on conditions, and since at different times people come to be in different

---

125 Frag. 568 Kock.

conditions, it is no doubt easy to say what each existing object appears to be like to each person, but not to say what it *is* like, since the anomalies are in fact undecidable.

For anyone who decides them is either in some of these conditions or in absolutely no condition at all. But to say that he is in no condition whatsoever (i.e. neither healthy nor sick, neither moving nor at rest, of no particular age, and free from the other conditions) is perfectly incongruous. But if he is in some condition as he judges the appearances, he will be a part of the dispute. [113] And again, he will not be an unbiassed judge of external existing objects because he will have been contaminated by the conditions he is in. So a waking person cannot compare the appearances of sleepers with those of people who are awake, or a healthy person those of the sick with those of the healthy; for we assent to what is present and affects us in the present rather than to what is not present.

[114] And there is another reason why the anomalies among the appearances are undecidable. Anyone who prefers one appearance to another and one circumstance to another does so either without making a judgement and without proof or making a judgement and offering a proof. But he can do so neither without these (for he will be unconvincing) nor yet with them. For if he judges the appearances he will certainly judge them by means of a standard. [115] Now he will say of this standard either that it is true or that it is false. If false, he will be unconvincing. But if he says that it is true, then he will say that the standard is true either without proof or with proof. If without proof he will be unconvincing. But if with proof, he will certainly need the proof to be true – otherwise he will be unconvincing. Then when he says that the proof which he adopts to make the standard convincing is true, will he do so after judging it or without judging it? [116] If he has not judged it he will be unconvincing. But if he has judged it, then clearly he will say that he has judged it by means of a standard – but we shall demand a proof of that standard, and then a standard for that proof. For a proof always requires a standard in order to be confirmed, and a standard always requires a proof in order to be shown to be true. A proof cannot be sound if there is no standard there already, nor can a standard be true if a proof has not already been made convincing. [117] In this way standards and proofs fall into the

reciprocal mode, by which both of them are found to be unconvincing: each waits to be made convincing by the other,[x] and so each is as unconvincing as the other.[126]

If, then, one cannot prefer one appearance to another either without a proof and a standard or with them, the different appearances which come about depending on different conditions will be undecidable. Hence so far as this mode too goes suspension of judgement about external existing objects is introduced.

[118][127] The fifth argument is the one depending on positions and intervals and places – for depending on each of these the same objects appear different.

For example, the same colonnade appears foreshortened when seen from one end, but completely symmetrical when seen from the middle. The same boat appears from a distance small and stationary, but from close at hand large and in motion. The same tower appears from a distance round, but from close at hand square.[128] [119] These depend on intervals.

Depending on places: lamplight appears dim in sunlight but bright in the dark. The same oar appears bent in water but straight when out of it. Eggs appear soft in the bird but hard in the air. Lyngurion[129] appears liquid inside the lynx but hard in the air. Coral appears soft in the sea but hard in the air. And sound appears different when produced in a pipe, in a flute, or simply in the air.

[120] Depending on positions: the same picture when laid down appears flat, but when put at a certain angle seems to have recesses and projections. Doves' necks appear different in colour depending on the different ways they turn them.

[121] Since, then, all apparent things are observed in some place and from some interval and in some position, and each of these produces a

---

[x] Reading τὴν ⟨ἐκ⟩ θατέρου πίστιν (Heintz): Mutschmann–Mau print the MSS text.

[126] For the reciprocal mode see I 169; for this application of it compare *M* VII 341.
[127] With I 118–23 compare Diogenes Laertius IX 85–6; Philo, *ebr* 181–3; see ANNAS and BARNES [1985], pp. 101–9.
[128] See I 32.
[129] A semi-precious stone allegedly consisting of the solidified urine of the lynx.

great deal of variation in appearances, as we have suggested, we shall be forced to arrive at suspension of judgement by these modes too.[y]

For anyone wishing to give preference to some of these appearances over others will be attempting the impossible. [122] If he makes his assertion simply and without proof, he will not be convincing. But if he wants to use a proof, then if he says that the proof is false, he will turn himself about;[130] and if he says that the proof is true, he will be required to give a proof of its being true, and another proof of that (since it too has to be true), and so *ad infinitum*.[131] But it is impossible to establish infinitely many proofs. [123] And so he will not be able to prefer one appearance to another with a proof either.

But if no-one can decide among these appearances either without proof or with proof, the conclusion is suspension of judgement: we are no doubt able to say what each thing appears to be like in this position or from that interval or in this place, but we are not able, for the reasons we have given, to assert what it is like in its nature.

[124][132] Sixth is the mode depending on admixtures. According to it we conclude that, since no existing object makes an impression on us by itself but rather together with something, it is perhaps possible to say what the mixture is like which results from the external object and the factor with which it is observed, but we cannot say purely what the external existing object is like.

That no external object makes an impression by itself but in every case together with something, and that it is observed as differing in a way dependent on this is, I think, clear. [125] For instance, the colour of our skin is seen as different in warm air and in cold, and we cannot say what our colour is like in its nature but only what it is like as observed together with each of these. The same sound appears different together with clear air or with muggy air. Aromatic herbs

---

[y] Retaining the plural, τούτους τοὺς τρόπους (MSS and Latin translation): Mutschmann–Mau print τούτου τοῦ τρόπου (Bekker) – see ANNAS and BARNES [1985], p. 102.

[130] For 'turning about' or self-refutation, in Greek περιτροπή, see I 139, 200; II 64, 76, 88, 91, 128, 133, 179, 185, 188; III 19, 28; and see BURNYEAT [1976].

[131] For the mode *ad infinitum* see I 166.

[132] With I 124–8 compare Diogenes Laertius IX 84–5; Philo, *ebr* 189–92; see ANNAS and BARNES [1985] pp. 112–18.

are more pungent in the bathhouse and in the sun than in chilly air. And a body surrounded by water is light, surrounded by air heavy.

[126] But to leave aside external admixtures, our eyes contain membranes and liquids inside them. Since, then, what we see is not observed without these, it will not be apprehended accurately; for it is the mixture which we grasp, and for this reason people with jaundice see everything as yellow, while people with a blood-suffusion in the eye see things as blood-red.[133] And since the same sound appears different in open places and in narrow winding places, and different in pure and in contaminated air, it is likely that we do not have a pure grasp of sound; for our ears have winding passages and narrow channels, and are contaminated by vaporous effluvia which are said to be carried from the region of the head. [127] Further, since certain kinds of matter exist in our nostrils and in the regions of taste, it is together with these, not purely, that we grasp what we taste and smell.

So because of the admixtures our senses do not grasp what external existing objects are accurately like. [128] But our intellect does not do so either, especially since its guides, the senses, fail it.[134] And no doubt it too produces some admixture of its own to add to what is announced by the senses; for we observe the existence of certain humours[135] round each of the regions in which the Dogmatists think that the 'ruling part' is located – in the brain or the heart or in whatever part of the animal they want to locate it.[136]

According to this mode too, therefore, we see that we cannot say anything about the nature of external existing objects, and are forced to suspend judgement.

---

[133] Cf. I 44.
[134] Cf. I 99.
[135] Cf. I 46.
[136] On the 'ruling part' or intellect, the ἡγεμονικόν, and the celebrated dispute about its physical location in the body compare II 32, 58, 70–1, 81; III 169, 188; *M* VII 313; IX 119. The Stoics placed the ruling part in the heart, while the Platonists opted for the brain. The fullest account of the matter is in Galen, *PHP* II–III (see especially III i 10–15 (= v 252–3 K), quoting Chrysippus, who himself reports a dispute on the subject: see TIELEMAN [1992]). See ANNAS [1992a], ch. 2.

[129]¹³⁷ The seventh mode, we said, is the one depending on the quantities and preparations of existing objects – where by 'preparations' we mean compositions in general. That we are forced by this mode too to suspend judgement about the nature of objects is clear.

For instance, the shavings from a goat's horn appear white when observed simply, without composition, but when combined in the existing horn are observed as black. Silver filings appear black on their own, but together with the whole they make a white impression on us. [130] Pieces of Taenarian marble when polished are seen as white, but appear yellowish in the whole mass. Grains of sand scattered apart from one another appear rough, but when combined in a heap affect our senses smoothly. Hellebore produces choking when consumed as a fine powder, but not when grated coarsely. [131] Wine drunk in moderation fortifies us, but taken in greater quantity enfeebles the body. Food likewise displays different powers depending on the quantity: often, for instance, through being consumed in large amounts it purges the body by indigestion and diarrhoea.

[132] Here too, therefore, we shall be able to say what the fine piece of horn is like, and what the combination of many fine pieces is like; what the small piece of silver is like, and what the combination of many small pieces is like; what the minute piece of Taenarian marble is like, and what the combination of many small pieces is like; and so with the grains of sand and the hellebore and the wine and the food – we can say what they are like relatively, but we cannot say what the nature of the objects is like in itself because of the anomalies in the appearances which depend on their compositions.

[133] For in general, beneficial things seem harmful depending on their being used in immoderate quantity; and things which seem harmful when taken to excess seem to do no harm in minute quantities. The chief witness to this argument is what is observed in the case of medicinal powers: here the accurate mixing of simple drugs makes the compound beneficial, but sometimes when the smallest error is made in the weighing it is not only not beneficial but

---

¹³⁷ With I 129–34 compare Diogenes Laertius IX 86; Philo, *ebr* 184–5; see ANNAS and BARNES [1985], pp. 120–7.

extremely harmful and often poisonous. [134] To such an extent does the relation among quantities and preparations determine[z] the reality of external existing objects.

Hence it is likely that this mode too will bring us round to suspension of judgement, since we cannot make assertions purely about the nature of external existing objects.

[135][138] The eighth mode is the one deriving from relativity, by which we conclude that, since everything is relative, we shall suspend judgement as to what things are independently and in their nature. It should be recognized that here, as elsewhere, we use 'is' loosely, in the sense of 'appears',[139] implicitly saying 'Everything appears relative'.[140]

But this has two senses: first, relative to the subject judging (for the external existing object which is judged appears relative to the subject judging), and second, relative to the things observed together with it (as right is relative to left). [136] We have in fact already deduced that everything is relative,[141] i.e. with respect to the subject judging (since each thing appears relative to a given animal and a given human and a given sense and a given circumstance), and with respect to the things observed together with it (since each thing appears relative to a given admixture[aa] and a given composition and quantity and position).

[137] We can also conclude in particular that everything is relative, in the following way. Do relatives differ or not from things which are

---

z   Reading συνέχει, after the Latin translation, with Heintz: Mutschmann–Mau print συγχεῖ, 'confound', the reading of the MSS.

aa   After 'admixture' the MSS have the phrase καὶ τόνδε τὸν τρόπον, 'and a given mode'. Although Mutschmann–Mau print the phrase, it is a nonsense. We follow Kayser, who simply deletes the words. In any event, it is clear that Sextus means to allude to the fifth, sixth and seventh modes.

138 With I 135–40 compare Diogenes Laertius IX 87–8; Philo, *ebr* 186–8; see ANNAS and BARNES [1985], pp. 130–45; BARNES [1988b].

139 Cf. I 198; *M* XI 18.

140 Note that many readers, both ancient and modern, have ignored Sextus' warning and identified scepticism with relativism: e.g. Anonymus, *in Theaet* lxiii 1–40; Gellius XI v 7–8; see ANNAS and BARNES [1985], pp. 96–8; BARNES [1988b].

141 There are explicit references to relativity at I 103, 132; and see also I 38–9, where, however, a different taxonomy of the modes is produced (see ANNAS and BARNES [1985], pp. 141–3).

in virtue of a difference?[142] If they do not differ, then the latter are relatives too. But if they do differ, then, since everything which differs is relative (it is spoken of relative to what it differs from), things in virtue of a difference will be relative. [138] Again, according to the Dogmatists, some existing things are highest genera, others lowest species, and others both genera and species. But all of these are relative. Everything, therefore, is relative. Further, some existing things are clear, others unclear, as they themselves say, and what is apparent is a signifier while what is unclear is signified by something apparent (for according to them 'the apparent is the way to see the unclear'[143]). But signifier and signified are relative. Everything, therefore, is relative. [139] Further, some existing things are similar, others dissimilar, and some are equal, others unequal. But these are relative. Everything, therefore, is relative.

And anyone who says that not everything is relative confirms that everything is relative. For by opposing us he shows that the very relativity of everything is relative to us and not universal.[144]

[140] So, since we have established in this way that everything is relative, it is clear that we shall not be able to say what each existing object is like in its own nature and purely, but only what it appears to be like relative to something. It follows that we must suspend judgement about the nature of objects.

[141][145] As for the mode based on frequent or rare encounters (which was said to be ninth in order), we shall set out the following cases.

The sun is surely a great deal more striking than a comet; but since we see the sun frequently and comets only rarely, we are so struck by comets that we actually think them to be portents, but are not struck at all by the sun. However, if we conceive of[146] the sun as appearing rarely and setting rarely, and as lighting up everything all at once and

---

[142] 'Things in virtue of a difference', τὰ κατὰ διαφοράν, are absolute or non-relative items; see e.g. M VIII 161–2 (cf. 37); X 263–5; Simplicius, *in Cat* 165. 32–166.30.

[143] Anaxagoras, frag. 21a Diels–Kranz; see below, III 78.

[144] A typical 'turn about' argument: cf. I 122.

[145] With I 141–4 compare Diogenes Laertius IX 87; see ANNAS and BARNES [1985], pp. 147–50.

[146] For imaginary examples see I 34.

suddenly plunging everything into darkness, then we shall consider the thing very striking. [142] Earthquakes, too, do not similarly upset people experiencing them for the first time and those who have grown accustomed to them. How striking the sea is to someone who sees it for the first time! Again, the beauty of a human body when seen for the first time, and suddenly, excites us more than it would if it became a customary sight.

[143] Again, what is rare is thought to be valuable, but not what is familiar and easily available. For instance, if we conceive of water as being rare, how much more valuable would it then appear to us than everything which seems valuable! Or if we imagine gold as simply strewn in quantity over the ground like stones, who do we think would find it valuable then, or worth locking away?

[144] Since, therefore, the same objects seem now striking and valuable, now not, depending on whether they impress us frequently or rarely, we deduce that we will no doubt be able to say what each of these things appears like given the frequency or rarity of the impressions they make on us, but we will not be able to state baldly what each external existing object is like. Because of this mode too, therefore, we suspend judgement about them.

[145][147] The tenth mode, which especially bears on ethics, is the one depending on persuasions and customs and laws and beliefs in myth and dogmatic suppositions. A persuasion is a choice of life or of a way of acting practised by one person or by many (for example, by Diogenes or by the Spartans). [146] A law is a written contract among citizens, transgressors of which are punished. A custom or usage (there is no difference) is a common acceptance by a number of people of a certain way of acting, transgressors of which are not necessarily punished. For example, there is a law against adultery, but with us it is a custom not to have sex with a woman in public. [147] A belief in myth is an acceptance of matters which did not occur and are fictional – examples include the myths about Cronus, which many people find convincing. A dogmatic supposition is an acceptance of a

---

[147] With I 145–63 compare Diogenes Laertius IX 83–4; Philo, *ebr* 193–202; below, III 198–234; see ANNAS and BARNES [1985], pp. 156–71; ANNAS [1986], [1993a], [1993b], [1993c].

matter which seems to be supported by abduction or proof of some kind, for example, that there are atomic elements of things, or homoeomeries, or least parts, or something else.

[148] We oppose each of these sometimes to itself, sometimes to one of the others.

For example, we oppose custom to custom like this: some of the Ethiopians tattoo their babies, while we do not;[148] the Persians deem it becoming to wear brightly-coloured full-length dresses, while we deem it unbecoming;[149] Indians have sex with women in public, while most other people hold that it is shameful.[150] [149] We oppose law to law like this: in Rome anyone who renounces his father's property does not repay his father's debts, while in Rhodes he repays them come what may; among the Tauri in Scythia there was a law that strangers should be sacrificed to Artemis, while among us killing a human at a religious rite is prohibited.[151] [150] We oppose persuasion to persuasion when we oppose the persuasion of Diogenes to that of Aristippus, or that of the Spartans to that of the Italians. We oppose belief in myth to belief in myth when we say in one place that the mythical father of gods and men is Zeus, and in another that he is Ocean, citing

Ocean, source of the gods, and Tethys, their mother ...[152]

[151] We oppose dogmatic suppositions to one another when we say that some people assert that there is one element, others infinitely many; some that the soul is mortal, others immortal; some that human affairs are directed by divine providence, others non-providentially.[153]

[152] We oppose custom to the others – for example, to law, when we say that in Persia homosexual acts are customary, while in Rome they are forbidden by law;[154] that among us adultery is forbidden,

---

[148] Cf. III 202.
[149] Cf. III 202.
[150] Cf. III 200.
[151] Cf. III 208, 221.
[152] Homer, *Iliad* XIV 201.
[153] See II 5; III 9–12.
[154] Cf. III 199.

while among the Massagetae it is accepted by custom as indifferent[155] (as Eudoxus of Cnidus narrates in the first book of his *Journey round the World*[156]); that among us it is forbidden to have sex with your mother, while in Persia it is the custom to favour such marriages; and in Egypt they marry their sisters, which among us is forbidden by law.[157] [153] Custom is opposed to persuasion: most men have sex with their own women in private, while Crates did it with Hipparchia in public;[158] Diogenes went round in a sleeveless tunic, while we dress normally. [154] Custom is opposed to belief in myth: the myths say that Cronus ate his own children, while among us it is the custom to provide for our children;[159] and among us it is the usage to revere the gods as good and as unaffected by evils, while they are represented by the poets as suffering wounds and envying one another. [155] Custom is opposed to dogmatic supposition: with us it is the custom to ask for good things from the gods, while Epicurus says that the divinity pays no attention to us;[160] and Aristippus[161] thinks that it is indifferent whether you wear women's clothes, whereas we hold that this is shameful.

[156] We oppose persuasion to law: although there is a law that a free man of a good family may not be struck, the all-in wrestlers strike one another because that is the persuasion in their way of life; and gladiators kill one another for the same reason, although man-slaughter is prohibited.[162] [157] We oppose belief in myth to persuasion when we say that the myths say that in Omphale's house Heracles

carded wool and endured slavery[163]

and did things which nobody would have done by choice even in moderation, whereas Heracles' persuasion was noble. [158] We oppose persuasion to dogmatic supposition: athletes pursue glory as a

---

155 Cf. III 209.
156 frag. 278b Lasserre.
157 Cf. III 205.
158 Cf. III 200; see e.g. Diogenes Laertius VI 97.
159 Cf. III 210–11.
160 Cf. III 9–12.
161 Cf. III 204.
162 Cf. III 212.
163 Homer, *Odyssey* XXII 423.

good and take on for its own sake a persuasion full of exertion, while many philosophers hold the belief that glory is a bad thing.

[159] We oppose law to belief in myth: the poets represent the gods as committing adultery and indulging in homosexual acts, while with us the law forbids these things. [160] We oppose law to dogmatic supposition: Chrysippus[164] says that it is indifferent whether or not you have sex with your mother or sister, while the law forbids this.

[161] We oppose belief in myth to dogmatic supposition: the poets say that Zeus came down and had sex with mortal women, while the Dogmatists deem this to be impossible; [162] and Homer says that Zeus because of his grief for Sarpedon

> rained drops of blood upon the earth,[165]

whereas it is a belief of the philosophers that the divinity is unaffected; and[ab] they deny the myth of the centaurs, presenting the centaur to us as an example of what is unreal.

[163] We could have taken many other examples for each of these oppositions, but in a brief account[166] this will suffice.

Thus, since so much anomaly has been shown in objects by this mode too, we shall not be able to say what each existing object is like in its nature, but only how it appears relative to a given persuasion or law or custom and so on. Because of this mode too, therefore, it is necessary for us to suspend judgement on the nature of external existing objects.

In this way, then, by means of the ten modes we end up with suspension of judgement.

xv The Five Modes[167]

[164] The more recent Sceptics[168] offer the following five modes of suspension of judgement: first, the mode deriving from dispute;

[ab] Mutschmann–Mau mark a lacuna in the text, supposing Sextus to have written something of the form 'and ⟨X says that so-and-so, while⟩ they deny . . .'.

[164] See III 206, note.

[165] *Iliad* XVI 459.

[166] For claims to brevity compare I 231; II 1, 219, 236; III 151, 222, 233; see I 4, note.

[167] With I 164–9 compare Diogenes Laertius IX 88–9 (cf. BARNES [1992], pp. 4263–8); on the chapter see especially BARNES [1990d].

[168] They contrast with 'the older Sceptics' of I 36 and are identified with Agrippa by Diogenes Laertius IX 88.

second, the mode throwing one back *ad infinitum*; third, the mode deriving from relativity; fourth, the hypothetical mode; fifth, the reciprocal mode.

[165][169] According to the mode deriving from dispute, we find that undecidable dissension about the matter proposed has come about both in ordinary life and among philosophers. Because of this we are not able either to choose or to rule out anything, and we end up with suspension of judgement. [166] In the mode deriving from infinite regress, we say that what is brought forward as a source of conviction for the matter proposed itself needs another such source, which itself needs another, and so *ad infinitum*, so that we have no point from which to begin to establish anything, and suspension of judgement follows. [167] In the mode deriving from relativity, as we said above,[170] the existing object appears to be such-and-such relative to the subject judging and to the things observed together with it, but we suspend judgement on what it is like in its nature. [168] We have the mode from hypothesis when the Dogmatists, being thrown back *ad infinitum*, begin from something which they do not establish but claim to assume simply and without proof in virtue of a concession. [169] The reciprocal mode occurs when what ought to be confirmatory of the object under investigation needs to be made convincing by the object under investigation; then, being unable to take either in order to establish the other, we suspend judgement about both.

That every object of investigation can be referred to these modes we shall briefly show as follows.

[170] What is proposed is either an object of perception or an object of thought, and whichever it is it is subject to dispute. For according to some, only objects of perception are true, according to others, only objects of thought, and according to yet others, some objects of perception and some objects of thought are true. Now, will they say that the dispute is decidable or undecidable?[171] If undecidable, we have it[ac] that we must suspend judgement; for it is not possible to

---

[ac] Retaining ἔχομεν with the MSS and Latin translation: Mutschmann–Mau print λέγομεν.

[169] On I 165 see BARNES [1990c].
[170] See I 135–6, with ANNAS and BARNES [1985], pp. 142–3; BARNES [1992], pp. 4274–5.
[171] For this question compare II 19, 32.

make assertions about what is subject to undecidable dispute. But if decidable, we shall ask where the decision is to come from. [171] For instance, is an object of perception (for we shall rest the argument on this first) to be decided by an object of perception or by an object of thought? If by an object of perception, then since we are investigating objects of perception, this too will need something else to make it convincing; and if this further thing also is an object of perception, it too will again need something further to make it convincing, and so *ad infinitum*. [172] But if the object of perception needs to be decided by an object of thought, then, since objects of thought are also in dispute, it too, being an object of thought, will need to be judged and made convincing. Now where will it get its conviction from? If from an object of thought, the business will proceed *ad infinitum* in the same way; but if from an object of perception then, since an object of thought was adduced to make the object of perception convincing and an object of perception for the object of thought, we have brought in the reciprocal mode.

[173] If to avoid this our interlocutor claims to assume something by way of concession and without proof in order to prove what comes next, then the hypothetical mode is brought in, and there is no way out. For[172] if he is convincing when he makes his hypothesis, we will keep hypothesizing the opposite and will be no more unconvincing. and if he hypothesizes something true, he makes it suspect by taking it as a hypothesis rather than establishing it; while if it is false, the foundation of what he is trying to establish will be rotten. [174] Again, if hypothesizing something achieves anything towards making it convincing, why not hypothesize the object of investigation itself rather than something else through which he is supposed to establish the object about which he is arguing? If it is absurd to hypothesize the object under investigation, it will also be absurd to hypothesize what is superordinate to it.

[175] That all objects of perception are relative is clear: they are relative to those perceiving them. It is thus evident that whatever perceptible object is proposed to us may easily be referred to the Five Modes.

---

[172] With the following arguments compare *M* VIII 369–78; *M* III 6–17; see BARNES [1990d], pp. 99–112.

We make similar deductions about objects of thought. For if the dispute about them is said to be undecidable, they will have granted us that we must suspend judgement about them. [176] But if the dispute is to be decided, then if this comes by way of an object of thought, we will throw them back *ad infinitum*, while if by an object of perception, we will throw them back on the reciprocal mode. For the object of perception is itself subject to dispute, and, being unable to be decided through itself because of the infinite regress, it will require an object of thought in just the same way as the object of thought required an object of perception. [177] Anyone who, for these reasons, assumes something as an hypothesis will again turn out to be absurd. And objects of thought are relative too: they are called objects of thought relative to the thinker,[ad] and if they were by nature such as they are said to be there would have been no dispute about them.[173] Thus objects of thought too are referred to the Five Modes – and for that reason it is absolutely necessary for us to suspend judgement about the object proposed.

Such are the Five Modes which have been handed down by the more recent Sceptics. They put them forward not as rejecting the Ten Modes but in order to refute the rashness of the Dogmatists in a more varied way by using both sets together.

xvi What are the Two Modes?[174]

[178] They also offer two other modes of suspension of judgement. Since everything apprehended is thought to be apprehended either by means of itself or by means of something else, they are thought to introduce puzzlement about everything by suggesting that nothing is apprehended either by means of itself or by means of something else.

That nothing is apprehended by means of itself is, they say, clear from the dispute which has occurred among natural scientists over, I suppose, all objects of perception and of thought – a dispute which is undecidable, since we cannot use either an object of perception or an

---

[ad]   Retaining νοοῦντα with the MSS: Mutschmann–Mau, following the Latin translation, print νοῦν νοητά.

[173]   Cf. III 193, 222, 226; M VIII 322–4 (and see below, III 179, note).
[174]   On the Two Modes see BARNES [1990d], pp. 116–19; JANÁČEK [1970].

object of thought as a standard because anything we may take has been disputed and so is unconvincing.

[179] And[ae] for the following reason they do not concede either that anything can be apprehended by means of something else. If that by means of which something is apprehended will itself always need to be apprehended by means of something else, they throw you into the reciprocal or the infinite mode;[175] and if you should want to assume that that by means of which another thing is apprehended is itself apprehended by means of itself, then this is countered by the fact that, for the above reasons, nothing is apprehended by means of itself.

We are at a loss as to how what is in conflict[176] could be apprehended either from itself or from something else, since the standard of truth or of apprehension is not apparent, while signs – quite apart from proof – are overthrown, as we shall learn in what follows.[177]

This discussion of the modes of suspension of judgement will suffice for the present.

xvii What are the modes which overthrow those who offer causal explanations?[178]

[180] Just as we offer the modes of suspension of judgement, so some also set out modes in accordance with which we bring the Dogmatists to a halt by raising puzzles about their particular causal explanations – we do this because they pride themselves on these especially.[179] Aenesidemus, indeed, offers eight modes in accordance with which he thinks he can refute and assert to be unsound every dogmatic causal explanation.[180]

[ae] Placing a full stop rather than a comma after ... εἶναι ἄπιστον.

[175] See I 169, 166.
[176] I.e. (presumably) something over which there is conflict or dispute.
[177] See II 104–33.
[178] See BARNES [1990a], pp. 2656–68.
[179] See e.g. Democritus, frag. 118 Diels–Kranz; Strabo, II.3.8 (on Posidonius). But by and large the Hellenistic philosophers did *not* concern themselves greatly with causal explanations. For other sources of special dogmatic pride see II 194, 205; *M* VII 27.
[180] Cf. Photius, *bibl* 212, 170b17–22.

[181] The first of these, he says, is the mode in accordance with which causal explanations, which are all concerned with what is unclear, have no agreed confirmation from what is apparent. According to the second, some people often give an explanation in only one way, although there is a rich abundance enabling them to explain the object of investigation in a variety of ways. [182] According to the third, they assign causes which reveal no order to things which take place in an ordered way. According to the fourth, when they have grasped how apparent things take place, they deem that they have apprehended how non-apparent things take place. But perhaps[181] unclear things are brought about similarly to apparent things, perhaps not similarly but in a special way of their own. [183] According to the fifth, just about all of them give explanations according to their own hypotheses about the elements, not according to any common and agreed approaches. According to the sixth, they often adopt what is concordant with their own hypotheses but reject what runs counter to them, even when this has equal plausibility. [184] According to the seventh, they often assign causes which conflict not only with what is apparent but also with their own hypotheses. According to the eighth, often when what seems to be apparent is just as puzzling as what is being investigated, they rest their exposition about what is puzzling upon what is just as puzzling.

[185] He says that it is not impossible that some should fail in their causal explanations in virtue of certain mixed modes deriving from the ones I have just described.

Perhaps the five modes of suspension of judgement will also suffice against causal explanations. For the explanation which is offered will either be in agreement with all the philosophical schools as well as with Scepticism and what is apparent or it will not. No doubt it cannot be in agreement; for both what is apparent and what is unclear are all subject to dispute. [186] But if it is subject to dispute, we shall ask for an explanation of this explanation as well; and if he gives an apparent explanation of an apparent explanation or an unclear of an unclear, he will be thrown back *ad infinitum*, whereas if he gives his explanation crosswise he will fall into the reciprocal mode. If he takes

---

181 For the Pyrrhonian use of 'perhaps' see I 194–5.

a stand somewhere, then either he will say that the explanation holds so far as what he has said goes, and will introduce something relative, rejecting what is by nature, or else he will assume something as a hypothesis and be led to suspend judgement.

Thus it is no doubt possible to refute the rashness of the Dogmatists in their causal explanations through these modes too.

xviii The Sceptical phrases[182]

[187] When we use one of these modes or one of the modes of suspension of judgement, we utter certain phrases which manifest a sceptical disposition and our feelings – we say, for example, 'No more', 'Nothing should be determined', and so on. So it will be apposite to deal next with these. Let us begin with 'No more'.

xix The phrase 'No more'

[188][183] This phrase, then, we utter sometimes in the form I have given and sometimes in the form: 'In no way more'. It is not the case, as some suppose, that we use 'No more' in specific investigations and 'In no way more' in generic ones; rather, we utter 'No more' and 'In no way more' indifferently, and will here discuss them as a single phrase.

This phrase, then, is elliptical. Just as when we say 'A thoroughbred' we implicitly say 'A thoroughbred horse' and when we say 'An annual' we implicitly say 'An annual flower',[184] so when we say 'No more' we implicitly say 'No more this than that'.[af]

[189]Now some of the Sceptics use the phrase in the sense of the question 'How come this rather than that?'[ag] and they use 'How

---

[af] Omitting ἄνω κάτω: cf. I 83.

[ag] The text is uncertain. Most MSS read ἀντὶ πύσματος τοῦ τὸ τί μᾶλλον κτλ. This makes no sense. Various conjectures have been made. We read: ἀντὶ πύσματος τοῦ τί μᾶλλον κτλ.

[182] With this and the following chapters compare Diogenes Laertius IX, 74–6.
[183] With I 188–91 compare I 14–15. On 'no more' see DE LACY [1958].
[184] The Greek examples are διπλῆ for ἑστία διπλῆ (if the text may stand) ['a double' for 'a double hearth'] and πλατεῖα for πλατεῖα ὁδός ['a broad' for 'a broad street'].

come?' here to ask for an explanation, so as to say: 'Why this rather than that?'[185] It is normal to use questions for statements, e.g.:

What mortal does not know the wife of Zeus?[186]

and statements for questions, e.g. 'I'm inquiring where Dio lives' and:

I'm asking why one should admire a poet.[187]

Again, 'How come?' is used in the sense of 'Why?' by Menander:

How come I have been abandoned?[188]

[190] 'No more this than that' makes clear our feelings: because of the equipollence of the opposed objects we end in equilibrium. (By 'equipollence' we mean equality in what appears plausible to us; by 'opposed' we mean in general conflicting;[189] and by 'equilibrium' we mean assent to neither side.) [191] Thus,[ah] although the phrase 'In no way more' exhibits the distinctive character of assent or denial, we do not use it in this way: we use it indifferently and in a loose sense, either for a question or for 'I do not know which of these things I should assent to and which not assent to',[ai][190] Our intention is to make clear what is apparent to us, and as to what phrase we use to make this clear we are indifferent.[191] Note too that when we utter the phrase 'In no way more' we are not affirming that it is itself certainly true and firm: here too we are only saying how things appear to us.[192]

xx Non-assertion

[192] About non-assertion we have this to say. 'Assertion' is used in two senses, one general and one specific. In the general sense it is a

---

[ah] Retaining οὖν with the MSS (γοῦν is printed by Mutschmann–Mau after earlier editors).

[ai] Retaining συγκατατίθεσθαι, with the Greek MSS: Mutschmann–Mau, following the Latin translation, omit the word.

[185] In Greek the word τί (which we render by 'How come?') may be used to mean either 'What?' or 'Why?'

[186] Euripides, *Hercules Furens* 1.

[187] Aristophanes, *Frogs* 1008.

[188] frag 900 Kock.

[189] Cf. 1 10.

[190] Cf. 1 213; *M* 1 315.

[191] Cf. 1 195, 207.

[192] Cf. 1 4.

phrase meaning the positing or denying of something – e.g. 'It is day', 'It is not day'. In the specific sense it means only the positing of something (in this sense negations are not called assertions). Now non-assertion is refraining from assertion in the general sense (which we say covers both affirmation and negation), so that non-assertion is the feeling we have because of which we say that we neither posit nor reject anything.[193]

[193] Hence it is clear that we do not use 'non-assertion' to mean that objects are in their nature such as to move us necessarily to non-assertion, but rather to make it clear that now, when we utter it, we feel in this way with regard to these matters under investigation. Remember too that we say we neither posit nor reject anything which is said dogmatically about what is unclear; for we do yield to things which passively move us and lead us necessarily to assent.[194]

xxi 'Perhaps', 'Maybe' and 'Possibly'

[194] We take 'Perhaps' and 'Perhaps not' in the sense of 'Perhaps it is and perhaps it is not'; 'Maybe' and 'Maybe not' for 'Maybe it is and maybe it is not'; 'Possibly' and 'Possibly not' for 'Possibly it is and possibly it is not'. (Thus for the sake of brevity we take 'Maybe not' in the sense of 'Maybe it is not', 'Possibly not' for 'Possibly it is not' and 'Perhaps not' for 'Perhaps it is not'.[195]) [195] Here again we do not fight about phrases, nor do we investigate whether the phrases make these things clear by nature, but (as I have said) we use them indifferently.[196] Now it is, I think, clear that these phrases are indicative of non-assertion. For instance, someone who says 'Perhaps it is' implicitly posits what is thought to conflict with it, namely 'Perhaps it is not', insofar as he does not make an affirmation about its being so. Similarly with the other phrases too.

---

[193] Cf. I 10.

[194] Cf. I 13, note.

[195] 'We use μὴ ἐξεῖναι for ἐξεῖναι μὴ εἶναι'. In Greek οὐκ ἔξεστι would normally be taken to mean 'It is not possible that ...' rather than 'It is possible that not ...': Sextus is excusing the ambiguity of his formulae (which does not appear in the English) by urging the advantage of brevity.

[196] Cf. I 191.

xxii 'I suspend judgement'

[196] We use 'I suspend judgement' for 'I cannot say which of the things proposed I should find convincing and which I should not find convincing', making clear that objects appear to us equal in respect of convincingness and lack of convincingness. Whether they are equal, we do not affirm: we say what appears to us about them, when they make an impression on us. Suspension of judgement gets its name from the fact that the intellect is suspended[197] so as neither to posit nor to reject anything because of the equipollence of the matters being investigated.[198]

xxiii 'I determine nothing'

[197] About 'I determine nothing' we have this to say. Determining we deem to be not merely saying something but making an utterance about an unclear object and assenting to it. For in this sense Sceptics will perhaps be found to determine nothing – not even 'I determine nothing' itself.[199] For this is not a dogmatic supposition (i.e. assent to something unclear) but a phrase which shows our feeling. Thus when Sceptics say 'I determine nothing', what they say is this: 'I now feel in such a way as neither to posit dogmatically nor to reject any of the things falling under this investigation'. When they say this they are saying what is apparent to them about the subject proposed – not dogmatically making a confident assertion, but describing and reporting how they feel.[aj]

xxiv 'Everything is undetermined'

[198] Indeterminacy is an intellectual feeling in virtue of which we neither deny nor posit anything investigated in dogmatic fashion, i.e. anything unclear. Thus when a Sceptic says 'Everything is undeter-

aj Reading οὐ δογματικῶς ..., ἀλλ' ἀπαγγελτικῶς ὅ (Heintz): the Greek MSS have οὐκ ἀπαγγελτικῶς ..., ἀλλ' ὅ; Mutschmann–Mau follow the Latin translation and print ἀπαγγελτικῶς, οὐ δογματικῶς ..., ἀλλ' ὅ.

197 ἐποχή, 'suspension of judgement', comes from ἐπέχειν 'to hold back', 'to check' (used of e.g. holding your breath, suspending payment).
198 Cf. I 10.
199 Cf. Diogenes Laertius IX 74, 104; Photius, bibl 212, 170a12 (Aenesidemus).

mined', he takes 'is' in the sense of 'appears to me';[200] by 'everything' he means not whatever exists but those unclear matters investigated by the Dogmatists which he has considered; and by 'undetermined' he means that they do not exceed what is opposed to – or, in general, conflicts with[201] – them in convincingness or lack of convincingness. [199] And just as someone who says 'Go away' implicitly says 'You, go away',[202] so someone who says 'Everything is undetermined' also signifies according to us[ak] 'relatively to me' or 'as it appears to me'. Hence what is said is this: 'Those of the matters investigated by the Dogmatists which I have considered appear such to me that none of them seems to me to exceed in convincingness or lack of convincingness what conflicts with it.'

xxv 'Everything is inapprehensible'

[200] Our attitude is similar when we say 'Everything is inapprehensible': we explain 'everything' in the same way, and we supply 'to me'. Thus what is said is this: 'All of the unclear matters investigated in dogmatic fashion which I have inspected appear to me inapprehensible.' This is not to make an affirmation that the matters investigated by the Dogmatists are of such a nature as to be inapprehensible; rather, it is to report our feeling 'in virtue of which', we say, 'I suppose that up to now I have not apprehended any of these things because of the equipollence of their opposites.' Hence everything brought forward to turn us about seems to me to be at variance with what we profess.[al] [203]

[ak] Reading συσσημαίνει καθ᾽ ἡμᾶς τὸ ὡς πρὸς ἐμέ κτλ. Mutschmann prefers ἤ (after T) to τό, and he then takes καθ᾽ ἡμᾶς as the first of three disjunctive objects of the verb. The textual reading makes little difference; but Mutschmann's construe of καθ᾽ ἡμᾶς is surely wrong.

[al] Reading ἐπαγγελλομένων (Heintz) for ἀπαγγελλομένων (mss, Mutschmann–Mau).

[200] Cf. I 135.
[201] Cf. I 10.
[202] Sextus' example is περιπατῶ and ἐγὼ περιπατῶ, '(I) go for a walk': in Greek, the verbal ending indicates the person, and the pronoun is only used for emphasis.
[203] For complaints of being misunderstood see I 19. Here the point is not clear. If 'turn about' is being used in its technical sense (see I 122, note), then perhaps Sextus means this: 'When we say that we do not hold beliefs, the Dogmatists think that they can show our view to be self-refuting – for are we not thereby indicating that *we believe* that we have no beliefs? But there is no turn about: our remarks do not state beliefs but merely manifest feelings.'

xxvi 'I have no apprehension' and 'I do not apprehend'

[201] The phrases 'I have no apprehension' and 'I do not apprehend' also show the Sceptic's own feeling, in virtue of which he refrains, for the moment, from positing or rejecting any of the unclear matters being investigated. This is clear from what we have said above about the other phrases.

xxvii 'Opposed to every account there is an equal account'[204]

[202] When we say 'Opposed to every account there is an equal account', we mean by 'every' every one we have inspected; we speak not of accounts in an unqualified sense but of those which purport to establish something in dogmatic fashion (i.e. about something unclear) – which purport to establish it in any way, and not necessarily by way of assumptions and consequence;[205] we say 'equal' with reference to convincingness and lack of convincingness;[206] we take 'opposed' in the sense of 'conflicting' in general;[207] and we supply 'as it appears to me'. [203] Thus when I say 'Opposed to every account there is an equal account', I am implicitly saying this: 'To every account I have scrutinized[am] which purports to establish something in dogmatic fashion, there appears to me to be opposed another account, purporting to establish something in dogmatic fashion, equal to it in convincingness or lack of convincingness'. Thus the utterance of this remark is not dogmatic but a report of a human feeling which is apparent to the person who feels it.

[204] Some utter the phrase in the form 'There is to be opposed to every account an equal account', making the following exhortatory

---

[am] Reading ἐξητασμένῳ (Heintz): Mutschmann–Mau print ζητουμένῳ after earlier editors; the MSS have ἐζητημένῳ or ἐζητουμένῳ or ἐξητουμένῳ.

[204] Cf. I 12.

[205] The word λόγος sometimes means 'argument': by alluding to the Stoic definition of an argument (see II 135), Sextus indicates that here he is taking the word λόγος in a more general sense – for any consideration in favour of a dogmatic claim you can find an equally convincing consideration in favour of something conflicting with it.

[206] Cf. I 10.

[207] Cf. I 10.

request: 'To every account purporting to establish something in dogmatic fashion let us oppose an account which investigates in dogmatic fashion, equal in convincingness or lack of convincingness and conflicting with it.' For they mean what they say to be directed to the Sceptics, though they use the infinitive 'to be opposed' for the imperative 'let us oppose'.[208] [205] They make this exhortation to the Sceptics to prevent them from being seduced by the Dogmatists into abandoning their investigation[an] and thus through rashness missing the tranquillity apparent to them, which (as we suggested above[209]) they deem to supervene on suspension of judgement about everything.

xxviii Rules for the sceptical phrases

[206] Those will be enough of the phrases to deal with in an outline,[210] especially since it is possible to discuss the rest on the basis of what we have said here.

In the case of all the sceptical phrases, you should understand that we do not affirm definitely that they are true – after all, we say that they can be destroyed by themselves, being cancelled along with what they are applied to, just as purgative drugs do not merely drain the humours from the body but drive themselves out too along with the humours.[211]

[207] We say too that we do not use the phrases strictly, making clear the objects to which they are applied, but indifferently and, if you like, in a loose sense – for it is unbecoming for a Sceptic to fight over phrases,[212] especially as it works to our advantage that not even these phrases are said to signify anything purely but only relatively, i.e. relatively to the Sceptics.[213]

[an] Excising περὶ αὐτοῦ (MSS) – Heintz proposes περὶ αὐτούς, but this is little better.

[208] In the Greek 'There is to be opposed' is represented simply by the infinitive, ἀντικεῖσθαι.

[209] I 25–9.

[210] Cf. I 4, note.

[211] Cf. I 14–15, and – for the metaphor – II 188; *M* VIII 480; Diogenes Laertius IX 76; Aristocles, apud Eusebius, *PE* XIV xviii 21.

[212] Cf. I 191.

[213] Cf. I 122.

[208] Besides, you must remember that we do not use these phrases about all objects universally, but about what is unclear and investigated in dogmatic fashion, and that we say what is apparent to us and do not make firm assertions about the nature of externally existing things.

For these reasons, every sophism brought against a sceptical phrase can, I think, be overthrown.[214]

[209][215] We have now examined the concept of scepticism, its parts, its standard, its aim, and also the modes of suspension of judgement, and we have spoken about the sceptical phrases. Thus we have exhibited the distinctive character of Scepticism. It is thus apposite, we think, to consider briefly the distinction between it and its neighbouring philosophies, in order that we may understand more clearly the suspensive persuasion. Let us begin with the philosophy of Heraclitus.

xxix That the Sceptical persuasion differs from the philosophy of Heraclitus

[210] That it differs from our own persuasion is clear: Heraclitus makes dogmatic assertions on many unclear matters, while we, as I have said,[216] do not. But Aenesidemus and his followers used to say that the Sceptical persuasion is a path to the philosophy of Heraclitus, because the idea that contraries appear to hold of the same thing leads to the idea that contraries actually do hold of the same thing; and while the Sceptics say that contraries appear to hold of the same thing, the Heracliteans go on from there to the idea that they actually do hold.[217]

Against this we say that the idea that contraries appear to hold of the same thing is not a belief of the Sceptics but a fact which makes an impression not only on Sceptics but on other philosophers too – and indeed on everyone. [211] For example, no-one would venture to say

---

[214] Cf. I 19, 200.
[215] Cf. I 5.
[216] See I 208.
[217] For the 'Unity of Opposites' in Heraclitus cf. II 63; texts in BARNES [1987], pp. 102–4, 114–17.

that honey does not affect healthy people sweetly or sufferers from jaundice bitterly.[218] Thus the Heracliteans start from a preconception common to all men – just as we do and no doubt the other philosophies too. Now, had it been from something said in Sceptical fashion (such as 'Everything is inapprehensible' or 'I determine nothing' or the like[219]) that they took the idea that contraries hold of the same thing, then perhaps they would have proved their point; but since they start from items which impress themselves not only on *us* but also on other philosophers – and on ordinary life too – why should anyone say that our persuasion rather than any of the other philosophies – or indeed ordinary life – is a path to the philosophy of Heraclitus? We all make use of common material

[212] Perhaps the Sceptical persuasion not only does not work in favour of recognition of the philosophy of Heraclitus but actually works against it. For Sceptics decry all the beliefs advanced by Heraclitus as rash assertions: they oppose the conflagration,[220] they oppose the idea that contraries hold of the same thing, and in the case of every Heraclitean belief they disparage its dogmatic rashness and (as I said before) repeat their refrains: 'I do not apprehend', 'I determine nothing'. All this is in conflict with the Heracliteans; but it is absurd to call a conflicting persuasion a path to the school it conflicts with: therefore it is absurd to call the Sceptical persuasion a path to the philosophy of Heraclitus.

xxx How does the Sceptical persuasion differ from the philosophy of Democritus?

[213] The philosophy of Democritus is also said to have something in common with Scepticism,[221] since it is thought to make use of the same materials as we do. For from the fact that honey appears sweet to some and bitter to others, they say that Democritus deduces that it

---

[218] Cf. II 51 (and I 20; *M* VIII 53–4).

[219] See I 200, 197.

[220] ἐκπύρωσις, or the theory that the world is periodically consumed by fire, was regularly (and perhaps wrongly) ascribed to Heraclitus.

[221] Cf. Diogenes Laertius IX 72, which ascribes this view to the Sceptics themselves; Numenius, apud Eusebius, *PE* XIV vi 4. For the 'sceptical' fragments of Democritus see BARNES [1987], pp. 251–7.

is neither sweet nor bitter,[222] and for this reason utters the phrase 'No more', which is Sceptical.

But the Sceptics and the Democriteans use the phrase 'No more' in different senses. The latter assign it the sense that neither is the case, we the sense that we do not know whether some apparent thing is both or neither.[223] [214] Hence even in this respect we differ. But the clearest distinction is made when Democritus says 'In verity[224] there are atoms and void.'[225] For by 'In verity' he means 'In truth' – and I think it is superfluous to remark that he differs from us in saying that atoms and void in truth subsist, even if he does begin from the anomaly in what is apparent.

xxxi How does Scepticism differ from Cyrenaicism?

[215] Some say that the Cyrenaic persuasion is the same as Scepticism, since it too says that we only apprehend[ao] feelings.[226] But it differs from Scepticism since it states that the aim is pleasure and a smooth motion of the flesh,[227] while we say that it is tranquillity, which is contrary to the aim they propose – for whether pleasure is present or absent, anyone who affirms that pleasure is the aim submits to troubles, as we argued in the chapter on 'The Aim'.[228] Further, we suspend judgement (as far as the argument goes) about external existing things, while the Cyrenaics assert that they have an inapprehensible nature.[229]

---

ao Retaining καταλαμβάνειν (MSS and the Latin translation): Mutschmann–Mau print καταλαμβάνεσθαι (Pohlenz).

222 Cf. II 63 (and I 101). But Democritus' views were notoriously hard to interpret: see Plutarch, *adv Col* 1108E–1111F.
223 Cf. I 191.
224 ἐτεῆ, a somewhat archaic word.
225 frag. 9 Diels–Kranz; cf *M* VII 135.
226 Cf. *M* VII 190–8. The testimonia to the Cyrenaics are collected in GIANNANTONI [1990]; on Cyrenaic epistemology see TSOUNA MCKIRAHAN [1992].
227 See *M* VII 199–200.
228 Cf. I 25–30.
229 Cf. I 3.

xxxii How does Scepticism differ from the Protagorean persuasion?

[216] Protagoras has it that human beings are measure of all things, of those that are that they are, and of those that are not that they are not.[230] By 'measure' he means the standard, and by 'things' objects; so he is implicitly saying that human beings are the standard for all objects, of those that are that they are and of those that are not that they are not. For this reason he posits only what is apparent to each person, and thus introduces relativity. [217] Hence he is thought to have something in common with the Pyrrhonists.[231]

But he differs from them, and we shall see the difference when we have adequately explained what Protagoras thinks.[232]

He says that matter is in a state of flux, and that as it flows additions continually replace the effluxes;[233] and that our senses are rearranged and altered depending on age and on the other constitutions of the body. [218] He also says that the reasons[234] for all apparent things are present in matter, so that the matter can, as far as it itself is concerned, be all the things it appears to anyone to be. Men grasp different things at different times, depending on their different conditions: someone in a natural state apprehends those things in the matter which can appear to those in a natural state, someone in an unnatural state apprehends what can appear to those in an unnatural state. [219] And further, depending on age, and according to whether we are sleeping or waking, and in virtue of each sort of condition, the same account holds.[235] According to him, then, man is the standard for what is; for all things that are apparent to men actually are, and what is apparent to nobody is not.

We see, then, that he holds beliefs about matter being in flux and

---

[230] Cf. *M* VII 60 = frag. 1 Diels–Kranz, from the opening of his book Καταβάλλοντες or Overthrowers.

[231] See BARNES [1988b].

[232] With the following account of Protagoreanism compare *M* VII 60–4; see DECLEVA CAIZZI [1988].

[233] Cf. III 82.

[234] 'Reasons' translates λόγοι: the general sense of the view ascribed (no doubt falsely) to Protagoras is clear, but the precise sense of λόγοι is obscure.

[235] Cf. I 100, the fourth of the Ten Modes.

about the presence in it of the reasons for all apparent things. But these things are unclear and we suspend judgement about them.

xxxiii How does Scepticism differ from the Academic philosophy?

[220] Some say that the philosophy of the Academy is the same as Scepticism; so it will be apposite for us to deal with that too.[236]

There have been, so most people say, three Academies: one – the oldest – was Plato's; a second was the Middle Academy of Arcesilaus, Polemo's pupil; and the third was the New Academy of Carneades and Clitomachus. Some add a fourth, the Academy of Philo and Charmidas, and some reckon as a fifth the Academy of Antiochus.[237] [221] Beginning with the Old Academy, then, let us see the difference between us and these philosophies.[238]

As for Plato,[239] some have said that he is dogmatic, others aporetic, others partly aporetic and partly dogmatic (for in the gymnastic works,[240] where Socrates is introduced either as playing with people or as contesting with sophists, they say that his distinctive character is gymnastic and aporetic; but that he is dogmatic where he makes assertions seriously through Socrates or Timaeus or someone similar).

[222] It would be superfluous to say anything here about those who say that Plato is dogmatic, or partly dogmatic and partly aporetic; for they themselves agree on his difference from us. As to whether he is purely sceptical, we deal with this at some length in our *Comment-*

---

236 The relationship between Academics and Pyrrhonians was discussed by Aenesidemus (see Photius, *bibl* 212, 169b18–170b3) and became a standard topic of debate. On the issue see STRIKER [1981]; ANNAS [1988].

237 On the problems raised by this doxographical account (repeated by Eusebius, *PE* XIV iv 12–16, and [Galen] *hist phil* 3 (= XIX 230 K (cf. 2, XIX 226–7 K))) see GLUCKER [1978], pp. 344–56.

238 The testimonia to the Middle and New Academies are collected by METTE [1984], [1985].

239 On Plato the sceptic see ANNAS and BARNES [1985], pp. 13–14; WOODRUFF [1986]; ANNAS [1988], [1992b].

240 I.e. the works allegedly written as training manuals for budding philosophers: the ancient categorizations of Plato's dialogues classified several dialogues – among them *Meno* and *Theaetetus* – as 'gymnastic' in this sense (see e.g. Diogenes Laertius III 49).

aries.[241] Here, in an outline,[242] we say,[ap] in opposition to Meno-dotus[aq] and Aenesidemus (who were the main proponents of this position), that when Plato makes assertions about Forms or about the existence of Providence or about a virtuous life being preferable to a life of vice, then if he assents to these things as being really so, he is holding beliefs; and if he commits himself to them as being more plausible, he has abandoned the distinctive character of Scepticism, since he is giving something preference in point of convincingness and lack of convincingness – and that even this is foreign to us is clear from what I have already said.[243] [223] Even if he does make some utterances in sceptical fashion when, as they say, he is exercising, this will not make him a Sceptic. For anyone who holds beliefs on even one subject, or in general prefers one appearance to another in point of convincingness or lack of convincingness, or makes assertions about any unclear matter, thereby has the distinctive character of a Dogmatist.

Timon makes this clear in what he says about Xenophanes. [224] For although he praised him in many passages, even dedicating his *Lampoons* to him, he represented him lamenting and saying:

> If only I had had a share of shrewd thought
>> and looked in both directions! But I was deceived by the treacherous
>> path,
> being a man of the past and having no care for any
> inquiry. For wherever I turned my thought,

[ap] Reading λέγομεν (after the Latin translation): Mutschmann–Mau print διαλεξόμεθα (Nebe); the Greek mss have διαλαμβάνομεν.

[aq] At this notorious textual crux we do not disagree with the text of Mutsch-mann–Mau.

[241] Elsewhere Sextus refers to his *Sceptical Commentaries* (*M* I 29, probably referring to *M* VIII, as the parallel at *M* XI 232 indicates; II 106, probably referring to *M* VIII; and VII 52); at *M* VII 446 and VIII 1 he uses the word 'commentary' to refer to *M* VII; at *M* III 116 the 'commentaries against the natural scientists' are perhaps *M* IX. All this makes it likely that the *Commentaries* to which Sextus here refers are the work of which *M* VII–XI is the surviving torso (see above, p. xii). – The reference to the commentaries on the soul at *M* VI 55 is puzzling: there is no obvious text in *M* VII–XI. The *Empirical Commentaries* (*M* I 61) and the *Medical Commentaries* (*M* VII 202) are no doubt distinct from the *Sceptical Commentaries*.

[242] See I 4, note.

[243] See e.g. I 10.

everything resolved into one and the same; and everything, existing always,

was drawn back all about and came to a stand in one homogeneous nature.[244]

Hence he calls him half-conceited – not perfectly unconceited – when he says:

Half-conceited Xenophanes, mocker of Homeric deceit,
who feigned an inhuman god,[ar] equal all about,
unmoving, unharmed, more thought-like than thought.[245]

He calls him 'half-conceited' as being partly unconceited, and 'mocker of Homeric deceit' because he disparaged the deceit in Homer. [225] Xenophanes held as beliefs, contrary to the preconceptions of other men, that everything is one, that god is united with everything, and that he is spherical, impassive, unchanging and rational.[246] Hence it is easy to display the difference between Xenophanes and us.[247]

Thus it is clear from what we have said that even if Plato is aporetic about some things, he is not a Sceptic; for in some matters he appears to make assertions about the reality of unclear objects or to give certain unclear items preference in point of convincingness.

[226][248] The members of the New Academy, if they say that everything is inapprehensible, no doubt differ from the Sceptics precisely in saying that everything is inapprehensible. For they make affirmations about this, while the Sceptic expects it to be possible for some things actually to be apprehended.[249] And they differ from us clearly in their judgements of good and bad. For the Academics say that things are good and bad not in the way we do, but with the conviction that it is plausible that what they call good rather than its

---

ar   Reading ὅς (Roeper): the MSS have ἔα; Mutschmann–Mau print εἰ (Diels). And retaining the MS readıng ἀπάνθρωπον: Mutschmann–Mau print ἀπ' ἀνθρώπων (Fabricius).

244 Timon, frag. 833 Lloyd–Jones–Parsons.
245 frag. 834 Lloyd–Jones–Parsons (see below, III 218).
246 This reflects the account of Xenophanes' theology found in e.g. [Aristotle], *On Melissus, Xenophanes, Gorgias* 977a14–b20.
247 For Xenophanes as a Sceptic see *M* VII 49–52 (cf. VIII 325–6; Diogenes Laertius IX 72); for the dispute over how to interpret his epistemological position see *M* VII 110.
248 With the account of the New Academy in I 226–8 compare *M* VII 159–89.
249 Cf. I 3.

contrary really is good (and similarly with bad), whereas we do not call anything good or bad with the thought that what we say is plausible – rather, without holding opinions we follow ordinary life in order not to be inactive.[250]

[227] Further, we say that appearances are equal in convincingness or lack of convincingness (as far as the argument goes), while they say that some are plausible and others implausible.[251] Even among the plausible ones they say there are differences: some, they think, really are just plausible, others plausible and inspected, others plausible and scrutinized and undistractable. For example, suppose a coil of rope is lying in a certain way in a dark room. When someone comes in suddenly, he receives a merely plausible appearance from it as if from a snake. [228] But to someone who has looked round carefully and inspected its features (e.g. it does not move, it has a certain colour, and so on) it appears as a rope, in virtue of an appearance which is plausible and scrutinized. Appearances which are in addition un-distractable are like this: Heracles is said to have brought Alcestis, who had died, back from Hades and to have shown her to Admetus. He received an appearance of Alcestis which was plausible and inspected; but since he knew that she had died, his intellect was distracted from assent and inclined to lack of conviction.[as][252] [229] The members of the New Academy, then, prefer plausible and scrutinized appearances to those which are merely plausible and to both they prefer appearances which are plausible and scrutinized and undistractable.

Even if both Academics and Sceptics say that they go along with certain things, the difference even here between the two philosophies

---

[as] Mutschmann–Mau mark a lacuna here; but see n. 252.

[250] Cf. I 23.

[251] On 'plausibility' in the New Academy see BETT [1989].

[252] The appearance of Alcestis is not undistractable but, on the contrary, distracted. The example reappears at *M* VII 254–6 as a case of a *non*-plausible appearance; there it is coupled with the appearance of Helen to Menelaus – and this, implausible, appearance occurs at *M* VII 180–1 in the explanation of what an *un*distractable appearance is. Thus both in *PH* and in *M* Sextus explains undistractableness by adducing a case of distraction. The procedure is in itself unimpeachable (but it must be admitted that Sextus hardly makes it clear that he is following the procedure); and the text need not be altered. For problems with the examples see ANNAS [1990].

is clear. [230] For 'go along with' is used in different senses.[253] It means not resisting but simply following without strong inclination or adherence (as a boy is said to go along with his chaperon); and it sometimes means assenting to something by choice and, as it were, sympathy (as a dissolute man goes along with someone who urges extravagant living). Hence, since Carneades and Clitomachus say that they go along with things and that some things are plausible in the sense of having a strong wish[at] with a strong inclination, whereas we say so in the sense of simply yielding without adherence, in this respect too we differ from them.

[231] We also differ from the New Academy with regard to what leads to the aim. For those who profess to belong to the Academy make use of the plausible in their lives, while we follow laws and customs and natural feelings, and so live without holding opinions.[254]

We would say more about the distinction were we not aiming at brevity.[255]

[232] Arcesilaus, who we said was champion and founder of the Middle Academy, certainly seems to me to have something in common with what the Pyrrhonists say – indeed, his persuasion and ours are virtually the same.[256] For he is not found making assertions about the reality or unreality of anything, nor does he prefer one thing to another in point of convincingness or lack of convincingness, but he suspends judgement about everything. And he says that the aim is suspension of judgement, which, we said, is accompanied by tranquillity.[257] [233] He also says that particular suspensions of judgement are good and particular assents bad.

Yet someone might say that we say these things in accordance with

---

[at] Following Heintz, we transpose the words κατὰ τὸ σφόδρα βούλεσθαι to follow Κλειτόμαχον.

[253] 'Go along with' translates the verb πείθεσθαι: πείθεσθαι + dative means either (i) 'obey' or (ii) 'believe'. According to Sextus, the Academics go along with things in sense (ii), whereas the Sceptics only go along with things in sense (i). Sextus here alludes to the fact that the Sceptic will 'yield' or 'assent' to items forced upon us: see I 13.

[254] See I 23–4.

[255] See I 163.

[256] On the scepticism of Arcesilaus see e.g. MACONI [1988].

[257] See I 10; and note I 30 for the remark that some *Sceptics* say that the aim is suspension of judgement.

what is apparent to us, not affirmatively, whereas he says them with reference to the nature of things – so he says that suspension of judgement is a good thing and assent a bad thing. [234] And if one is to be convinced by what is said about him, they say that he appeared superficially to be a Pyrrhonist but in truth was a Dogmatist. Because he used to test his companions by his aporetic skill, to see if they were gifted enough to receive Platonic beliefs, he seemed to be aporetic; but to the gifted among his companions he would entrust[au] Plato's views.[258] Hence Aristo called him

> Plato in front, Pyrrho behind, Diodorus in the middle

because he made use of dialectic in Diodorus' fashion but was an out-and-out Platonist.

[235][259] Philo and his followers say that as far as the Stoic standard (i.e. apprehensive appearance) is concerned objects are inapprehensible, but as far as the nature of the objects themselves is concerned they are apprehensible.[260] And Antiochus brought the Stoa into the Academy, so that it was said of him that he did Stoic philosophy in the Academy; for he tried to show that Stoic beliefs are present in Plato. So the difference between the sceptical persuasion and what are called the Fourth and Fifth Academies is quite clear.

xxxiv Is Medical Empiricism the same as Scepticism?

[236] Some say that the Sceptical philosophy is the same as the Empiric school in medicine. But you must realize that if this form of Empiricism makes affirmations about the inapprehensibility of unclear matters, then it is not the same as Scepticism, nor would it be appropriate for Sceptics to take up with that school.[261]

---

au Reading παρεγχειρίζειν (Bekker) for παρεγχειρεῖν (MSS, Mutschmann–Mau).

258 Cf. e.g. Cicero, *Luc* 60; Anonymus, *in Theaet* liv 14; Numenius, apud Eusebius, *PE* XIV vi 6; Augustine, *Against the Academics* III 38 (see GLUCKER [1978], pp. 296–306).

259 On the accounts of Philo and Antiochus given here see TARRANT [1985]; BARNES [1989].

260 See Cicero, *Luc* 34; Photius, *bibl* 212, 170a22 (Aenesidemus).

261 On Medical Empiricism see e.g. EDELSTEIN [1964]; FREDE [1985], [1988]. Sextus himself was a doctor (texts in DEICHGRÄBER [1965], pp. 216–18) and an Empiric: see [Galen], *Introduction* XIV 683 K (other texts in DEICHGRÄBER

They might rather adopt, as it seems to me, what is called the Method;[262] [237] for this alone of the medical schools seems to practise no rashness in unclear matters and does not presume to say whether they are apprehensible or inapprehensible, but it follows what is apparent, taking thence, in line with Sceptical practice, what seems to be expedient.

We said above[263] that ordinary life, which the Sceptics too participate in, is fourfold, consisting in guidance by nature, necessitation by feelings, handing down of laws and customs, and teaching of kinds of expertise. [238] By the necessitation of feelings Sceptics are conducted by thirst to drink, by hunger to food, and so on. In the same way Methodic doctors are conducted by feelings to what corresponds to them: by contraction to dilatation (as when someone seeks refuge in heat from the compression due to intense cold[264]) and by flux to checking[265] (as when those in the baths who are dripping with sweat and relaxed come to check it and so seek refuge in the cold air). And it is clear that things foreign to nature force us to proceed to remove them: even a dog will remove a thorn which has got stuck in his paw.[266] [239] And – not to overstep the outline character of my essay[267] by discussing each case – I think that everything which the Methodics say in this vein can be brought under the necessitation of feelings, either natural or unnatural.

Furthermore, lack of opinion and indifference in the use of words is common to the two persuasions. [240] Just as Sceptics, without holding opinions, use the phrases 'I determine nothing' and 'I do not apprehend anything' (as we have said),[268] so the Methodics talk about 'common features' and 'pervading' and the rest in a straightforward way; and similarly they take the word 'indication', without holding any opinions, in the sense of being conducted from apparent

---

[1965], pp. 40–1) – hence his modern name. How, then, are we to explain I 236?

262 On Medical Methodism see e.g. FREDE [1982].

263 I 23–4.

264 Cf. II 239.

265 The word is ἐποχή, which normally means 'suspension of judgement': a pun.

266 Cf. I 70.

267 See I 4, note.

268 See I 197, 201.

feelings, both natural and unnatural, to what seems to correspond to them (as I suggested for thirst and hunger and so on).[269]

[241] Hence, judging by these and similar points, we should say that the medical persuasion of the Methodics has some affinity with Scepticism – not absolutely but more so than the other medical schools and in comparison with them.[av]

So much for what seem to be neighbours of the Sceptical persuasion. Here we bring to a close both the general account of Scepticism and the first Book of our *Outlines*.[270]

[av] Punctuating with Bury, i.e. omitting the brackets in Mutschmann–Mau.

[269] With Methodic 'indications' compare the Dogmatic notion of an indicative sign: below, II 101.

[270] See I 4, note.

BOOK II

These are the Contents of the Second Book of the *Outlines of Scepticism*:

i Can Sceptics investigate what the Dogmatists talk about?

[1] Since we have reached[a] our investigation of Dogmatism, let us inspect, concisely and in outline,[1] each of the parts of what they call philosophy, having first answered those who persistently allege that Sceptics can neither investigate nor, more generally, think about the items on which they hold beliefs.[2]

[2] They say that Sceptics either apprehend what the Dogmatists talk about or do not apprehend it. If they apprehend it, how can they be puzzled about what they say they apprehend? If they do not apprehend it, they do not even know how to talk about what they have not apprehended.[3] [3] For just as someone who does not know what, for example, the removal argument[4] or the theorem in two complexes[5] is cannot even say anything about them, so someone who does not recognize any of the items the Dogmatists talk about cannot conduct an investigation in opposition to them about things which he does not know. In neither case, therefore, can Sceptics investigate what the Dogmatists talk about.

[4] Now those who put this argument forward must tell us how they are here using the word 'apprehend' – does it mean simply 'think of', without any further affirmation of the reality of the things about which we are making our statements? Or does it also include[b] a positing of the reality of the things we are discussing?

If they say that 'apprehend' in their argument means 'assent to an

---

[a] Reading ἐπεὶ δ᾽ ⟨ἐπὶ⟩ . . .
[b] Omitting νοεῖν with Heintz: Mutschmann–Mau print μετὰ τοῦ νοεῖν; the MSS offer τὸ νοεῖν μετὰ τοῦ.

[1] See I 4, note.
[2] The persistent allegation is not referred to elsewhere. Its ultimate origin lies in Plato (*Meno* 80DE – cf. Aristotle, *Posterior Analytics* A 1, 71a29).
[3] Compare the parallel argument ascribed to the Epicureans at *M* VIII 337 (and see below, III 268).
[4] τὸ καθ᾽ ὃ περιαιρουμένου: Sextus alludes to some technical notion (perhaps, like the second example, a notion drawn from Stoic logical theory). We do not catch the allusion, either because the text is corrupt (as the Latin tradition suggests) or simply because no other occurrence of the phrase has survived.
[5] 'Complex' [τροπικόν] is a term of art from Stoic logic, where it designates a compound proposition (cf. II 202; *M* VIII 440–2; Galen, *inst log* vii 1). The 'theorem in two complexes' is the argument-schema: 'If P, then Q; if P, then not-Q: therefore not-P' (see Origen, *c Cels* VII xv).

apprehensive appearance'[6] (an apprehensive appearance comes from something real, is imprinted and stamped in accordance with the real object itself, and is such as would not come from anything unreal[7]), then they themselves will perhaps be unwilling to allow that they cannot investigate things which they have not apprehended in this way. [5] For example, when a Stoic conducts an investigation in opposition to an Epicurean who says that substance is divided or that god does not show providence for things in the universe or that pleasure is good,[8] has he apprehended these things or has he not apprehended them? If he has apprehended them, then in saying that they are real he utterly rejects the Stoa; and if he has not apprehended them, then he cannot say anything against them. [6] And similar things are to be said against those who come from the other schools, when they want to investigate the beliefs of those who hold different views from themselves. Thus they cannot investigate anything in opposition to one another.

Or rather – not to put too fine a point on it – pretty well all of their dogmatic philosophy will be confounded and the Sceptical philosophy vigorously advanced if it is granted that you cannot investigate what has not been apprehended in this way. [7] For anyone who makes assertions and holds beliefs about any unclear object will say that he is making an assertion about it either having apprehended it or not having apprehended it. If not having apprehended it, he will not carry conviction. If having apprehended it, he will say that he has apprehended it either directly and in itself and by an evident impression, or else by way of some inquiry and investigation. [8] If the unclear object is said to have made an immediate and evident impression on him in itself and so to have been apprehended, then in this case it will not in fact be unclear – rather, it will be equally apparent to everyone and agreed upon and not disputed.[9] (On

---

[6] See III 241; *M* VIII 397.

[7] For this Stoic definition see e.g. *M* VII 248, 402, 426; Diogenes Laertius VII 46; Cicero, *Luc* XXIV 77–8 – cf. ANNAS [1990]; FREDE [1983].

[8] Three central tenets of Epicureanism, all rejected by the Stoics. 'Substance is divided' expresses Epicurean atomism (for 'substance', οὐσία, in the sense of 'matter' see III 2): the Stoics held that matter (within the cosmos) is continuous, the Epicureans that it consists of atoms separated by void. On providence see I 151; on pleasure, III 181.

[9] Cf. e.g. II 182; III 254, 266.

everything unclear there has been an interminable dispute among them.) Thus a Dogmatist who makes affirmations and assertions about the reality of something unclear will not have apprehended it as a result of its having made an evident impression on him in itself. [9] But if by way of some inquiry, how – on the hypothesis before us – could he have investigated it before accurately apprehending it? For the investigation requires that what is going to be investigated should first have been accurately apprehended and then be investigated; and the apprehension of the object under investigation in turn demands that the object has already been investigated. Thus, by the reciprocal mode of perplexity,[10] it becomes impossible for them to investigate and hold beliefs about what is unclear: if any of them wish to start from apprehension, we face them with the demand that they should have already investigated the object before apprehending it; and if they wish to start from investigation, we face them with the demand that they should have apprehended what is to be investigated before investigating it. Thus for these reasons they can neither apprehend anything unclear nor make any firm assertion about it. And from this, I think, it will directly result that the subtleties of the Dogmatists are destroyed and the philosophy of suspension is introduced.

[10] If they say they mean that it is not apprehension of this sort but rather mere thinking which ought to precede investigation, then investigation is not impossible for those who suspend judgement about the reality of what is unclear. For a Sceptic is not, I think, barred from having thoughts, if they arise from things which give him a passive impression and appear evidently to him[c] and do not at all imply the reality of what is being thought of – for we can think, as they say, not only of real things but also of unreal things. Hence someone who suspends judgement maintains his sceptical condition while investigating and thinking; for it has been made clear[11] that he assents to any impression given by way of a passive appearance insofar as it appears to him.

[11] And consider whether in actual fact the Dogmatists are not barred from investigation. For those who agree that they do not

---

c   Omitting λόγῳ (for which the main MSS read λόγων).

10   See I 169.
11   See I 13.

know how objects are in their nature may continue without inconsistency to investigate them: those who think they know them accurately may not. For the latter, the investigation is already at its end, as they suppose, whereas for the former, the reason why any investigation is undertaken – that is, the idea that they have not found the answer – is fully present.[12]

[12] We must investigate each part of what they call philosophy – briefly on the present occasion.[13] And since there has been much dispute among the Dogmatists about the parts of philosophy[14] (some saying that it has one part, some two, some three), a dispute which it would not be appropriate to deal with in more detail here, we shall set down impartially the opinion of those who seem to have dwelt upon the matter more fully and advance our argument on this basis.

ii Where should the investigation of Dogmatism begin?

[13] The Stoics and some others say that there are three parts of philosophy – logic, physics, ethics – and they begin their exposition with logic (although there has indeed been much dissension even about where one should begin.)[15] We follow them without holding any opinion on the matter; and since what is said in the three parts requires judgement and a standard and the account of standards seems to be included in the logical part, let us begin with the account of standards and with the logical part,[16]

iii Standards[17]

[14][18] first remarking that although they call a standard both that by which they say reality and unreality are judged and that by attending

---

[12] Cf. I 2–3.

[13] See I 163.

[14] See *M* VII 1–19; Diogenes Laertius VII 39–41; Plutarch, *Stoic rep* 1035A. The tripartite division of philosophy was in fact accepted by pretty well all later Greek philosophy; see HADOT [1979].

[15] Cf. *M* VII 20–3.

[16] Cf. *M* VII 24. Note that Zeno and Chrysippus both began with logic: Diogenes Laertius VII 40.

[17] On the notion of a standard or κριτήριον see STRIKER [1974]; HUBY and NEAL [1989].

[18] Cf. *M* VII 29–30.

to which we live our lives, it is now our purpose to discuss what is said to be the standard of truth. (We have dealt with standards in the other sense in our account of Scepticism.[19])

[15][20] The standards with which our account is concerned are spoken of in three senses – a general, a special and a very special. In the general sense, every measure of apprehension is a standard – it is in this sense that we talk of 'natural standards' such as seeing. In the special sense, every technical measure of apprehension is a standard – such as a ruler or a pair of dividers. In the very special sense, every technical[d] measure of apprehension of an unclear object is a standard[21] – this sense applies not to everyday standards but only to logical standards and those which the Dogmatists bring forward in order to judge the truth.

[16][22] We propose to deal principally with logical standards. But logical standards are spoken of in three senses[23] – that by which, that through which, and that in virtue of which. For example, that by which – a human; through which – either perception or intellect; in virtue of which – the impact of an appearance in virtue of which humans set themselves to make judgements through one of the means we have mentioned.

[17] It was no doubt appropriate to make these preliminary remarks in order to have a conception of what our account is about. For the rest, let us proceed to our counterargument against those who rashly say that they have apprehended the standard of truth. We begin with the dispute.

---

[d] Adding τεχνικόν after καταλήψεως with three MSS; but see the parallel at *M* VII 33, where the word appears in no MSS (and is restored by Heintz).

[19] See I 21–4.

[20] Cf. *M* VII 31–3.

[21] But see II 95 (cf. I 178) and – more clearly – *M* VII 25 (cf. VIII 141–2), where standards, in contrast to signs and proofs, are said to bear upon 'the things which make an impression on us directly in perception or thought'. The problem is discussed by BRUNSCHWIG [1988a].

[22] Cf. *M* VII 33–7.

[23] Cf. Diogenes Laertius I 21 (Potamo); Albinus, *The Doctrines of Plato* IV, p. 154 H; Ptolemy, *On the Standard* 1–2.

iv Is there a standard of truth?[24]

[18][25] Of those who have discussed standards, some have asserted that there is one (e.g. the Stoics and certain others), some that there is not (among them, Xeniades of Corinth[26] and Xenophanes of Colophon who says: 'but belief is found over all'[27]); and we suspend judgement[e] as to whether there is one or not.

[19] Now they will say either that this dispute is decidable or that it is undecidable.[28] If undecidable, they will immediately grant that one must suspend judgement; if decidable, let them say by what it will be judged when we neither possess an agreed standard nor even know if there is one but are investigating the matter.

[20][29] Again, in order for the dispute that has arisen about standards to be decided, we must possess an agreed standard through which we can judge it; and in order for us to possess an agreed standard, the dispute about standards must already have been decided. Thus the argument falls into the reciprocal mode and the discovery of a standard is blocked – for we do not allow them to assume a standard by hypothesis, and if they want to judge the standard by a standard we throw them into an infinite regress.

Again, since a proof needs a standard which has been proved and a standard needs a proof which has been judged, they are thrown into the reciprocal mode.[30]

[21] Now, although we think that these considerations are actually enough to show the rashness of the Dogmatists in their account of standards, nevertheless, so that we may be able to bring some variety into our refutation of them, it is not absurd to persevere with the topic. Not that we propose to contest each of their opinions about standards one by one – for the dispute is vast, and in that way we too

---

[e] Reading ἐπίσχομεν: the mss have ἐπίσχωμεν, Mutschmann–Mau print ἐπέσχομεν (Kayser).

[24] On this chapter see LONG [1978a].

[25] Cf. *M* VII 47–54.

[26] Known only from Sextus, who ascribes to him the view that 'everything is false, i.e. every appearance and belief is false' (*M* VII 53; see below II 76, 85).

[27] See note to I 223; for the context of the quotation see *M* VII 49–52.

[28] Cf. I 170.

[29] For the modes of Agrippa which Sextus here deploys see I 164–9.

[30] Cf. II 183.

would necessarily fall into giving an unmethodical account.[31] But since the standard we are investigating is thought to be threefold – that by which, that through which, and that in virtue of which[32] – we shall tackle each of these in turn and establish its inapprehensibility; for in this way our account will be at once methodical and complete.

Let us begin with the standard by which; for along with it the others too seem in a way to reach an impasse.[33]

v That by which

[22] Humans – so far as what the Dogmatists say goes – seem to me to be not only inapprehensible but actually inconceivable. After all, we hear Plato's Socrates explicitly confessing that he does not know whether he is a human or something else.[34] And when they wish to establish the concept, first they are in dispute and secondly what they say is actually unintelligible.

[23] Democritus says that a human being is what we all know.[35] But as far as this goes, we shall not be acquainted with humans; for we also know dogs – and for that reason dogs will be humans. And there are some humans we do not know – so they will not be humans. Or rather, as far as this conception goes, no-one will be a human; for if Democritus says that a human must be known by everyone, and no human is known by all humans, then no-one will be a human according to him. [24] That this point is not sophistical but[f] in line with his own views is apparent. For our author says that the only things that are truly real are the atoms and the void, and these, he says, belong not only to animals but to *all* compounds.[36] Thus, as far as these items are concerned, we shall not conceive of what is peculiar to humans (since they are common to everything); and yet nothing else exists apart from them. Therefore we shall not have anything through

---

f   Adding ἀλλ᾽ after λέγομεν (Heintz).

31   Cf. II 48; III 37; *M* VIII 337a.
32   Cf. II 16.
33   Cf. *M* VII 263.
34   A willful misreading of *Phaedrus* 230A (paraphrased at *M* VII 264).
35   Cf. *M* VII 265–6 (Democritus, frag. 165 Diels–Kranz).
36   Cf. Plutarch, *adv Col* 1110E: see Democritus, frag. 125 Diels–Kranz (cf. also above, I 214).

which we shall be able to distinguish humans from other animals and to think purely of them.

[25]³⁷ Epicurus says that a human being is a figure of *that* sort, together with vitality. So, according to him, since humans are shown by pointing, anyone who is not being pointed to is not a human; and if someone is pointing to a woman, men will not be humans, and if to a man, women will not be humans. (We shall argue along the same lines from difference in circumstances, which we know from the fourth mode of suspension.³⁸)

[26] Others³⁹ have said that human beings are mortal rational animals, capable of understanding and knowledge. Now since we show in the first mode of suspension⁴⁰ that no animal is irrational but that all are capable both of understanding and of knowledge, then – so far as what the Dogmatists say goes – we shall not know what on earth they mean. [27] Moreover, the attributes contained in the definition are meant either as actual or as potential. If as actual, then you are not a human unless you have already acquired perfect knowledge and are perfect in point of reason and are in the very process of dying (for that is what being actually mortal is). If as potential, then you will not be a human if you possess perfect reason or have acquired understanding and knowledge – and this is more absurd than the former alternative. It is apparent, then, that the concept of a human being cannot be constituted in this way either. [28] As for Plato, when he asserts that human beings are broad-nailed two-footed featherless animals capable of political knowledge,⁴¹ he does not himself claim to be setting this out affirmatively. For if humans are among the things which, according to him, are coming into being but never really exist, and if it is impossible, according to him, to assert anything affirmatively about things which never exist,⁴²

---

³⁷ Cf. *M* VII 267–8.
³⁸ Above I 100–17. Sextus means that if you point to, e.g., a drunk or a sleeper, then the sober and the wakeful will not be men.
³⁹ Cf. *M* VII 269. The 'others' include Peripatetics (e.g. Aristotle, *Top* 133b2) and probably Stoics (e.g. Seneca, *ep* lxxvi 9–10).
⁴⁰ See above, I 62–78.
⁴¹ Cf. *M* VII 281 (see [Plato], *Definitions* 415A; Diogenes Laertius VI 40); cf. below, II 211.
⁴² See *Theaet* 152D, *Tim* 27E (cf. below, III 54).

then Plato will claim to set out[g] the definition not as affirming it but rather as speaking – as was his custom[43] – in accordance with plausibility.

[29] Even if we grant by way of concession that humans can be conceived of, we shall find that they are inapprehensible. For they are composed of soul and body; but neither bodies nor souls perhaps are apprehended: nor, therefore, are humans. [30] That bodies are not apprehended is clear from the following considerations.[44] The attributes of a thing are different from that of which they are attributes. Thus, when a colour or something of that sort makes an impression on us, it is likely that the attributes of a body make the impression but not the body itself. At any rate, they say that bodies are extended in three dimensions.[45] We ought then to apprehend length, breadth and depth if we are to apprehend bodies. ⟨But we do not apprehend depth.⟩[h] For if this made an impression on us, we should recognize silver-gilt for what it is.[46] Therefore, bodies do not make an impression on us.

[31] But to leave aside the controversy about body, humans are again found to be inapprehensible because souls are inapprehensible. That souls are inapprehensible is clear from the following considerations. Of those who have discussed the soul,[i] some have said that there are no souls (e.g. Dicaearchus of Messene[47]), others that there are, while others have suspended judgement.

[32] Now if the Dogmatists say that this dispute is undecidable,[48] they will immediately grant the inapprehensibility of the soul; and if they say that it is decidable, let them tell us what they will decide it with. They cannot decide it with perception, since souls are said by them to be objects of thought; but if they say they will decide it with

---

g Omitting δοκεῖν.
h Adding οὐδέ γε τὸ βάθος καταλαμβάνομεν (Kayser), *exempli gratia*.
i Omitting ἵνα τὴν πολλὴν καὶ ἀνήνυτον μάχην παραλίπωμεν: the clause makes no sense in its present position, and perhaps arose as a variant reading for the first clause of this section.

43 See I 221.
44 Cf. *M* VII 294–5; on body in general see III 38–49; *M* IX 359–440.
45 Cf. III 39.
46 Cf. *M* VII 299.
47 A pupil of Aristotle: see *M* VII 349 and esp. Cicero, *Tusculan Disputations* I x 21.
48 Cf. I 170.

intellect, we shall reply that, since the intellect is the most unclear part of the soul – this is shown by the fact that some people agree about the reality of the soul and yet differ about the intellect[49] – [33] then if it is with the intellect that they want to apprehend the soul and decide the dispute about it, they want to decide and confirm what is less a matter of investigation by what is more a matter of investigation – which is absurd. Thus the dispute about the soul will not be decided with the intellect. Therefore with nothing. But if this is so, souls are actually inapprehensible. Hence humans cannot be apprehended either.

[34][50] But even if we grant that humans are apprehended, it is surely not possible to show that it is by humans that objects must be judged. For anyone who says that objects should be judged by humans will say this either without proof or with proof. Not with proof; for the proof must be true and must have been judged – and so have been judged by something. Now since we cannot say on the basis of agreement by what the proof itself can be judged (for we are investigating the standard by which), we shall not be able to decide the proof; and for this reason we shall not be able to prove the standard, with which our account is now concerned. [35] But if it is said without proof that it is by humans that objects must be judged, this will be unconvincing. Thus we shall not be able to affirm that humans are the standard by which.

And by what will it be judged that humans are the standard by which? If they state the point without giving a judgement, they will not be found convincing. But if they say that it will be judged by humans, they take for granted the matter under investigation; [36] and if by another animal, how will this animal be adduced to judge whether humans are the standard? If without giving a judgement, it will not be found convincing. If with a judgement, then it ought in turn to be judged by something: if by itself, the same absurdity remains (the matter under investigation will be judged through the matter under investigation); if by humans, the reciprocal mode[51] is introduced; if by something else apart from these, we shall again ask

---

[49] See I 128.
[50] With 34–6 compare *M* VII 315–16 (see also above, I 59–61).
[51] Cf. I 169.

for the standard by which for that – and so *ad infinitum*.[52] For this reason too, therefore, we will not be able to say that it is by humans that objects must be judged.

[37] But suppose it to be the case, and to have been made convincing, that objects must be judged by humans. Now, since there are many differences among humans,[53] let the Dogmatists first agree with one another that we should attend to this human, and only then let them bid us give him our assent. But if they are going to dispute about this 'as long as water flows and trees grow tall' (as the saying goes[54]), how can they urge us rashly to give our assent to anyone?

[38] If they say that we should find the Sage convincing,[55] we shall ask them which Sage – the Sage according to Epicurus, or according to the Stoics, or the Cyrenaic Sage, or the Cynic? They will not be able to agree on an answer. [39][56] And if someone claims that we should abandon our search for the Sage and simply find convincing whoever is cleverest at present, then, first, they will also dispute about who is cleverer than the others; and secondly, even if it is granted that they can agree in determining who among everyone present and past is cleverest, even so he should not be found convincing. [40] For since there are many – indeed, pretty well infinitely many – grades and degrees of cleverness, we say that it is possible[57] that someone else should be born who is even cleverer than the one we say is cleverest of everyone past and present. Then just as we are required to find convincing because of his cleverness the one who is now said to be the most intelligent of everyone present and past, so we should rather find convincing the cleverer one who will exist after him. And when he is born, we should expect in turn that someone else will be born, cleverer than him; and someone else cleverer than him; and so *ad infinitum*. [41] (It is unclear whether these people will agree with one another or dispute in what they say.) Hence, even if someone is allowed to be the cleverest of everyone past and present, still, since we

---

[52] Cf. I 166.
[53] See the second mode of suspension, above I 79–81.
[54] The line, from an anonymous epigram on Midas (see Plato, *Phaedrus* 264D) is quoted again by Sextus at *M* VIII 184 and *M* I 28.
[55] See I 91.
[56] With II 39–42 compare II 61–2.
[57] For the appeal to possible cases see I 34, note.

cannot say affirmatively that there will be no-one shrewder than him (for that is unclear), we shall always have to wait for the judgement of the cleverer person who will exist later, and never assent to the one who is now superior.

[42] Even if we grant by way of concession that there neither is nor was nor will be anyone cleverer than this hypothetical clever person, even so it is not right to find him convincing. For clever people, when they try to establish something, are especially prone to champion what is unsound and make it seem sound and true;[58] so when our shrewd person says something we shall not know whether he is describing the object as it is in its nature or whether he is presenting it as true although it is false and persuading us to consider it as though it were true – for he is the cleverest of all and for that reason cannot be refuted by us. Hence we shall not give even him our assent as judging objects truly; for while we think that he is speaking the truth,[j] we also think that, because of his excessive shrewdness, he says what he does from a desire to present false objects as truths. For these reasons, in judging objects one should not find convincing even someone who seems to be shrewdest of all.

[43] If someone says that we should attend to the agreement of the majority, we shall say that that is idle. For, first, what is true is no doubt rare, and for this reason it is possible for one person to be more intelligent than the majority.[59] Secondly, for *every* standard there are more people opposed to it than in agreement about it; for those who admit any standard different from the one which some people seem to agree upon are opposed to it and are far more numerous than those who agree about it.[60]

[44][61] Besides, those who agree either exhibit different conditions or share a single condition. Now they do not exhibit different conditions so far as the matter in question goes – how then would

---

[j] Reading οἴεσθαι μὲν with the mss; Mutschmann–Mau print οἷόν τε μὲν εἶναι (Apelt).

[58] Cf. *M* VII 325.
[59] Cf. *M* VII 329.
[60] Cf. *M* VII 330–2.
[61] Cf. *M* VII 333–4 (and see the fourth of the Ten Modes, above, I 100–17).

they say the same thing about it?[k] But if they share a single condition, then, since the one person who says something different has a single condition and all of these who agree have a single condition, we will find no difference in number so far as the conditions we are attending to go. [45] For this reason we should not attend to the majority any more than to one person. Moreover, as we suggested in the second[l] mode of scepticism,[62] numerical difference among judgements is actually inapprehensible; for there are infinitely many individual humans and we cannot survey all their judgements and assert what the majority of all humans assert and what the minority. For this reason too, then, preference among judges on the basis of number is absurd.

[46] But if we do not attend to number either, we shall find no-one by whom objects will be judged, even though we have granted so much by way of concession. Hence on all these grounds the standard by which objects are to be judged is found to be inapprehensible.

[47] Since the other standards too are cancelled along with this one (for each of them is either a part or a feeling or an activity of humans[63]), it would no doubt be apposite to proceed in our account to one of the topics next in order, on the grounds that the other standards too have been sufficiently discussed;[m] but so that we may not seem to be reluctant to make a specific counterargument against each of them, we shall for good measure[64] say a few words about them too. And first we shall discuss the standard called 'through which'.

vi That through which

[48][65] The dispute among the Dogmatists on this subject is great – indeed, pretty well infinite; but, with methodical procedure again in view,[66] we say that, since according to them humans are that by

---

[k] Retaining the MS reading περὶ αὐτοῦ: Mutschmann–Mau emend to περὶ ταὐτοῦ.
[l] Reading δευτέρῳ (τετάρτῳ MSS).
[m] Reading εἰρημένον (Chouet: εἰρημένων MSS, Mutschmann–Mau).

[62] Above I 89.
[63] Cf. M VII 263.
[64] Cf. I 62.
[65] Cf. M VII 343.
[66] See II 21.

which objects are judged and humans – as they themselves agree – have nothing through which they can judge except the senses and the intellect, then if we show that they can judge neither through the senses alone nor through intellect alone nor through both of them together, we shall have spoken concisely against all their particular opinions; for they all seem to be traceable back to these three positions.

[49] Let us begin with the senses. Since some say that the senses are affected vacuously (for none of the things they seem to grasp exists), while others assert that everything by which they think they are moved exists, and yet others that some of these things exist and some do not exist,[67] we shall not know to whom to give our assent. For we shall not decide the dispute with the senses (since we are investigating whether they are affected vacuously or truly apprehend things), nor yet with anything else (for there is no other standard through which we should judge, according to the hypothesis before us). [50] It will therefore be undecidable and inapprehensible whether the senses are affected vacuously or apprehend something; from which it follows that we must not attend to the senses alone in judging objects – for we cannot say of them whether they apprehend anything at all.

[51][68] But suppose it to be the case, by way of concession, that the senses are capable of grasping things. Even so, they will nonetheless be found unconvincing with regard to judging external existing objects. After all, the senses are moved in contrary ways by external objects[69] – e.g. taste, by the same honey, is now affected bitterly, now sweetly, and sight takes the same colour to be now blood-red, now white. [52] Nor does smell agree with itself – after all, people with headaches say that myrrh is unpleasant and people not in this state say that it is pleasant. People who are possessed or mad think that they hear others talking to them when we do not hear anything. The same water seems unpleasant to the feverish because of excessive heat, but lukewarm to others. [53] Now whether one should say that all

---

[67] Cf. *M* VIII 213, 354–5 (where Sextus' paradigms for the three groups are Democritus, Epicurus and Zeno the Stoic).

[68] With II 51–2 compare *M* VII 345–6.

[69] The following illustrations are taken from the fourth of the Ten Modes, I 101 (with the exception of the colours, for which see I 44). Note that *M* VII 345 refers explicitly to the Ten Modes of Aenesidemus.

appearances are true, or that these are true and those false, or that all are false, it is impossible to say; for we have no agreed standard through which to judge which we are to prefer, nor are we equipped with a proof which is both true and judged because we are still investigating the standard of truth through which true proofs should properly be decided.

[54] For these reasons, anyone who requires us to find convincing people who are in a natural state[70] and not those who are unnaturally disposed will be saying something absurd. If he says this without proof he will not be convincing, and for the reason just given he will not possess a proof that is true and judged. [55] Yet even if one were to concede that the appearances of those in a natural state were convincing and the appearances of those unnaturally disposed unconvincing, even so it will be found impossible to judge external existing objects by the senses alone. After all, sight, even in its natural state, says of the same tower now that it is round, now that it is square; taste says of the same foods in the case of the sated that they are unpleasant, in the case of the hungry that they are pleasant; hearing similarly grasps the same sound at night as loud, in the daytime as faint; [56] smell takes the same things to be malodorous in the case of most people, not at all so in the case of tanners; the same touch is warmed by the vestibule as we enter the baths, chilled as we leave.[71] For this reason, since the senses conflict with themselves even when they are in a natural state, and since the dispute is undecidable (for we have no agreed standard through which they can be judged), the same impasse must follow.

To establish the point, we can also adduce several of the other things we said earlier in discussing the modes of suspension. Hence it is no doubt not true that the senses alone can judge external existing objects.

[57] Let us now turn our account to the intellect. Those who require us to attend to intellect alone in judging objects will, first, be unable to show that the existence of intellect is apprehensible. For

---

[70] See I 102–3.
[71] The examples for taste and touch are again taken from the fourth mode (I 109–10); the example for sight comes from the fifth mode (I 118), for hearing perhaps from the sixth (see I 125); the example for smell is new.

since Gorgias, in stating that nothing exists,[72] says that intellect does not exist, while some assert that it is real, how will they decide the dispute? Neither with intellect (for then they will be taking for granted the matter under investigation) nor with anything else (for they say, according to the hypothesis now before us, that there is nothing else through which objects are judged). It will therefore be undecidable and inapprehensible whether intellect exists or not; from which it follows that in judging objects we must not attend to the intellect alone, which has not yet been apprehended.

[58][73] But suppose that intellect has been apprehended and that it has been agreed, by way of hypothesis, that it exists: I say that it cannot judge objects. For if it does not even see itself accurately but disputes about its own substance and the way in which it is produced and the place in which it is located,[74] how can it apprehend anything else accurately?

[59][75] Even granted that intellect is capable of judging objects, we shall not discover how we are to judge in virtue of it. For there are many differences in intellect – the intellect of Gorgias, in virtue of which he says that nothing exists, is one thing, that of Heraclitus, in virtue of which he says that everything exists,[76] is another, and yet another is that of those who say that some things exist and others do not: we shall not know how we are to decide among the different intellects, nor shall we be able to say that it is right to follow this person's intellect but not that person's. [60] For if we venture to judge with one intellect, then by assenting to one part of the dispute we shall be taking for granted what is under investigation; and if with something else, we shall be mistaken in saying that we must judge objects with the intellect alone.

[61] Finally, on the basis of what we said about the standard by which,[77] we shall be able to show that we cannot discover an intellect

---

[72] See the paraphrase of Gorgias' essay *On Nature or that which is not* at *M* VII 65–87.

[73] Cf. *M* VII 348–50.

[74] Cf. I 128, note.

[75] With II 59–60 compare *M* VII 351.

[76] Heraclitus does not *say* this; rather, it was supposed to follow from his view – if such was his view – that contradictories can be true at the same time.

[77] See II 39–42.

more shrewd than the others; that even if we discover an intellect
more shrewd than any past or present intellect, we must not attend to
it, since it is unclear whether there will in turn come to exist another
more shrewd than this; [62] and that even if we hypothesize an
intellect than which none could be quicker, we shall not assent to the
person who judges through it, fearing that he might utter some false
statement and be able, because he has the sharpest of intellects, to
persuade us that it is true.

Thus we must not judge objects with the intellect alone.

[63] It remains to say that we should judge through both. And this,
in turn, is impossible. For not only do the senses not guide the
intellect to apprehension: they actually oppose it.[78] After all, because
honey appears bitter to some people and sweet to others, Democritus
said that it is neither sweet nor bitter,[79] and Heraclitus that it is
both.[80] And the same argument holds for the other senses and their
objects. In this way the intellect, if it takes its start from the senses, is
compelled to make different and conflicting assertions. And this is
foreign to a standard of apprehension.

Next we should say this: [64] they will judge objects either with all
the senses and everyone's intellects, or with some. If anyone says with
all, he will require the impossible; for there is plainly much conflict
among senses and intellects – and in particular, since Gorgias' intellect
asserts that one must attend neither to the senses nor to the intellect,[81]
the view will be turned about.[82] But if with some, how will they judge
that we must attend to these senses and intellects[n] but not to those,
when they do not possess an agreed standard through which to decide
among the different senses and intellects? [65] If they say that we will
judge[o] the senses and the intellects with intellect and the senses, so
that things are judged with some of these and not with others, they
take for granted what is under investigation; for we are investigating

---

[n] Reading ταῖς διανοίαις (Kayser): the MSS offer τῇ διανοίᾳ; Mutschmann–
 Mau print ⟨τῇδε⟩ τῇ διανοίᾳ (Bekker).

[o] Reading κρινοῦμεν with the majority of MSS: Mutschmann–Mau prefer the
 minority reading, κρινοῦσιν.

[78] See I 99.
[79] See I 213.
[80] See I 211.
[81] I.e. insofar as neither exists.
[82] See I 122, note.

whether anyone can judge through these. [66] Next we should say that either they will judge both senses and intellects with the senses, or both senses and intellects with intellects, or senses with the senses and intellects with intellects, or intellects with the senses and senses with intellect. Now if they want to judge both items with the senses or with the intellect, they will no longer be judging through the senses and intellect but through one of these, whichever they choose; and the impasses I mentioned earlier[83] will ensue for them. [67] If they decide among senses with the senses and among intellects with intellect, then, since senses conflict with senses and intellects with intellects, they will be taking for granted the matter under investigation, whichever of the conflicting senses they adopt to judge the other senses; for they will be adopting one part of the dispute, as though it were already convincing, in order to decide matters which are no less under investigation than it is. [68] (The same argument applies to intellects.) If they decide among intellects with the senses and among senses with the intellect, we find the reciprocal mode,[84] according to which, if we are to decide among the senses the intellects must already have been judged, and if the intellects are to be tested the senses must already have been carefully probed.

[69] Thus, since standards of a given kind cannot be decided by things of the same kind, nor both kinds by one kind, nor crosswise by things of the other kind, we shall not be able to prefer intellect to intellect or sense to sense. And for this reason we shall not have anything through which to judge; for if we can neither judge with all the senses and intellects, nor know with which we must judge and with which not, we shall not have anything through which to judge objects. Hence for these reasons too the standard through which will be unreal.

vii That in virtue of which

[70][85] Next in order, then, let us look at the standard in virtue of which they say objects are judged. The first thing to say about it is that

---

[83] See II 49–56, 57–62.
[84] See I 169.
[85] See *M* VII 371–3 (and cf. below, II 219).

appearances are inconceivable.[p] For they[86] say that an appearance is an imprinting on the ruling part. Since, then, the soul and its ruling part are, as they say, breath or something subtler than breath, you will not be able to conceive of an imprinting on it either in virtue of indentation and projection (of the sort we see on seals)[87] or in virtue of their mythical power of alteration.[88] For it could not contain memory of the numerous theorems which make up an expertise,[89] since those already there would be erased during the subsequent alterations. [71][90] But even if appearances could be conceived of, they will be inapprehensible; for since they are feelings of the ruling part, and the ruling part, as we have shown,[91] is not apprehended, we shall not apprehend its feelings either.

[72] Next, even if we grant that appearances are apprehended, objects cannot be judged in virtue of them; for the intellect, as they say, sets itself upon external objects and receives appearances not through itself[q] but through the senses, and the senses do not apprehend external existing objects but only – if anything – their own feelings.[92] An appearance, then, will actually be of the feeling of a sense – and that is different from an external existing object. For honey is not the same thing as my being affected sweetly, nor wormwood as my being affected bitterly: they are different.[93] [73] And if this feeling is different from the external existing object, an appearance will be not of the external existing object but of some-

p Mutschmann–Mau suppose a lacuna in the text; the sentence originally read something like '… appearances are ⟨not only inapprehensible but also⟩ inconceivable'.

q Omitting the second δι' αὑτῆς which Mutschmann–Mau add on the basis of the Latin translation.

86 'They' are the Stoics; the argument is repeated at III 188; for the 'ruling part' of the soul see I 128; for the notion of 'imprinting' see *M* VII 227–41, 372–80.

87 The view of Cleanthes: *M* VII 228, 372.

88 The view of Chrysippus: *M* VII 229–31, 372–3; Diogenes Laertius VII 50. See ANNAS [1992a], ch. 3.

89 For the standard definition of expertise, τέχνη, which was allegedly invented by Zeno (Olympiodorus, *Commentary on Plato's Gorgias* 12.1) and eventually became a commonplace, see III 188, 241, 251; *M* VII 373; *M* II 10.

90 Cf. *M* VII 380.

91 See II 57, although there Sextus does not speak explicitly of the ruling part.

92 Cf. *M* VII 354.

93 Cf. I 20.

thing else different from it.[94] So if the intellect judges in virtue of appearances, it judges badly and not in accordance with the existing object. Hence it is absurd to say that external objects are judged in virtue of appearances.

[74][95] Nor can we say that the soul apprehends external existing objects through its sensory feelings inasmuch as the feelings of the senses are similar to the external existing objects. For how will the intellect know whether the feelings of the senses are like the sense-objects, given that it does not itself come into contact with the external objects and that the senses make clear to it not the nature of these objects but their own feelings, as we deduced from the modes of suspension?[96] [75] Just as someone who does not know Socrates but has looked at a picture of him does not know whether the picture is like Socrates, so the intellect, studying the feelings of the senses but not observing the external objects, will not know whether the feelings of the senses are like the external existing objects. Therefore it cannot rely on similarity to judge them.

[76][97] But let us grant by way of concession not only that appearances are conceived of and are apprehended but also that they allow objects to be judged in virtue of them – even though our argument has suggested quite the contrary. Then either we shall find every appearance convincing and decide in virtue of it, or else we shall find only some convincing. If every, clearly we shall also find convincing Xeniades' appearance in virtue of which he said that all appearances are unconvincing,[98] and the argument will be turned about[99] to the position that not all appearances are convincing.[r] Hence objects cannot[s] be judged in virtue of them. [77] If some, how shall we judge that it is right to find these appearances convincing and those unconvincing? For if without an appearance, then they will grant that appearances are redundant for judging, since they will be

---

[r] Adding πιστάς before πάσας (Stephanus).
[s] Reading μή for καί (Mutschmann).

[94] Cf. M VII 357.
[95] With II 74–5 compare M VII 358.
[96] See I 59, 87, 93, 99, 117, etc: the senses show how things appear to us, and these appearances are πάθη or feelings.
[97] With II 76–7 compare M VII 388–90.
[98] Cf. II 18.
[99] See I 122, note.

saying that some objects can be judged apart from them. But if with
an appearance, how will they get hold of the appearance which they
are adducing for judging the other appearances? [78] And[t] they will
need another appearance in turn to judge this second appearance; and
another to judge that, and so *ad infinitum*.[100] But it is impossible to
make infinitely many decisions. Therefore it is impossible to discover
which appearances one must use as standards and which not. Since,
then, even if we grant that we must judge objects in virtue of
appearances, the account is turned about[101] in either way – whether
we find every one of them[u] convincing, or some convincing as
standards and others unconvincing – it may be concluded that we
must not adduce appearances as standards for judging objects.

[79][102] This is all we need to say here in an outline[103] about the
standard in virtue of which objects were said to be judged. You must
realize that it is not our intention to assert that standards of truth are
unreal (that would be dogmatic); rather, since the Dogmatists seem
plausibly to have established that there is a standard of truth, we have
set up plausible-seeming arguments in opposition to them, affirming
neither that they are true nor that they are more plausible than those
on the contrary side, but concluding to suspension of judgement
because of the apparently equal plausibility of these arguments and
those produced by the Dogmatists.

viii Truths and truth[104]

[80][105] Yet even if we grant as a hypothesis that there is a standard of
truth, it is found to be useless and vain once we suggest that, as far as
what is said by the Dogmatists goes, truth is unreal and truths
non-existent.

[81][106] We suggest it thus: truths are said to differ from the truth in

---

[t] Reading καί for ἤ.
[u] Reading πάσῃ (with the early editors) for πᾶσι (mss, Mutschmann–Mau).

100 See I 166.
101 See I 122.
102 With the content of II 79 compare II 103, 130, 192; *M* VII 444; VIII 159–160.
103 Cf. I 4, note.
104 On this chapter see LONG [1978b].
105 Cf. *M* VIII 2–3.
106 With II 81–3 compare *M* VII 38–45.

three ways – in substance, in constitution, in power. In substance, because truths are incorporeal (they are statements and sayables[107]) whereas the truth is corporeal (it is knowledge assertoric of all truths, and knowledge is the ruling part in a certain condition – just as a hand in a certain condition is a fist[108] – and the ruling part is corporeal, for according to them it is breath[109]). [82] In constitution, since truths are simple (e.g. I am conversing), whereas the truth is constituted by a recognition of many truths. [83] In power, because the truth is linked to knowledge, whereas truths are not necessarily so linked – that is why they say that the truth is present only in virtuous men[110] but truths are present in bad men as well (a bad man may say something true).

[84] That is what the Dogmatists say. We – thinking again of the plan of this essay[111] – will here produce arguments only against truths, since the truth is cancelled out together with them, being said to be composed from recognition of truths. Again, since some of our arguments are more general (with them we shake the very subsistence of truths) and others specific (with them we show that truths are not to be found in sounds or in sayables or in the movement of the intellect), we think it sufficient for the present to set out the more general ones only.[112] For just as, when the foundations of a wall are brought down, all the upper parts are brought down with them,[113] so, when the subsistence of truths is overthrown, the particular subtleties of the Dogmatists are cancelled out together with them.

ix Is anything true by nature?

[85][114] There is a dispute about truths among the Dogmatists; for some say that some things are true, and some that nothing is true.[115]

---

107 See II 104, note.
108 Cf. Alexander, *in Top* 360.11–13.
109 Cf. II 70.
110 See I 91, note.
111 See I 4, note.
112 For the 'specific' arguments see *M* VIII 55–139.
113 The simile recurs at *M* IX 2; the same point is made below, III 1; cf. *M* VII 216; *M* I 40; III 10, 12; V 50.
114 Cf. *M* VIII 3–10, 15–16.
115 The latter view was allegedly maintained by Xeniades (see II 18) and by Monimus (*M* VIII 5).

And it is not possible to decide the dispute; for if you say that some things are true, you will not be found convincing if you say it without proof, because of the dispute; and if you actually want to bring a proof, then if you confess that the proof is false you will be unconvincing, while if you say that the proof is true you fall into the reciprocal argument[116] and in addition you will be asked for a proof of the fact that it is true – and another proof for that, and so *ad infinitum*:[117] and it is impossible to prove infinitely many things. Therefore it is impossible to know that some things are true.

[86][118] Again, things, which they say constitute the most general class of all,[119] are either true, or false, or neither false nor true, or both false and true. Now if they say that things are false, they will be allowing that everything is false: since animals are alive, every particular animal is alive, and in just the same way, if the most general class of all – the class of things – is false, every particular will be false and nothing true. From which it may be concluded that nothing is false. For 'Some things are false',[v] being itself included among all things, will be false. And if things are true, everything will be true; from which it may in turn be concluded that nothing is true, since this itself – I mean, that nothing is true – being a thing, is true. [87] If things are both false and true, each of the particulars will be both false and true. From which it may be concluded that nothing is true by nature; for that which has a nature such as to be true will certainly not be false. If things are neither false nor true, it is agreed that all particular things too, being said to be neither false nor true, will not be true. For these reasons too, then, it will be unclear to us whether anything is true.

[88][120] In addition, truths are either apparent only or unclear only,

---

v   Omitting πάντα ἐστὶ ψευδῆ καὶ τὸ.

116   See I 169.
117   See I 166.
118   With II 86–7 compare *M* VIII 32–6.
119   Sextus alludes to the Stoic ontological classification, according to which 'things' [τὸ τί] form the highest genus which includes everything whatever: cf. II 223–5; III 124; Seneca, *ep* lviii 15; Alexander, *in Top* 301.19–25; see BRUN-SCHWIG [1988b].
120   With II 88–94 compare *M* VIII 17–31 (for the pattern of argument see below, II 124–9).

or else some truths are unclear and some apparent.[121] But none of these is true, as we shall show. Therefore nothing is true.

If truths are apparent only, they will say either that all apparent things are true or that some are. If all, the argument is turned about;[122] for it appears to some people that nothing is true.[123] If some, you cannot say without deciding the matter that these things are true and those false. But if you use a standard you will say either that this standard is apparent or that it is unclear. And you certainly will not say that it is unclear; for the present hypothesis has it that only apparent things are true. [89] But if you say that it is apparent, then since we are investigating which apparent things are true and which false, the apparent thing you assume in order to judge apparent things will itself in turn need another apparent standard – and that another, and so *ad infinitum*.[124] But it is impossible to make infinitely many decisions. It is therefore impossible to apprehend whether truths are apparent only.

[90] Similarly, too, anyone who says that unclear things alone are true will not say that they are all true (for he will not say that it is true both that the stars are even in number and[w] that they are odd[125]). But if he says that some are, with what shall we judge that these unclear things are true and those false? Certainly not with anything apparent; but if with something unclear, then since we are investigating which unclear things are true and which false, this unclear thing too will need some other unclear thing to decide it – and that another, and so *ad infinitum*. For that reason, truths are not unclear only.

[91] It remains to say that some truths are apparent and some unclear. But this too is absurd. For either all apparent things and all unclear things are true, or some apparent things and some unclear things. Now if all are, the argument will again be turned about,[126] it being granted that it is true that nothing is true. And it will be said

---

[w] Reading καί (Heintz) for ἤ (MSS, Mutschmann–Mau).

[121] The views, according to *M* VIII 6–10, of Epicurus, Plato and Democritus, and the Stoics.

[122] See I 122.

[123] Cf. II 85.

[124] See I 166.

[125] A stock example of something over which even a Stoic will suspend judgement: II 91, 97, 231; III 177; *M* VIII 147.

[126] See I 122.

that it is true both that the stars are even in number and that they are odd. [92] If some of the apparent things and some of the unclear things are true, how shall we decide that of the apparent things these are true and those false? If through something apparent, the argument is thrown back *ad infinitum*. If through something unclear, then since unclear things need judgement, through what will this unclear thing in its turn be judged? If through something apparent, the reciprocal mode turns up; if through something unclear, the mode which throws one back *ad infinitum*.[127] [93] We must say the same about unclear things too. If you attempt to judge them with something unclear, you are thrown back *ad infinitum*; if with something apparent, then either you always take something apparent and are thrown back *ad infinitum* or else you change over to something unclear and are thrown into the reciprocal mode. It is therefore false to say that some truths are apparent and some unclear.

[94] Thus if neither apparent things nor unclear things only are true, nor yet some apparent and some unclear things, then nothing is true. If nothing is true, and if standards are thought to have their utility in judging truths, then standards are useless and vain – even if we grant by way of concession that they[x] have some subsistence. And since we should suspend judgement about whether anything is true, it follows that those who say that dialectic is the science of what is false and true and neither[128] are rash.

[95][129] Standards of truth having appeared perplexing, it is no longer possible to make strong assertions, so far as what is said by the Dogmatists goes, either about what seems to be evident or about what is unclear. For since the Dogmatists deem that they apprehend the latter from what is evident, how, if we are compelled to suspend judgement about what they call evident,[130] could we be bold enough to make any assertion about what is unclear? [96] But for extra good

---

x   Reading αὐτό with most MSS for αὐτῷ, which Mutschmann–Mau prefer.

127 See I 166, 169.
128 See II 229 and 247 (cf. *M* XI 187), where the definition is ascribed to the Stoics. Diogenes Laertius (VII 62) attributes it more specifically to Posidonius. See LONG [1978c].
129 With II 95–6 compare *M* VIII 140–2.
130 See II 15, note.

measure[131] we shall also produce particular objections against unclear objects. And since they are thought to be apprehended and supported through signs and proofs, we shall suggest briefly that it is right to suspend judgement both about signs and about proofs. Let us begin with signs; for proofs are thought to be a species of sign.[132]

x Signs

[97][133] Some objects, then, according to the Dogmatists, are clear and some are unclear. And of the unclear, some are unclear once and for all, some are unclear for the moment, some are unclear by nature. What comes of itself to our knowledge, they say, is clear (e.g. that it is day); what does not have a nature such as to fall under our apprehension is unclear once and for all (e.g. that the stars are even in number[134]); [98] what has an evident nature but is made unclear for us for the moment by certain external circumstances is unclear for the moment (e.g. for me now, the city of the Athenians); and what does not have a nature such as to fall under our evident grasp is unclear by nature (e.g. imperceptible pores – for these are never apparent of themselves but would be deemed to be apprehended, if at all, by way of something else, e.g. by sweating or something similar[135]).

[99][136] Now, clear things, they say, do not need signs: they are apprehended of themselves.[137] Nor do things unclear once and for all, since they are not apprehended at all. But things unclear for the moment and things unclear by nature are apprehended through signs – but not through the same signs: things unclear for the moment are apprehended through recollective signs, things unclear by nature through indicative signs. [100] Thus some signs, according to them, are recollective, some indicative.[138] They call a sign recollective if,

---

131 See I 62.

132 See II 122, 131, 134; *M* VIII 277, 299.

133 With II 97–8 compare *M* VIII 144–7 (see also VIII 316–20).

134 See II 90.

135 A stock example; see e.g. II 140, 142; *M* VIII 306; [Galen], *def med* XIX 353 K; Diogenes Laertius IX 89.

136 With II 99–101 compare *M* VIII 148–55 (cf. 143); see e.g. BURNYEAT [1982]; GLIDDEN [1983]; EBERT [1987].

137 Cf. II 116, 126, 168.

138 For the distinction see also e.g. [Galen], *opt sect* I 149 K; *def med* XIX 396 K.

having been observed evidently together with the thing it signifies, at the same time as it makes an impression on us – and while the other thing remains unclear – it leads us to recall the thing which has been observed together with it and is not now making an evident impression on us (as in the case of smoke and fire). [101] A sign is indicative, they say,[139] if it signifies that of which it is a sign not by having been observed evidently together with the thing it signifies but from its proper nature and constitution (as bodily movements are signs of the soul[140]). That is why they also define this sign as follows:[141] An indicative sign is a pre-antecedent[142] statement in a sound conditional, revelatory of the consequent.[y]

[102][143] There being two different sorts of signs, as we have said, we argue not against all signs but only against indicative signs, which seem to be a fiction of the Dogmatists. For recollective signs are found convincing by everyday life: seeing smoke, someone diagnoses fire; having observed a scar, he says that a wound was inflicted. Hence not only do we not conflict with everyday life, but we actually join the struggle on its side, assenting without opinion to what it has found convincing and taking a stand against the private fictions of the Dogmatists.[144]

[103][145] It was no doubt appropriate to make these prefatory remarks in order to illuminate the subject of our investigation: now let us move to our counterargument, not endeavouring to show that indicative signs are unreal, but recalling the apparent equipollence of the arguments brought in favour of their reality and unreality.[146]

---

y   Mutschmann–Mau (after Natorp and Heintz) delete the last two sentences ('That is why ... the consequent').

139   Contrast the Methodics' account of 'indications': I 240.
140   Cf. I 85.
141   See II 104; *M* VIII 245.
142   See II 106.
143   Cf. *M* VIII 156–8.
144   For the Sceptics siding with ordinary life see I 23, note; on II 102 see e.g. BARNES [1992], pp. 4251–2.
145   Cf. *M* VIII 159–60 (and above, II 79).
146   See II 130.

xi Are there any indicative signs?

[104]¹⁴⁷ Signs, so far as what the Dogmatists say about them goes, are inconceivable.

Those who seem to have treated the matter accurately – the Stoics – wish to establish the concept of a sign by saying that a sign is a pre-antecedent statement in a sound conditional, revelatory of the consequent.¹⁴⁸ They say that a statement is a self-contained sayable¹⁴⁹ which is assertoric so far as it itself goes¹⁵⁰ and that a sound conditional is one which does not begin from a truth and end in a falsity. [105] For a conditional either begins from a truth and ends in a truth (e.g. If it is day, it is light), or begins from a falsity and ends in a falsity (e.g. If the earth is flying, the earth has wings), or begins from a truth and ends in a falsity (e.g. If the earth exists, the earth is flying), or begins from a falsity and ends in a truth (e.g. If the earth is flying the earth exists). Of these they say that only those beginning from a truth and ending in a falsity are unsound and that the others are sound. [106] They call pre-antecedent the antecedent in a conditional which begins from a truth and ends in a truth.¹⁵¹ It is revelatory of the consequent since 'This woman is lactating' is thought to make clear 'This woman has conceived' in the conditional 'If this woman is lactating, this woman has conceived.'¹⁵²

[107]¹⁵³ This is what they say. We say, first, that it is unclear whether there are any sayables. Among the Dogmatists the

---

¹⁴⁷ With II 104–6 compare *M* VIII 244–53; see EBERT [1991], pp. 29–44.

¹⁴⁸ See II 101.

¹⁴⁹ For the Stoic theory of 'sayables' or λεκτά (i.e. of what we say when we utter something significant) see *M* VIII 11–12, 70–4; Diogenes Laertius VII 63 (cf. above II 81, 84; below, III 52). See e.g. LONG [1971]; FREDE [1974], pp. 32–48; GRAESER [1978]; ANNAS [1992a], chh. 3–4.

¹⁵⁰ 'Assertoric' sayables contrast with imperatival, interrogatory, etc. sayables (cf. *M* VIII 71–4; Diogenes Laertius VII 66). The qualification 'so far as it itself goes' [ὅσον ἐφ' ἑαυτῷ] is obscure: perhaps it alludes to the fact that assertoric sentences can be used with non-assertoric force (see I 181–90). A statement is a complete sayable which is assertoric as far as its own form and structure go – though it may, for all that, be employed for non-assertoric ends.

¹⁵¹ Cf. II 115.

¹⁵² This stock example of a sign is already found in Aristotle: *Prior Analytics* 70a13–16.

¹⁵³ With II 107–8 compare *M* VIII 258–61 (cf. 76–7; *M* I 157).

Epicureans say that there are no sayables[154] and the Stoics that there are. Now, when the Stoics say that there are sayables, they either make a mere assertion or else use a proof.[155] If an assertion, the Epicureans will set in opposition to them the assertion which says that there are no sayables; and if they adduce a proof, then, since proofs are composed of statements,[156] which are sayables,[z] the proof, being composed[aa] of sayables, will not be able to be adduced to make it convincing that there are sayables – for how will anyone who does not grant that there are sayables concede that there are compounds of sayables? [108] Hence anyone who tries to establish that there are sayables by presupposing the reality of a compound of sayables wants to make what is being investigated convincing through what is being investigated. Thus if it is not possible to establish either simply or by way of a proof that there are sayables, it is unclear that there are any sayables.

Similarly, whether there are any statements; for statements are sayables. [109] And maybe even if it is granted by way of a hypothesis that there are sayables, statements turn out to be unreal, since they are composed of sayables which do not co-exist with one another.[157] Thus in the case of 'If it is day, it is light', when I say 'It is day', 'It is light' does not yet exist; and when I say 'It is light', 'It is day' no longer exists. Thus, if what is composed from certain things cannot exist if its parts do not co-exist with one another, and if the things from which statements are composed do not co-exist with one another, then statements will not exist.

[110][158] But to leave these matters too to one side, sound conditionals will be found inapprehensible. For Philo[159] says that a

---

z   Adding ὄντων before λεκτῶν (Kayser).
aa   Deleting δέ after λεκτῶν.

154   See *M* VIII 13, 258; Plutarch, *adv Col* 1119F.
155   Cf. II 121, 153.
156   See II 135–6 (cf. III 52).
157   Cf. *M* VIII 81–4, 135–6 (where the argument is applied to the parts of *simple* statements); note also the parallel argument below, at II 144. See BARNES [1988c].
158   With II 110–12 compare *M* VIII 112–17, 265 (cf. *M* I 310); Cicero, *Luc* xlvii 143. The different accounts of the conditional have been much discussed; see esp. FREDE [1974], pp. 80–93.
159   A pupil of Diodorus Cronus, testimonia in DÖRING [1972]; GIANNANTONI [1990].

sound conditional is one which does not begin from a truth and end in a falsity (e.g. – when it is day and I am conversing – 'If it is day, I am conversing'). Diodorus[160] says that it is one which neither could nor can begin from a truth and end in a falsity. According to him, the conditional just stated seems to be false, since if it is day but I shall be silent,[ab] it will begin from a truth but end in a falsity. [111] But 'If it is not the case that there are indivisible elements of existing things, there are indivisible elements of existing things' is true – for it will always begin from something false, viz. 'It is not the case that there are indivisible elements of existing things', and – according to him[161] – end in something true, viz. 'There are indivisible elements of existing things.' Those who introduce connectedness[162] say that a conditional is sound when the opposite of its consequent conflicts with its antecedent. According to them, the conditionals just stated will be unsound, but 'If it is day, it is day' will be true. [112] And those who judge by meaning say that a conditional is true when its consequent is contained implicitly in its antecedent. According to them, 'If it is day, it is day' – and every duplicated conditional statement[163] – will no doubt be false; for it is impossible for anything to be contained in itself.

[113][164] Now it will no doubt seem impossible for this dispute to be decided. For if we prefer one of these positions we shall be convincing neither without proof nor with proof. For a proof seems to be sound when its conclusion follows the conjunction of its assumptions as a consequent follows an antecedent: e.g. 'If it is day, it is light; but it is day: therefore it is light' – 'If if it is day it is light and it is day, it is light.'[165] [114] But since we are investigating how to judge whether a consequent follows its antecedent, the reciprocal mode turns up.[166] For if the judgement about the conditional is to be proved, the

---

[ab] Reading σιωπήσοντος for σιωπήσαντος (MSS, Mutschmann–Mau).

[160] Testimonia in DÖRING [1972]; GIANNANTONI [1990]; see SEDLEY [1977].
[161] See III 32; M IX 363.
[162] Probably Chrysippus: see Diogenes Laertius VII 73; Cicero, fat vi 12. But note that at II 104 the Stoics are given a 'Philonian' account of conditionals.
[163] On 'duplicated' statements see M VIII 108–10; Diogenes Laertius VII 68.
[164] With II 113–14 compare M VIII 118–23.
[165] Cf. II 137: the condition which Sextus states is necessary but not sufficient for a sound proof.
[166] See I 169.

conclusion must follow[ac] the assumptions of the proof, as we have just said; and if that in turn is to be found convincing, the conditional – i.e. whether the consequent follows – must have been decided.[167] And this is absurd. [115] Sound conditionals, therefore, are inapprehensible.

Pre-antecedents,[168] too, are puzzling. For a pre-antecedent, they say, is an antecedent in a conditional of the sort which begins from a truth and ends in a truth.[169] [116] But if signs are revelatory of their consequents, the consequents are either clear or unclear. Now if they are clear, they will not need the item which is meant to reveal them[170] – rather, they will be apprehended together with it: they will not be signified by it, and for that reason it will not be a sign of them. And if unclear, then since there has been an undecidable dispute about unclear things as to which of them are true and which false, and in general as to whether any of them are true, it will be unclear whether the conditional ends in a truth – which means that it will also be unclear whether its antecedent pre-antecedes.

[117][171] But to leave this too aside, they cannot be revelatory of their consequents, if the things signified are relative to their signs and for that reason are apprehended together with them. For relatives are apprehended together with one another;[172] and just as what is to the right cannot be apprehended as being to the right of what is to the left before what is to the left has been apprehended, and vice versa, and similarly in the case of the other relatives, so signs cannot be apprehended as signs of what is signified[ad] before what is signified has been apprehended. [118] But if signs are not apprehended before what is signified, they cannot be revelatory of them either, since they are apprehended together with them and not after them.

---

ac   Reading ἀκολουθεῖν δεῖ (Zimmermann): ἀκολουθεῖ MSS, Mutschmann–Mau.
ad   Adding σημεῖον before σημειωτοῦ (Mutschmann).

167   Cf. II 145.
168   Cf. *M* VIII 266–8.
169   See II 106.
170   Cf. II 99.
171   With II 117–20 compare *M* VIII 163–5 (cf. Diogenes Laertius IX 97).
172   Cf. II 125, 169, 179; III 7; *M* VIII 165, 174–5. Three analogous principles about relatives make their appearance in *PH*: (i) relatives are apprehended together (so here); (ii) relatives exist together (see II 126); (iii) relatives are conceived of together (see III 27). See BARNES [1988b].

Thus even as far as the more general remarks of those who belong to other schools go, signs are inconceivable.[173] For they say that they are both relative to something and revelatory of what is signified (to which they say they are relative). [119] Hence, if they are relative to something and relative to what is signified, they must necessarily be apprehended together with what is signified – just like what is to the left and what is to the right, what is up and what is down, and the other relatives. But if they are revelatory of what is signified, they must necessarily be apprehended before them, in order that, having been recognized beforehand, they may lead us to a conception of the object known on the basis of them. [120] But it is impossible to conceive of an object which cannot be recognized before something before which it must necessarily be apprehended.[174] Therefore it is impossible to conceive of something which is both relative to something and revelatory of that relative to which it is thought of. But they say that signs are both relative to something and revelatory of what is signified: therefore it is impossible to conceive of signs.[175]

[121][176] In addition, there is the following to be said. There has been a dispute among our predecessors, some saying that there are indicative signs, others[177] asserting that nothing is an indicative sign. Now anyone who says that there are indicative signs will speak either simply and without proof, making a mere assertion, or else with proof.[178] But if he makes a mere assertion he will be unconvincing; and if he wants to give a proof he will take for granted the matter under investigation. [122] For since proof is said to be a species of sign,[179] then as it is controversial whether there are any signs or not, there will be controversy too as to whether there are any proofs or not – just as, if you are investigating, say, whether there are any animals, you are also investigating whether there are any humans; for humans are animals. But it is absurd to try to prove what is under investigation through what is equally under investigation or through

---

[173] I.e. the argument in II 117–18 is not restricted to the technical Stoic account of indicative signs; note the 'general' definition of signs at *M* VIII 143: 'something which seems to make something clear'.

[174] Cf. III 28.   [175] Cf. II 132, 134.

[176] With II 121–3 compare *M* VIII 179–81.

[177] E.g. the Empiric doctors: see e.g. [Galen], *opt sect* I 149 K.

[178] Cf. II 107.   [179] See II 96.

itself; therefore no-one will be able by way of a proof to affirm that there are signs. [123] But if it is not possible to make a firm assertion about signs either simply or with a proof, it is impossible to make an apprehensive assertion about them; and if signs are not accurately apprehended, they will not be said to be significant of anything inasmuch as they themselves are not agreed upon – and for that reason they will not even be signs.[180] Hence in this way too we deduce that signs are non-existent and inconceivable.

[124] There is still the following to be said.[181] Either signs are apparent only or they are unclear only or some signs are apparent and some unclear. But none of these is sound. Therefore there are no signs.

Now, that it is not the case that all signs are unclear is shown as follows. What is unclear does not appear of itself, as the Dogmatists say, but makes an impression on us through something else. A sign, then, if it is unclear, will need another sign, which will be unclear – since, according to the hypothesis before us, nothing apparent is a sign –; and that will need another, and so *ad infinitum*.[182] But it is impossible to grasp infinitely many signs. Therefore it is impossible for signs to be apprehended if they are unclear.[183] And for that reason they will actually be non-existent; for they cannot signify anything or be signs, since they are not apprehended.[184]

[125] But if all signs are apparent, then since signs are relative to something and relative to what is signified, and relatives are apprehended together with one another,[185] what is said to be signified, being apprehended together with what is apparent, will be apparent. Just as, since right and left make an impression on us at the same time, right is no more said to be apparent than left nor left than right, so if a sign and what is signified are apprehended together, the sign should no more be said to be apparent than what is signified. [126] But if what is signified is apparent, it will not be a thing signified, having no

---

[180] See II 124, 128 (the same line of thought at II 184; III 26, 101).
[181] For the pattern of argument see II 88–94.
[182] See I 166.
[183] Cf. *M* VIII 178.
[184] See II 123.
[185] See II 117.

need for the item which is meant to signify and reveal it.[186] Hence, just as if right is rejected there is no left either, so if what is signified is rejected there cannot be any signs either.[187] Thus, signs turn out to be non-existent if anyone says that signs are apparent only.

[127] It remains to say that some signs are apparent and others unclear. But then the puzzles remain. For the things said to be signified by the apparent signs will be apparent, as we have already remarked, and, not needing what is meant to signify them, will not be things signified at all; hence the former will not be signs either, since they signify nothing. [128] And the unclear signs will require something to reveal them: if they are said to be signified by what is unclear, the account falls back *ad infinitum* and they turn out to be inapprehensible and for that reason unreal, as we have already remarked;[188] and if by what is apparent, they will be apparent, being apprehended together with their apparent signs, and for this reason they will also be unreal. For it is impossible for there to be any object which is both unclear by nature and apparent; and the signs with which our account is concerned, being supposed unclear, have been found to be apparent by the turning about of the argument.[189]

[129] If, then, neither are all signs apparent nor all unclear nor some signs apparent and some unclear, and if there are no other possibilities, as they themselves say, then what they call signs will be unreal.

[130] These few points, taken from many,[190] will suffice here to suggest that there are no indicative signs. Next we shall set out the suggestions that there are signs, so that we may establish the equipollence of the opposed accounts.[191]

The phrases brought against signs either signify something or signify nothing. If they are insignificant, how will they shake the reality of signs? And if they signify something, there are signs.[192]

[131][193] Again, the arguments against signs are either probative or

---

[186] Cf. II 99.
[187] For this principle (cf. II 117, note) see e.g. III 16, 25, 27, 101; *M* VIII 164; IX 234, 340.
[188] See II 123, 124.
[189] See I 122.
[190] See I 58.
[191] See II 103.
[192] Cf. *M* VIII 279.
[193] Cf. *M* VIII 277–8, 281–2 (see also below, II 185).

not probative. If they are not probative, they do not prove that there are no signs; and if they are probative, then, since proof is a species of sign,[194] being revelatory of the conclusion, there will be signs. Hence the following argument[195] is also put forward: If there are signs, there are signs; and if there are not signs, there are signs (for that there are not signs is shown through a proof which in fact is a sign); but either there are signs or there are not signs: therefore there are signs.

[132] This argument is matched by the following one:[196] If nothing is a sign, there are no signs; and if there are signs – of the sort which the Dogmatists say are signs – there are no signs (for the signs with which the argument is concerned, being said in their conception to be both relative and revelatory of what is signified, turn out to be unreal, as we have established[197]); [133] but either there are signs or there are not signs: therefore there are not signs. And as for the phrases concerning signs, let the Dogmatists themselves tell us whether they signify something or signify nothing. If they signify nothing, it is not convincing that there are signs; and if they signify, then what they signify will follow – but they signify that there are no[ae] signs, and it follows that there are no signs, as we have suggested, by the turning about of the argument.[198]

Thus, since such plausible arguments are adduced both for there being signs and for there not being, we should no more say that there are signs than that there are not.[199]

[ae] Adding μή before εἶναι (Heintz).

[194] See II 96.

[195] For the pattern see II 186.

[196] Cf. *M* VIII 296; on the technique of 'matching' arguments or παραβολή see SCHOFIELD [1983].

[197] See II 120.

[198] This last argument is perplexing (see esp. HEINTZ [1932], pp. 52–62). The text is certainly corrupt: Mutschmann–Mau add one 'not' and we add two; and deeper surgery may be required. We paraphrase thus: 'As for the Dogmatists' argument at II 130, let them answer their own question, "Do the Sceptics' phrases used against signs signify anything?" If they say No, then that certainly does not establish that signs exist; and if they say Yes, then what our phrases signify holds good and there are no signs. So the argument in II 130 is turned about [cf. I 122]: in either case, as we have been urging, there are no signs.' (There is a different reply to the Dogmatists' argument about the Sceptics' phrases at *M* VIII 290.)

[199] Cf. *M* VIII 298 (and below, II 192; III 29, 49, 65, 135). On 'no more' see above, I 188–91.

xii Proof

[134]²⁰⁰ It is clear from these considerations that proof too is an object of disagreement. If we suspend judgement about signs, and proofs are a sort of sign,²⁰¹ then it is necessary to suspend judgement about proofs too. For we shall find that the arguments we propounded about signs can also be applied to proofs: proofs are thought to be both relative to something and revelatory of their conclusions, and it was from these points²⁰² that pretty well everything we said against signs followed. [135] But if something must be said about proofs specifically, I shall consider briefly the argument about them, having first tried to explain in a few words what they say proofs are.

A proof, they say, is an argument which, by way of agreed assumptions and in virtue of yielding a conclusion, reveals an unclear consequence.²⁰³ What they mean will be plainer from the following considerations.

An argument is a compound of assumptions and consequence.²⁰⁴ [136]²⁰⁵ The statements assumed without dispute for the establishment of the conclusion are said to be the assumptions, and the statement purportedly established by way of the assumptions is said to be the consequence. E.g. in the following argument:

If it is day, it is light.
But it is day.
Therefore, it is light.

'It is light' is the consequence^af and the rest are assumptions.

[137]²⁰⁶ Some arguments are conclusive, others inconclusive. They are conclusive when the conditional which begins from the conjunc-

---

^af Reading ἐπιφορά for συμπέρασμα (cf. M VIII 302).

²⁰⁰ Cf. M VIII 299–300.
²⁰¹ See II 96.
²⁰² See II 120, 132.
²⁰³ Cf. II 143, 170; M VIII 314, 385; Diogenes Laertius VII 45; Cicero, Luc ix 26; Clement, strom VIII iii 5.1; see BRUNSCHWIG [1980]; EBERT [1991], pp. 219–86.
²⁰⁴ I.e. a structure consisting of premisses and conclusion: Sextus here uses the Stoic definition, and the Stoic terminology (λῆμμα or 'assumption' and ἐπιφορά or 'consequence', where the Peripatetics preferred πρότασις and συμπέρασμα). Cf. e.g. Diogenes Laertius VII 45, 76.
²⁰⁵ Cf. M VIII 301–2.
²⁰⁶ Cf. M VIII 303–5 (and 414–17).

tion of the assumptions of the argument and ends in its consequence is sound.[207] E.g. the argument just mentioned is conclusive, because in the conditional 'If it is day and if it is day it is light it is light', 'It is light' follows the conjunction of its assumptions, viz. 'It is day and if it is day it is light'. Arguments not of this character are inconclusive.

[138][208] Some conclusive arguments are true, others not true. They are true when not only (as we have said) is the conditional formed from the conjunction of the assumptions and the consequence sound, but also the conjunction of the assumptions, which is antecedent in the conditional, is true. (A conjunction is true when everything it contains is true.[209] E.g. 'It is day, and if it is day it is light'.) Arguments not of this character are not true. [139] This argument:

> If it is night, it is dark.
> But it is night.
> Therefore, it is dark.

is conclusive, since the conditional 'If it is night and if it is night it is dark, it is dark' is sound. But it is not true. For the conjunctive antecedent, 'It is night and if it is night it is dark', is false, since it contains in itself the false 'It is night'. For a conjunction which contains in itself something[ag] false is false. (Hence they also say that a true argument is one which concludes to a true conclusion by way of true assumptions.[210])

[140][211] Next, some true arguments are probative, others not probative. They are probative if they conclude to something unclear by way of things that are clear, and not probative if they are not of this sort. E.g. this argument:

> If it is day, it is light.
> But it is day.
> Therefore, it is light.

---

ag   Omitting ἕν, which Mutschmann–Mau add to the MSS text.

[207] See II 113, 145, 249; Diogenes Laertius VII 77.
[208] With II 138–9 compare M VIII 418–21 (and 311).
[209] See BRUNSCHWIG [1978a].
[210] See II 187, 248; M VIII 414; Diogenes Laertius VII 79; Galen, *an pecc dig* (FDS 1070) = V 72 K.
[211] Cf. M VIII 305–6, 422–3, neither of which passages is quite the same as ours.

is not probative; for its conclusion – that it is light – is clear. But this argument:[212]

> If sweat flows through the surface, there are imperceptible pores.
> But sweat flows through the surface.
> Therefore, there are imperceptible pores.

is probative; for its conclusion, 'Therefore there are imperceptible pores', is unclear.

[141][213] Of arguments which conclude to something unclear, some lead us through the assumptions to the conclusion in a manner which is merely progressive, others in a manner which is progressive and at the same time revelatory. E.g. progressively, those which are thought to depend on convincingness and memory, such as:

> If some god[ah] has told you that this man will be rich, then this man will be rich.
> But this god (I point, let us suppose, to Zeus) has told you that this man will be rich.
> Therefore, this man will be rich.

For we assent to the conclusion not so much because of the necessity of the assumptions as because we are convinced by the god's assertion. [142] Other arguments lead us to the conclusion in a manner which is not only progressive but also revelatory, such as:[214]

> If sweat flows through the surface, there are imperceptible pores.
> But the first.
> Therefore, the second.[215]

For that sweat flows is revelatory of the fact that there are pores, because it is a preconception that liquid cannot be carried through a solid body.

[143][216] A proof, then, ought to be an argument which is conclusive and true and has an unclear conclusion which is revealed by the

---

ah Adding θεῶν after τίς σοι (Fabricius).

212 Cf. II 98.
213 With II 141–2 compare M VIII 307–9.
214 Cf. II 98, 140.
215 The Stoics called such semi-schematic arguments λογότροποι (Diogenes Laertius VII 77; Suda, s.v. λογότοπος [sic]); cf. e.g. III 121.
216 Cf. M VIII 314.

power of the assumptions; and for this reason a proof is said to be an argument which, by way of agreed assumptions and in virtue of yielding a conclusion, reveals an unclear consequence.[217] This, then, is how they usually illuminate the concept of proof.

xiii Are there any proofs?

[144] That proofs are unreal can be deduced from the very things they say, by overturning everything contained in the concept.

Thus[218] arguments are composed of statements and compound objects cannot exist unless the things from which they are composed co-exist with one another (this is clear from beds and the like). But the parts of an argument do not co-exist with one another. For when we say the first assumption, neither the second assumption nor the consequence yet exists; when we say the second assumption, the first assumption no longer exists and the consequence does not yet exist; and when we utter the consequence, its assumptions no longer subsist. Therefore the parts of an argument do not co-exist with one another. Hence arguments will seem to be unreal.

[145][219] Apart from that, conclusive arguments are inapprehensible. For if they are judged by deciding whether the consequent of a conditional follows the antecedent,[220] and if this has been subject to undecidable dispute and is no doubt inapprehensible (as we have suggested in our remarks on signs[221]), then conclusive arguments too will be inapprehensible.

[146][222] The dialecticians say that inconclusive arguments are due either to disconnectedness or to deficiency or to being propounded in an unsound form or to redundancy. To disconnectedness[223] when the assumptions do not cohere[224] with one another or with the consequence, as in the following case:

---

[217] See II 135.
[218] Cf. II 109.
[219] Cf. *M* VIII 426–9.
[220] Cf. II 137.
[221] See II 114.
[222] With II 146–50 compare *M* VIII 429–34; see EBERT [1991], pp. 131–75.
[223] See also II 238.
[224] Here, and in II 152, 'cohere' renders ἀκολουθία: see I 16, note.

> If it is day, it is light.
> But wheat is being sold in the market.
> Therefore, Dio is walking.

[147] To redundancy[225] when an assumption is found to be redundant with regard to the argument's yielding a conclusion, e.g.:

> If it is day, it is light.
> But it is day.
> But Dio is walking.
> Therefore, it is light.

To being propounded in an unsound form when the form of the argument is not conclusive, e.g. whereas the following, they say, are deductions:[ai]

> If it is day, it is light.
> But it is day.
> Therefore, it is light.

and:

> If it is day, it is light.
> But it is not light.
> Therefore, it is not day.

the following argument is inconclusive:

> If it is day, it is light.
> But it is light.
> Therefore, it is day.

[148] For since the conditional announces that if its antecedent is the case then so too is its consequent,[226] it is likely that when the antecedent is taken as an additional assumption the consequent should be derived, and that when the consequent has been rejected, the antecedent too should be rejected – for if the antecedent were the case the consequent would also be the case. But if the consequent is taken as an additional assumption, the antecedent is not necessarily

---

[ai] Retaining the MS reading συλλογισμῶν which Mutschmann–Mau emend to συλλογιστικῶν.

[225] On which see BARNES [1980].
[226] See II 189; Diogenes Laertius VII 71.

posited; for the conditional did not promise that the antecedent follows the consequent, but only that the consequent follows the antecedent. [149] For this reason, then, an argument which concludes to the consequent from a conditional and its antecedent is said to be deductive, and so also is one which concludes to the opposite of the antecedent from a conditional and the opposite of its consequent. But an argument which concludes to the antecedent from a conditional and the consequent is said to be inconclusive, as in the case just given. (That is why it may conclude to something false even if its assumptions are true, when it is said at night by lamp-light. For the conditional 'If it is day, it is light' is true, and so is the additional assumption 'But it is light'; but the consequence, 'Therefore it is day', is false.)

[150] An argument is unsound in virtue of deficiency if one of the things needed for concluding to the conclusion is omitted. E.g. whereas, they think, the following argument is sound:

> Wealth is either good or bad or indifferent.
> But it is neither bad nor indifferent.
> Therefore, it is good.

the following argument is bad from deficiency:

> Wealth is either good or bad.
> But it is not bad.[aj]
> Therefore, it is good.

[151] Now if I show that according to them no difference can be discerned between inconclusive and conclusive arguments, I shall have shown that conclusive arguments are inapprehensible, so that the endless verbiage they devote to dialectic is superfluous. I show it as follows.

[152]²²⁷ Arguments which are inconclusive in virtue of disconnectedness were said to be recognized by the fact that their assumptions do not cohere²²⁸ with one another or with the consequence. Now,

---

[aj] Mau suggests the addition of ⟨ἢ ἀδιάφορος⟩, '... or indifferent': the result is indeed a non-conclusive argument, but *M* VIII 434 shows that the received text is correct.

227 With II 152–3 compare *M* VIII 435–7.
228 Cf. II 146.

since recognition of this coherence must be preceded by a judgement on conditionals, and conditionals are undecidable, as we have deduced,[229] arguments which are inconclusive in virtue of disconnectedness will also be indiscernible. [153] For anyone who says that a certain argument is inconclusive in virtue of disconnectedness will, if he merely makes a statement, have opposed to him the statement opposite to his own; and if he purports to prove it by way of an argument, he will be told that this argument must first be conclusive and only then prove that the assumptions of the argument said to be disconnected are in fact unconnected. But we shall not recognize whether the argument is probative if we do not possess an undisputed judgement on conditionals by which to judge whether the conclusion follows the conjunction of the assumptions of the argument. So for this reason we shall not be able to distinguish conclusive arguments from those said to be unsound in virtue of disconnectedness.

[154][230] We shall say the same against anyone who says that an argument is unsound because it is propounded in a bad form. For anyone trying to establish that a certain form is unsound will have no agreed conclusive argument through which he can conclude to what he says.

[155][231] By these considerations we have implicitly also argued against those who try to show that arguments are inconclusive because of deficiency. For if complete and finished arguments are indistinguishable, deficient arguments will also be unclear. And further, anyone who wishes to show by argument that a given argument is deficient will have no agreed judgement on conditionals through which he can judge the validity[232] of the argument he utters, and so he will not be able to say, correctly and after judging the matter, that it is deficient.

[156][233] Arguments said to be unsound by redundancy are also indistinguishable from probative arguments. For as far as redundancy

---

[229] See II 145.
[230] Cf. M VIII 444–5.
[231] Cf. M VIII 446.
[232] 'Validity' renders ἀκολουθία: see I 16, note.
[233] Cf. M VIII 438.

goes, even the unprovable arguments which the Stoics talk so much about [234] will be found to be inconclusive – and if they are rejected, the whole of dialectic is overthrown. For these are the arguments which they say need no proof[235] for their own construction and are probative of the fact that the other arguments reach a conclusion.[236] That they are redundant will be clear if we set out the unprovable arguments and then deduce what we are maintaining.

[157] They dream up many unprovable arguments, but they set out in particular the following five,[237] to which all the rest are thought to be referred. First, the argument which, from a conditional and the antecedent, concludes to the consequent, e.g.:

If it is day, it is light.
But it is day.
Therefore, it is light.

Secondly, the argument which, from a conditional and the opposite of the consequent, concludes to the opposite of the antecedent, e.g.:

If it is day, it is light.
But it is not light.
Therefore, it is not day.

[158] Thirdly, the argument which, from a negative conjunction and one of the conjuncts, concludes to the opposite of the other, e.g.:

It is not the case that it is day and it is night.
But it is day.
Therefore, it is not night.

---

[234] For the Stoic 'unprovable' or 'indemonstrable' argument-forms expounded in II 157–8, see also e.g. below, II 198–203; M VIII 223–7; Galen, *inst log* vi 6; Diogenes Laertius VII 79–81; see e.g. FREDE [1974], pp. 127–53.

[235] ἀναπόδεικτος, which we translate in the traditional fashion by 'unprovable', is in this context used to designate what does not *require* proof rather than what *cannot* be proved; cf. M VIII 223; Diogenes Laertius VII 79; Galen, *inst log* viii 1.

[236] Cf. II 166, 194.

[237] The five are the Chrysippean canon (see the texts listed above, n. 234). Some Stoics offered different lists (see Diogenes Laertius VII 79; Galen, *inst log* xiv 3); on the lists of seven unprovables (Cicero, *Topics* xii 53–xiv 57; Martianus Capella, IV 414–21; Boethius, *Commentary on Cicero's Topics* 355–8) see IERO-DIAKONOU [1993].

Fourthly, the argument which, from a disjunction and one of the disjuncts, concludes to the opposite of the other, e.g.:

> Either it is day or it is night.
> But it is day.
> Therefore, it is not night.

Fifthly, the argument which, from a disjunction and the opposite of one of the disjuncts, concludes to the other, e.g.:

> Either it is day or it is night.
> But it is not night.
> Therefore, it is day.

[159][238] These, then, are the unprovables which they talk so much about – and they all seem to me to be inconclusive by redundancy. For example (to begin from the first), either it is agreed that 'It is light' follows 'It is day', its antecedent in the conditional 'If it is day, it is light', or else it is unclear. But if it is unclear, we shall not grant the conditional as something agreed upon. And if it is clear that if 'It is day' is the case then of necessity 'It is light' will also be the case, then when we say that it is day it is concluded that it is light, so that the argument:

> It is day.
> Therefore, it is light.

is sufficient, and the conditional 'If it is day, it is light' is redundant.

[160] We proceed in the same way in the case of the second unprovable too. Either it is possible for the antecedent to be the case when the consequent is not the case, or else it is not possible. But if it is possible, the conditional will not be sound; and if it is not possible, then 'Not the antecedent' is posited at the same time as 'Not the consequent' is posited, and the conditional is again redundant, the argument coming to be propounded thus:

> It is not light.
> Therefore, it is not day.

[161] The same argument applies also to the third unprovable. Either it is clear that the conjuncts cannot co-exist with one another, or else it

238 With II 159–62 compare *M* VIII 440–2 (and see below, II 193).

is unclear. And if it is unclear, we shall not grant the negation of the conjunction; while if it is clear, then at the same time as the one conjunct is posited the other is rejected, and the negation of the conjunction is redundant, since we argue thus:

It is day.
Therefore, it is not night.

[162] We make similar remarks in the case of the fourth and the fifth unprovables. Either it is clear that in the disjunction the one disjunct is true and the other false with complete conflict[239] (that is what the disjunction announces[240]), or else it is unclear. But if it is unclear, we shall not grant the disjunction; and if it is clear, then when one of the disjuncts is posited it is plain that the other is not the case, and when one is rejected it is clear that the other is the case, so that it is enough to propound the arguments as follows:

It is day.
Therefore, it is not night.

and:

It is not day.
Therefore, it is night.

– and the disjunction is redundant.

[163] We can make similar remarks about the so-called categorical deductions which are used especially by the Peripatetics.[241] Thus, for example, in this argument:

The just is fine.
The fine is good.
Therefore, the just is good.

either it is agreed and is clear that the fine is good, or else it is controverted and unclear. But if it is unclear, then it will not be granted when the argument is propounded, and for that reason the

---

[239] Two propositions are in 'complete' conflict if exactly one of them must be true; they are in 'partial' conflict if at most one of them can be true: see Galen, *inst log* IV 1–2 (cf. below, II 191; *M* VIII 283).
[240] See II 191; Diogenes Laertius VII 72.
[241] See ANNAS [1992c].

deduction will not reach a conclusion; and if it is clear that anything fine is necessarily also good, then at the same time as it is said that this individual thing is fine, it may be concluded that it is also good, so that it is enough to propound the argument as follows:

> The just is fine.
> Therefore, the just is good.

– and the other assumption, in which the fine was said to be good, is redundant.[242] [164] Similarly, too, in the argument:

> Socrates is human.
> Everything human is an animal.
> Therefore, Socrates is an animal.

If it is not directly clear that anything which is human is also an animal, the universal proposition is not agreed upon and we shall not grant it when it is propounded. [165] But if being an animal follows being human,[ak] and for that reason the proposition 'Everything human is an animal' is agreed to be true, then at the same time as it is said that Socrates is human, it may be concluded that he is an animal, so that it is enough to propound the argument thus:

> Socrates is human.
> Therefore, Socrates is an animal.

and the proposition 'Everything human is an animal' is redundant. [166] And similar methods can be used – not to dwell on the matter now – in the case of the other primary[al] categorical deductions.

Since these arguments which the dialecticians place as the foundations of their deductions[243] are redundant, then as far as redundancy goes, the whole of dialectic is overthrown, given that we cannot distinguish arguments which are redundant and for that reason inconclusive from the deductions they call conclusive. [167] And if some refuse to allow that there are arguments with a single

---

[ak] Reading τῷ ἄνθρωπον εἶναι (Mau): the MSS offer different readings, all of them unsatisfactory; Mutschmann–Mau print τοῦ ἀνθρώπου τῷ εἶναι.

[al] Retaining the MS reading, πρώτων: Mutschmann–Mau print τρόπων τῶν (Heintz).

[242] Cf. Alexander, *in Top* 13.25–14.2.
[243] See II 156.

assumption, they deserve to be found no more convincing than Antipater who does not rule out such arguments.[244]

For[245] these reasons, then, what the dialecticians call conclusive arguments are undecidable. But in addition, true arguments are undiscoverable, both for the reasons given above[246] and because they ought certainly to end in a truth. Now the conclusion which is said to be true is either apparent or unclear. [168] But it is surely not apparent; for it would not need to be revealed by way of the assumptions if it made an impression by itself and were no less apparent than its assumptions.[247] And if it is unclear, then since there has been an undecidable dispute about what is unclear (as we have already suggested[248]), so that unclear things are actually inapprehensible, the conclusion of an argument said to be true will be inapprehensible. And if this is inapprehensible, we shall not know whether what is being concluded is true or false. We shall be ignorant, then, whether the argument is true or false, and true arguments will be undiscoverable.

[169] But to pass over this too, arguments concluding to something unclear by way of what is clear are undiscoverable. For if the consequence follows the conjunction of the assumptions, and if what follows and the consequent are relative to something, i.e. relative to the antecedent, and if relatives are apprehended together with one another, as we established,[249] then if the conclusion is unclear the assumptions too will be unclear, and if the assumptions are clear the conclusion too will be clear inasmuch as it is apprehended together with them and they are clear;[250] so that what is unclear is not after all concluded from what is clear. [170] Nor, for these reasons, is the

---

244 Cf. *M* VIII 443; Alexander, *in Top* 8.16–18; Apuleius, *int* 184.20–3. Antipater, head of the Stoa in the middle of the second century BC, opposed the orthodox Chrysippean view. Sextus mentions the matter here in order to avoid the following rejoinder to his argument: 'But I *can* distinguish conclusive from non-conclusive arguments – conclusive arguments have only one premiss.'
245 With this paragraph compare *M* VIII 448–52.
246 See II 85–94 (where truth in general is attacked) or 145–66 (for if there are no conclusive arguments, there are *a fortiori* no true arguments)?
247 Cf. II 99.
248 See II 116.
249 See II 117.
250 Cf. III 7.

consequence revealed by the assumptions. It is either unclear and not apprehended or else clear and not needing anything to reveal it.

Thus if a proof is said to be an argument which in virtue of yielding a conclusion[am] reveals an unclear consequence by way of items agreed to be true,[251] and if we have suggested that there are no arguments and none that are conclusive or that are true or that conclude to something unclear by way of what is clear or that are revelatory of the conclusion, then it is plain that proofs are non-existent.

[171][252] By way of the following assault too we shall find proof to be unreal or even inconceivable. Anyone who says that there are proofs posits either generic proof or some specific proof; but it is not possible to posit either generic or specific proofs, as we shall suggest, and it is not possible to think of any others apart from them: you cannot therefore posit proofs as existing. [172] Generic proof is non-existent for the following reasons. Either it has assumptions and a consequence, or it does not. And if it does not, it is not a proof at all; but if it has assumptions and a consequence, then since everything which is proved and proves in this way is particular, it will be a specific proof. Therefore there are no generic proofs.

[173] Nor are there specific proofs either. For they will say either that a proof is the compound of the assumptions and the consequence or that it is the compound of the assumptions alone; but a proof is neither of these, as I shall establish: therefore there are no specific proofs. [174] Now the compound of the assumptions and the consequence is not a proof, first because it contains an unclear part, namely the consequence, and so will be unclear. But that is absurd; for if a proof is unclear, it will itself need something to prove it rather than be probative of other things. [175] Secondly, since they say that proofs are relative to something,[253] i.e. relative to their consequences, and relatives are thought of, as they themselves say, in relation to other things, then what is being proved must be something other than the proof. Then, if what is being proved is the conclusion, proofs will not be thought of as including their conclusions. And either the

---

[am] Omitting τουτέστι συνακτικός (Bekker).

[251] See II 135.
[252] With II 171–6 compare *M* VIII 382–90 (and see 338–47; *M* II 110–11).
[253] See II 179; *M* VIII 335; 453–62.

conclusion contributes something towards its own proof or it does not. But if it does contribute, it will be revelatory of itself, while if it does not contribute but is redundant, it will not be a part of the proof since we shall say that the proof itself is unsound by redundancy. [176] But the compound of the assumptions alone will not be a proof either. For who would say that something stated like this:

If it is day, it is light.
But it is day.

either is an argument or finishes a thought at all? Therefore the compound of the assumptions alone is not a proof.

Therefore specific proofs have no subsistence either. And if neither specific nor generic proofs subsist, and it is not possible to conceive of any proofs apart from these, then proofs are non-existent.

[177][254] Again, it is possible to suggest the non-existence of proofs by the following considerations. If there are proofs, they are either apparent and revelatory of what is apparent, or unclear and revelatory of what is unclear, or unclear and revelatory of what is apparent, or apparent and revelatory of what is unclear. But proofs cannot be conceived of as revelatory in any of these ways: therefore they are inconceivable. [178] If a proof is apparent and revelatory of what is apparent, then what is revealed will be at the same time both apparent and unclear – apparent, since it was hypothesized to be so, and unclear, since it needs something to reveal it and does not make a plain impression on us by itself. If a proof is unclear and revelatory of what is unclear, then it will itself need something to reveal it and will not be revelatory of anything else – and that departs from the concept of a proof. [179] For these reasons there cannot be unclear proofs of what is clear either. Nor can there be clear proofs of what is unclear. For since proofs are relative to something[255] and relatives are apprehended at the same time as one another,[256] what is said to be proved, being apprehended at the same time as the clear proof, will be clear, so that the account is turned about[257] and the proof is not found to be

---

[254] With II 177–9 compare *M* VIII 391–5.
[255] See II 175.
[256] See II 17, note.
[257] See I 122.

clear itself and probative of something unclear. If, then, there are neither apparent proofs of what is apparent, nor unclear proofs of what is unclear, nor unclear of what is clear, nor clear of what is unclear, and if they say that there is nothing apart from these, then they must say that proof is nothing.

[180][258] In addition, we should make the following remark. There has been a dispute about proofs. Some say that they do not even exist (for example, those who state that nothing at all exists[259]), others that they do exist (most of the Dogmatists), and we say that they no more exist than not exist. [181] And again, proofs certainly include beliefs, and they have disputed about every belief, so that there must be dispute about every proof. For if the proof that, say, there is void, is agreed to, it is also agreed that there is void: clearly, then, those who controvert the existence of void also controvert the proof. And the same argument goes for the other beliefs which are subjects of proof. Hence every proof is controverted and under dispute.

[182] Since proofs are unclear, then, because of the dispute about them (for disputed items, insofar as they have been subject to dispute, are unclear[260]), they are not manifest in themselves but ought to be recommended to us by a proof. Now the proof by way of which proofs are established will not be agreed upon and manifest (for we are now investigating whether proofs exist at all); but, being disputed and unclear, it will need another proof, and that another, and so *ad infinitum*.[261] But it is impossible to prove infinitely many things. Therefore, it is impossible to establish that there are proofs. [183] Nor can they be revealed by way of signs. For the existence of signs is under investigation, and signs require proof to show their own reality, so that the reciprocal mode turns up,[262] proofs needing signs and signs in turn needing proofs[263] – which is absurd.

And for the following reasons it is not possible to decide the dispute about proof: the decision requires a standard and, as there is

[258] With II 180–1 compare *M* VIII 327–34.
[259] E.g. Gorgias: II 57. At *M* VIII 327 the Empiric doctors 'and perhaps Democritus' are cited as denying proof (cf. Galen, *On Sects, for beginners* 5, I 72 K).
[260] See II 116.
[261] See I 166.
[262] See I 169.
[263] See II 122.

an investigation as to whether there are any standards (as we have established[264]) and standards therefore need a proof to show that there are standards, the reciprocal mode of impasse again turns up.[265] [184] If, then, it cannot be suggested either by a proof or by a sign or by a standard that there are proofs, and if proofs are not clear in themselves, as we have established, then it will be inapprehensible whether there are any proofs. And for that reason proofs will actually be unreal; for they are conceived of together with the notion of proving, and they cannot prove if they are not apprehended.[266] Hence they will not actually be proofs.

[185][267] This, in an outline,[268] will be enough against proofs. The Dogmatists, attempting to establish the contrary, say that the arguments propounded against proofs are either probative or not probative. But if they are not probative, they cannot show that there are no proofs; and if they are probative, then they themselves, by a turning about,[269] introduce the subsistence of proof. [186] Hence they also propound the following argument:

> If there are proofs, there are proofs.
> If there are not proofs, there are proofs.
> But either there are proofs or there are not proofs.
> Therefore, there are proofs.

They propound the following argument too, with the same force:

> Whatever follows opposites is not only true but also necessary.
> These things – there are proofs, there are not proofs – are opposite to one another, and that there are proofs follows each of them.
> Therefore, there are proofs.

[187] Now we may argue against this by saying, for example, that since we do not deem any arguments to be probative, we do not necessarily say that the arguments against proof are probative, but that they appear plausible to us – and plausible arguments are not

---

[264] See II 18–79.
[265] Cf. II 20; *M* VIII 380; Diogenes Laertius IX 91.
[266] Cf. II 123.
[267] With II 185–6 compare *M* VIII 465–7 (and above, II 131).
[268] See I 4, note.
[269] See I 122.

probative of necessity.[270] But if they actually are probative (which we do not affirm), they are certainly also true. But true arguments are those which conclude to a truth by way of truths.[271] Thus their consequence is true – and that was: There are no proofs. 'There are no proofs' is therefore true, by being turned about.[272] [188] Arguments, like purgative drugs which evacuate themselves along with the matters present in the body, can actually cancel themselves along with the other arguments which are said to be probative.[273] This is not incongruous, since the phrase 'Nothing is true' not only denies everything else but also turns itself about[274] at the same time.

And the following argument can be shown to be inconclusive:

> If there are proofs, there are proofs.
> If there are not proofs, there are proofs.
> Either there are or there are not.
> Therefore, there are.

The point can be made in several ways, but for present purposes the following attack will be enough.[275] [189] If the conditional 'If there are proofs, there are proofs' is sound, the opposite of its consequent, viz. 'There are no proofs', must conflict with 'There are proofs'; for this is the antecedent of the conditional.[276] But it is impossible, according to them, for a conditional composed of conflicting statements to be sound. For a conditional announces that if its antecedent is the case, then so too is its consequent,[277] and conflicting statements announce the contrary – that if either one of them is the case, it is impossible for the other to hold. If, therefore, this conditional – 'If there are proofs, there are proofs' – is sound, then the conditional 'If there are not proofs, there are proofs' cannot be sound. [190] Again, if we concede by way of hypothesis that the conditional 'If there are not proofs, there are proofs' is sound, then 'There are proofs' can co-exist with 'There are not proofs'. But if it can co-exist with it, it does not

---

[270] Cf. *M* VIII 473.
[271] See II 139.
[272] See I 122.
[273] Cf. *M* VIII 480; and see above, I 14–15, 206.
[274] See I 122.
[275] See STOPPER [1983]; NASTI DE VINCENTIS [1984].
[276] See II III.
[277] See II 148.

conflict with it. Therefore in the conditional 'If there are proofs, there are proofs' the opposite of its consequent does not conflict with its antecedent. Thus, in its turn the latter conditional is not sound [191] if the former is posited by way of concession as sound. And if 'There are no proofs' does not conflict with 'There are proofs', then the disjunction, 'Either there are proofs or there are not proofs', will not be sound either. For a sound disjunction announces that one of its elements is sound[an] and the other or others false and conflicting.[278] Or, if the disjunction is sound, the conditional 'If there are no proofs, there are proofs' again turns out to be bad, being composed of conflicting elements. Thus the assumptions in the argument just mentioned are discordant and destroy one another; [192] and for that reason the argument is not sound. Nor can they even show that anything follows the opposites, since, as we have deduced,[279] they have no standard for implication.[280]

This we say for good measure.[281] For if the arguments on behalf of proofs are plausible – and let them be so – and the attacks we have made on proofs are also plausible, then we must suspend judgement about proofs too, saying that there no more are than are not proofs.[282]

xiv Deductions

[193] For this reason it is no doubt superfluous to deal with the deductions which they talk so much about – they are turned about [283] together with the reality of proofs (for it is plain that if there are no proofs, then probative arguments have no place either); and we have also implicitly argued against them in our earlier remarks[284] when, discussing redundancy, we described a procedure by way of which it is possible to show that all the probative arguments both of the Stoics

---

[an] Retaining the MS reading ὑγιές: Mutschmann–Mau print ἀληθές (Heintz).

278 See II 162.
279 See II 110–14.
280 'Implication' renders ἀκολουθία: see I 16, note.
281 See I 62.
282 See II 133 (and I 188–91 on 'no more').
283 I 122.
284 See II 159–66.

and of the Peripatetics are in fact inconclusive. [194] But for good measure[285] it is no doubt no bad idea to discuss them in their own right too, since they particularly pride themselves on them.[286] Many things can be said to suggest their non-existence; but in an outline[287] it is enough to use the following procedure against them. Here too I shall talk about the unprovables – for if they are rejected, all the other arguments too are overthrown, since it is on the unprovables that the proof of their conclusiveness depends.[288]

[195][289] Now this proposition – Everything human is an animal – is confirmed inductively [290] from the particulars; for from the fact that Socrates, being human, is also an animal, and similarly with Plato and Dio and each of the particulars, it is thought possible to affirm that everything human is an animal. For if even one of the particulars were to appear contrary to the others, the universal proposition is not sound – e.g. since most animals move their lower jaw but the crocodile alone moves its upper jaw, the proposition 'Every animal moves its lower jaw' is not true.[291] [196] Thus when they say:

> Everything human is an animal.
> But Socrates is human.
> Therefore, Socrates is an animal.

and wish to conclude from the universal proposition 'Everything human is an animal' to the particular proposition 'Therefore Socrates is an animal', which (as we have suggested) is actually confirmatory of the universal proposition in virtue of the inductive mode, they fall into the reciprocal argument,[292] confirming the universal proposition inductively by way of each of the particulars and the particular deductively from the universal.[ao] [197] Similarly in the case of the following argument:

[ao] There is a lacuna in the text: we follow Bury and read: τῶν κατὰ μέρος ⟨ἐπαγωγικῶς, βεβαιοῦντες, τὴν δὲ κατὰ μέρος⟩ ἐκ τῆς καθόλου.

285 See I 62.
286 See I 180.
287 See I 4, note.
288 See II 156.
289 With II 195–7 compare II 163–5.
290 See II 204.
291 A stock example (e.g. Apuleius, *int* 185.15–20; Alexander, *in APr* 43.28–44.2): see BARNES, BOBZIEN, FLANNERY and IERODIAKONOU [1991], p. 104, n. 12.
292 See I 169.

Socrates is human.
But nothing human is a quadruped.
Therefore, Socrates is not a quadruped.

Wishing to confirm the proposition 'Nothing human is a quadruped' inductively from the particulars and wanting to deduce each of the particulars from 'Nothing human is quadruped', they fall into the impasse of reciprocity.

[198] The rest of the arguments which the Peripatetics call unprovable[293] should be gone through in a similar way. And so too with arguments such as:[294]

If it is day, it is light.
But it is day.
Therefore, it is light.[ap]

For 'If it is day, it is light' leads to the conclusion, as they say, that when it is day it is light,[aq] and 'It is light' together with 'It is day' is confirmatory of 'If it is day, it is light'. For this conditional would not be deemed sound if 'It is light' had not been earlier observed always to co-exist with 'It is day'. [199] Thus one must first apprehend that when it is day it is necessarily also light, in order to construct the conditional 'If it is day, it is light', and by way of this conditional it is concluded that when it is day it is light. Hence, since the conditional 'If it is day, it is light' concludes – so far as the unprovable before us goes – to the co-existence of its being day and its being light, while the co-existence of these items confirms the conditional, here too the reciprocal mode of impasse[295] overturns the subsistence of the argument.

[200] Similarly with the following argument:

If it is day, it is light.
But it is not light.
Therefore, it is not day.

[ap] Reading εἰ ἡμέρα ἔστι φῶς ἔστιν, ⟨ἀλλὰ μὴν ἡμέρα ἔστιν· φῶς ἄρα ἔστιν⟩.
[aq] Reading τοῦ ⟨ὅτι ἡμέρας οὔσης⟩ φῶς ἔστιν (Heintz).

[293] For the Peripatetic appropriation of the term 'unprovable' see e.g. Alexander, *in APr* 54.12.
[294] For the Stoic unprovables see II 157–8.
[295] See I 169.

For it is from the fact that day is not observed without light that the conditional 'If it is day, it is light' would be deemed to be sound – since if, let us suppose, day were at some time to appear but light not, the conditional would be said to be false. But as far as the unprovable just mentioned goes, there not being day when there is no light is concluded by way of 'If it is day, it is light'. Hence each of them requires for its own confirmation that the other has been firmly grasped in order that it may thereby become convincing, and both are found undecidable by the reciprocal mode.[ar][296]

[201] Again, it is from the fact that certain things cannot co-exist with one another (e.g. day, as it might be, and night) that both the negation of the conjunction – 'It is not the case that it is day and it is night' – and the disjunction – 'Either it is day or it is night' – would be deemed to be sound. But they deem that the fact that they do not co-exist is confirmed by both the negation of the conjunction and the disjunction, saying:

> It is not the case that it is day and it is night.
> But it is night.
> Therefore, it is not day.

and:

> Either it is night or it is day.
> But it is night.
> Therefore, it is not day.

(or:

> But it is not night.
> Therefore, it is day.)

[202] Hence we again deduce that if in order to confirm the disjunction and the negation of the conjunction we require to have previously apprehended that the statements contained in them do not co-exist, while they think they conclude that they do not co-exist both by the disjunction and by the negation of the conjunction, then the

---

[ar] Retaining the MS reading χρῆζον (Mutschmann–Mau print χρήζει) and supposing a lacuna after τρόπον containing e.g. ἀνεπίκριτον εὑρίσκεται.

[296] See I 169.

reciprocal mode is introduced.[297] For we cannot find these com-plexes[298] convincing without apprehending the non-co-existence of the statements contained in them nor can we confirm their non-co-existence before propounding the deductions which use these com-plexes. [203] That is why, not knowing where to begin to find conviction because of the circularity, we shall say that, so far as these considerations go, neither the third nor the fourth nor the fifth of the unprovables has any subsistence.

So much will suffice for the present on the subject of deductions.

xv Induction[299]

[204] It is easy, I think, to reject the method of induction.[as] For since by way of it they want to make universals convincing on the basis of particulars,[300] they will do this by surveying either all the particulars or some of them. But if some, the induction will be infirm, it being possible that some of the particulars omitted in the induction should be contrary to the universal; and if all, they will labour at an impossible task, since the particulars are infinite and indeterminate.[301] Thus in either case it results, I think, that induction totters.

xvi Definitions

[205] The Dogmatists also take great pride[302] in their technique of definition, which they list in the logical part of what they call philosophy. Let us then make some remarks – a few for the present[303] – about definitions.

While the Dogmatists think that definitions are useful for many purposes, you will no doubt find that the main heads which they say cover all their indispensable uses are two in number: [206] they

---

[as] Omitting περί (after the Latin translation).

[297] See I 169.
[298] τροπικά: see above, II 3.
[299] On this chapter see VON SAVIGNY [1975].
[300] See II 195; cf. e.g. Aristotle, *Top* 105a13–16.
[301] See II 210.
[302] See I 180.
[303] See I 58.

always present definitions as indispensable either for apprehension or for teaching.[304] If, then, we suggest that they are useful for neither of these things, we shall, I think, turn about [305] all the vain effort which the Dogmatists have bestowed on them.

[207] For example, if someone who is ignorant of the *definiendum* cannot define what is unknown to him, while someone who knows a thing and then defines it has not apprehended the *definiendum* from the definition but has first apprehended it and then put together the definition, then definitions are not indispensable for the apprehension of objects. Again, if we want to define everything we shall define absolutely nothing because of the infinite regress, and if we agree that some things can be apprehended without their definitions, we show that definitions are not indispensable for apprehension (for we can apprehend everything without its definition in the way the things which were not defined were apprehended). [208] Hence either we shall define absolutely nothing because of the infinite regress[at] or we shall show that definitions are not indispensable.

And for the following reason we shall find that they are not indispensable for teaching either. Just as the first person to recognize an object recognized it without a definition, in the same way someone who is being taught it can be taught it without a definition.

[209] Again, they decide definitions on the basis of the *definienda*, and they say that unsound definitions are those which include something which does not belong to all or some of the *definienda*. That is why, when someone says that a human is an immortal rational animal or a literate mortal rational animal – in the one case no humans being immortal, in the other some not being literate – they say that the definition is unsound.[306] [210] But perhaps definitions are actually undecidable because of the infinity of the particulars on the basis of which they ought to be decided.[307] And again, they will not be capable of apprehending or of teaching those things on the basis of

---

at Retaining the MS reading διὰ τὴν εἰς ἄπειρον ἔκπτωσιν, words which Mutschmann–Mau (after Bekker) excise.

304 See Diogenes Laertius VII 42.
305 See I 122.
306 See Diogenes Laertius VII 60; Alexander, *in Top* 42.27–43.8, for the Stoic account of definition.
307 Cf. II 204.

which they are decided and which must clearly be recognized and apprehended beforehand if at all.

It would surely be ridiculous to say that definitions are useful for apprehension or for teaching or, generally, for illumination when they involve us in such obscurity. [211] For example[308] – if we may indulge in a little ridicule[309] – suppose someone wanted to ask you if you had met a human on horseback leading a dog, and were to pose the question like this: 'O mortal rational animal receptive of thought and knowledge, have you met[au] a broad-nailed animal capable of laughter and receptive of political knowledge, resting his buttocks on a neighing mortal animal, leading a barking quadruped animal?' – wouldn't he be mocked for casting such a familiar subject into obscurity[av] because of his definitions?

As far as these considerations go, then, we should say that definitions are useless – [212] whether they are said to be accounts which, by a brief reminder, lead us to a conception of the objects denoted by the phrases (as is clear – isn't it? – from what we said a little earlier[310]), or rather accounts which show what it is for something to be a certain thing, or what you will.[311] For when they want to establish what a definition is, they fall into an interminable dispute which, because of the plan of my work,[312] I here pass over, even if it seems to overthrow definitions.[aw]

So much is enough for definitions.

[au] Reading ἀπήντηται after the Latin translation: ἀπήντητο MSS, Mutschmann–Mau.

[av] Reading ἀσάφειαν (Mutschmann) for ἀφασίαν (MSS, Mutschmann–Mau); emending γνωρίμου πράγματος to γνώριμον πρᾶγμα, and excising τὸν ἄνθρωπον.

[aw] We translate the text given in the Greek MSS. Mutschmann–Mau append a phrase based on the Latin translation, thus: ' ... even if ⟨what we have said here about the uselessness of definitions⟩ seems to overthrow definitions'.

[308] From Epicurus: see Anonymus, *in Theaet* xxii 39–47.

[309] Cf. I 62.

[310] An ironical reference to the joke in II 211?

[311] The second account of definition is standard Aristotelianism; the first (which reappears at [Galen], *def med* XIX 348 K) perhaps coincides with what Galen calls 'conceptual' definitions: *On Differences in Pulses* VIII 708 K; cf. Scholia to Dionysius Thrax, 107.1–21.

[312] See I 4, note.

xvii Division

[213] Since some of the Dogmatists[313] say that logic is a science of deduction, induction, definition and division, and we have already discussed deduction and induction and definitions (after our arguments about standards and signs and proofs), we think it not out of place briefly to discuss division too. Now they say that divisions are made in four ways: either a word is divided into significations, or a whole is divided into parts, or a genus into species, or a species into individuals. It is no doubt easy to see that in none of these cases is there a science of division.

xviii The division of a word into significations

[214] For example, they say – and reasonably – that sciences deal with what holds by nature and not with what holds by convention. For a science is supposed to be a firm and unchangeable object, and what holds by convention is open to easy and ready change, being altered by the variations of conventions, which are up to us. Thus, since words signify by convention and not by nature[314] (for then everyone, Greeks and foreigners alike, would understand everything signified by our phrases; and besides, it is up to us to show and signify what is signified by whatever words we want to – and by different words at any time[315]), how could there be a science of the division of names into significations? Or how could dialectic be, as some think,[316] a science of what signifies and what is signified?

xix Whole and part

[215] We shall discuss wholes and parts in our remarks on what is called physics;[317] for the present, we should make the following remarks about the so-called division of a whole into its parts.[318]

---

313 See e.g. Albinus, *didascalicus* 156 H; Ammonius, *in Int* 15.16–18.
314 Cf. II 256; III 267; *M* XI 241; *M* I 37, 144–7. The thesis was denied by the Stoics: e.g. Origen, *c Cels* I xxiv.
315 Sextus may be thinking of the famous story about Diodorus, who named his slaves 'But' and 'Therefore': see e.g. Ammonius, *in Int* 38.17–20.
316 So e.g. Chrysippus: Diogenes Laertius VII 62.
317 See III 98–101; BARNES [1988c].
318 The material is recycled at III 85–93.

When someone says that ten is divided into one and two and three and four, ten is not divided into these things. For as soon as its first part, i.e. one, is removed – to grant this for the moment by way of concession – ten is no longer present, but rather nine – and in general something different from ten. [216] Thus the subtraction and division of the rest is made not on ten but on other things which alter at each subtraction. Perhaps, then, it is not possible to divide a whole into what are said to be its parts.

Again,[319] if a whole is divided into parts, the parts ought to be included in the whole before the division; but no doubt they are not included. For example – to rest our argument again on ten – they say that nine is necessarily a part of ten; for ten is divided into one and nine. And the same goes for eight; for ten is divided into eight and two. And the same for seven and six and five and four and three and two and one. [217] Now if all these are included in ten, and if, taken together with it, they make fifty-five, then fifty-five is included in ten – which is absurd. Thus what are said to be the parts of ten are not included in it, nor can ten be divided into them as a whole into parts, since they are not observed in it at all.

[218] The same things will meet us in the case of magnitudes, if someone wants to divide as it might be a ten-foot length. Thus it is no doubt impossible to divide a whole into parts.

xx Genera and species

[219] There remains, then, the argument about genera and species. We shall discuss it at more length elsewhere,[320] here making the following summary remarks.

If they say that genera and species are conceptions,[321] then the assaults made on the ruling part and on appearances overthrow them;[322] and if they allow them a subsistence of their own, what will they say to the following argument? [220] If genera exist, either they are as many as the species or there is one genus common to all the

---

[319] With this paragraph compare III 87.
[320] No lengthier discussion is found in Sextus' surviving works.
[321] So the Stoics: Diogenes Laertius VII 60.
[322] See II 70–1.

species that are said to fall under it. Now if the genera are as many as their species, there will no longer be a common genus to be divided into them. But if it is said that there is one genus in all its species, then each of its species either shares in it as a whole or shares in a part of it.[323] Certainly not as a whole; for it is impossible that, being a single thing, a genus should be included in the same way in different things and be observed as a whole in each of the things in which it is said to be. But if in a part, then first the whole genus will not follow the species, as they suppose it to, and a human will not be an animal but part of an animal – e.g. a substance but neither animate nor perceptive. [221] Secondly, all the species will be said to share either in the same part of their genus or each in a different part. Now they cannot share in the same part, for the reasons just mentioned. But if in different parts, the species will not be similar to one another in respect of genus (something they will not admit), and each genus will be infinite, being cut into infinitely many pieces – for it is divided not only into the species but also into the individuals, in which the genus together with its species is to be seen (Dio is said to be not only a human but also an animal).

If this is absurd, then the species do not share in their genus, which is one thing, by parts. [222] But if each species shares neither in the genus as a whole nor in part of it, how can it be said that there is one genus in all the species and that it is divided into them? Perhaps no-one could say this unless he were concocting a romance[324] – which will be turned about[325] under sceptical attack by their own undecidable disputes.

[223] In addition we should make the following point. If[ax] the species are such-and-such or thus-and-so, then their genera are either both such-and-such and thus-and-so, or such-and-such but not thus-and-so, or neither such-and-such nor thus-and-so. E.g. since of things[326] some are bodies and others incorporeal, and some true and others false, and some white – as it might be – and others black, and

---

ax Adding ὤν before τὰ εἴδη (Heintz).

323 A similar pattern of argument at III 158–62 – the origin is to be found in Plato, *Parm* 131AC.
324 See III 155.
325 See I 122.
326 On 'things' [τὸ τί], see II 86.

some vast and others minute, and similarly in other cases, then things (for the sake of argument), which some say form the highest genus, will be either all or some or none of these. [224] But if things are none of them at all, then the genus does not exist and[ay] the inquiry comes to an end. And if it is said to be all of them, then – in addition to the fact that this is impossible – each of the species and individuals in which it is present will have to be all of them. For since animal, as they say, is an animate perceptive substance, each of its species is said to be a substance and animate and perceptive: in the same way, if the genus is both body and incorporeal, both false and true, both black – as it might be – and white, both minute and vast, and all the rest, then each of the species and each of the individuals will be all of them – and this is not observed to be the case. Thus this too is false. [225] But if it is some of them only, the genus of these will not be the genus of the rest. E.g. if things are bodies, things will not be the genus of the incorporeals, if animals are rational, animal will not be the genus of irrational things, so that there will be no incorporeal things and no irrational animals.[az] And similarly in other cases. And that is absurd.

Thus a genus can be neither both such-and-such and thus-and-so, nor such-and-such but not thus-and-so, nor neither such-and-such nor thus-and-so. And if this is so, there cannot be any genera at all.

If someone says that a genus is all of them potentially, we shall say that what is potentially something must also be actually something – e.g. a man is not potentially literate unless he is actually something.[ba] Thus if a genus is potentially all of them, we ask them what it is actually – and so the same impasses remain. It cannot be all the contraries actually. [226] Nor can it be some of them actually and others only potentially – e.g. body actually and incorporeal potentially. For it is potentially what it is capable of being actually; and what is body actually cannot become incorporeal in actuality – so that if (for the sake of argument) it is body[bb] actually, it is not

---

[ay] Mutschmann–Mau mark a lacuna after γένος: we translate as though nothing more than a καί filled it.

[az] Reading μήτε ἄλογον ζῷον (Pappenheim): ζῷον μήτε ἄλογον MSS, Mutschmann–Mau.

[ba] Reading εἰ μή τι καί after the Latin translation (nisi et): the Greek MSS offer μή τις, which Mutschmann–Mau print.

[bb] Omitting the τι which Mutschmann–Mau add to the received text.

incorporeal potentially, and vice versa. Thus a genus cannot be some of them actually and others only potentially. And if it is nothing at all actually, it does not even subsist. Thus genera, which they say they divide into species, are nothing.

[227] Again, it is worth considering the following point. If Alexander is the same as Paris, it is not possible for 'Alexander is walking' to be true and 'Paris is walking' false: in the same way, if being a human is the same for Theo as for Dio, the noun 'human', when it is brought into the construction of a statement, will make the statement either true in both cases or false in both cases. But this is not observed to hold; for when Dio is sitting and Theo is walking, 'A human is walking' is true if said of one of them and false of the other. Therefore the noun 'human' is not common to both, nor the same for both, but – if anything – peculiar to each.

xxi Common attributes

[228] Similar remarks are also made about the common attributes. If seeing is one and the same attribute both for Dio and for Theo, then if we suppose that Dio has died and that Theo survives and sees, either they will say that the seeing of the dead Dio remains undestroyed (which is incongruous), or they will say that the same seeing both has been destroyed and has not been destroyed (which is absurd). Therefore Theo's seeing is not the same as Dio's, but – if anything – it is peculiar to each. Again, if breathing is the same attribute both for Dio and for Theo, it is not possible for the breath in Theo to exist and that in Dio not to exist; but it is possible – if one is dead and the other survives. Therefore it is not the same.

On these matters, then, it will be enough for the present to have said this much by way of summary.[327]

xxii Sophisms[328]

[229] It is no doubt not out of place to spend a little time too on the question of sophisms, since those who extol dialectic say that it is

---

[327] See I 4. [328] On this chapter see EBERT [1991], pp. 176–208.

indispensable for their solution.[329] For, they say, if dialectic is the science which distinguishes between true and false arguments, and if sophisms are false arguments, then dialectic will be capable of discriminating these things which sully the truth with apparent plausibility. That is why the dialecticians, as though coming to the aid of tottering common sense, earnestly try to teach us the concept and the varieties and the resolutions of sophisms.

They say that a sophism is a plausible and treacherous argument leading one to accept the consequence which is either false or similar to something false or unclear or in some other way unacceptable. [230] False, as in the case of this sophism:

> No-one requires you to drink a predicate.
> But to drink wormwood is a predicate.
> Therefore, no-one requires you to drink wormwood.

Similar to something false, as in this case:

> What neither was nor is possible is not nonsense.
> But 'The doctor *qua* doctor kills' neither was nor is possible.
> Therefore, 'The doctor *qua* doctor kills' is not nonsense.

[231] Unclear, thus:

> It is not the case both that I have propounded something to you already and that the stars are not even in number.
> But I have propounded something to you already.
> Therefore, the stars are even in number.[330]

Unacceptable in some other way, as in what are called solecistic arguments, e.g.:

> What you see exists.
> But you see unclearly.
> Therefore, unclearly exists.

Or:

---

[329] See Plutarch, *Stoic rep* 1034F, on Zeno the Stoic; cf. e.g. Cicero, *fin* III xxi 72; Galen, *an pecc dig* V 72–3 (*FDS* 1199).
[330] Cf. II 90.

What you perceive exists.
But you perceive inflamed spots.
Therefore inflamed spots exists.[331]

[232] Next they attempt to establish their resolutions. In the case of the first sophism they say that one thing has been conceded in the assumptions and another inferred. For it has been conceded that predicates are not drunk and that to drink wormwood – not wormwood itself – is a predicate. Hence, whereas one ought to infer 'Therefore no-one drinks to drink wormwood', which is true, it is inferred that no-one drinks wormwood, which is false – and which may not be concluded from the assumptions which have been conceded.

[233] In the case of the second sophism they say that while it seems to lead to something false and makes the inexpert shrink from assenting to it, it actually concludes to something true, viz. 'Therefore "The doctor *qua* doctor kills" is not nonsense'. For no statement is nonsense, and 'The doctor *qua* doctor kills' is a statement. Hence it is not nonsense.

[234] Reduction to the unclear depends, they say, on items which change.[332] Since nothing has already been propounded (let us suppose), the negation of the conjunction turns out true; for the conjunction is false by virtue of containing the false conjunct 'I have propounded something to you already'. But after the negation of the conjunction has been propounded, the further assumption – But I have propounded something to you already – comes to be true because the negation of the conjunction was propounded before the further assumption;[bc] and the proposition of the negation of the conjunction comes to be false, since what was false in the conjunction comes to be true. Hence the conclusion can never be reached, since the negation of the conjunction does not co-exist with the further assumption.

[bc] Removing the comma before διὰ τὸ ἠρῶτασθαι and placing one after συμπλοκῆς (Heintz).

[331] The translations present solecisms of the same type as the ones in Sextus' Greek.

[332] I.e. on statements which change their truth-value: see Diogenes Laertius VII 76; Epictetus, *Diatribes* I vii 13–21; Simplicius, *Commentary on Aristotle's Physics* 1299.36–1300.10.

[235] As for the last arguments – the solecistic ones – some say that they are advanced nonsensically and contrary to ordinary usage.

Such, then, are the things some dialecticians say about sophisms (others say other things). These remarks may perhaps tickle the ears of the superficial, but they are unnecessary, and the effort spent on them is vain. It is no doubt possible to see this even on the basis of what we have already said; for we suggested that, according to the dialecticians, truths and falsities cannot be apprehended,[333] and to this end we used a variety of arguments and in particular we overthrew the evidence for their deductive prowess, namely proofs and unprovable arguments.[334]

[236] Many other things can be said which bear specifically on the present topic; but let us now briefly[335] make the following point.

In those cases where it is dialectic in particular which is able to refute a sophism, the resolution is useless; and where a resolution is useful, it is not the dialecticians who can resolve them but those who, in each expertise, have grasped the interconnexions among the objects. [237] Thus – to recall one or two examples – suppose the following sophism is propounded by a doctor:[bd]

> In diseases a varied diet and wine are to be recommended at the abatement.
> But in every type of disease, abatement usually[be] occurs before the first third day.
> Therefore, it is necessary that a varied diet and wine be usually taken before the first third day.

A dialectician would have nothing to say towards the resolution of this argument, useful though one would be; [238] but a doctor will resolve the sophism. For he knows that there are two sorts of abatement, the abatement of the disease as a whole and the tendency of each particular intensification to be allayed after its crisis; and he knows that while abatement of particular intensifications usually

---

bd Retaining the MS reading ἰατρῷ which Mutschmann–Mau delete.
be Reading ὡς τὸ πολύ for πάντως (MSS, Mutschmann–Mau).

333 See II 85–96.
334 See II 144–84.
335 See I 163.

occurs before the first third day, we recommend a varied diet not at this abatement but at the abatement of the disease as a whole. Hence the doctor will say that the assumptions of the argument are disconnected,[336] one abatement, i.e. that of the affliction as a whole, being taken in the first assumption, another, i.e. the particular abatement, in the second. [239] Again, suppose that, in the case of someone suffering from a fever due to intensified compression,[337] the following argument is propounded:

> Contraries cure contraries.[338]
> But cold is contrary to the fever which is present.
> Therefore, cold is appropriate to the fever which is present.

[240] A dialectician will remain quiet; but a doctor, who knows what are the principal and primary afflictions and what are their symptoms, will say that the argument should attend not to the symptoms (indeed, on the application of cold the fever increases) but to the primary afflictions, and that the constriction is primary and demands not compression but a relaxing mode of treatment, whereas the consequential heating is not principal and primary – nor, therefore, is what seems appropriate to it.

[241] In this way, in sophisms which usefully demand a resolution, a dialectician will have nothing to say. Rather, he propounds arguments to us of the following sort:

> If it is not the case that you have beautiful horns and you have horns, then you have horns.
> But it is not the case that you have beautiful horns and you have horns.
> Therefore, you have horns.[339]

[242]

> If anything moves, it moves either in a place in which it is or in a place in which it is not.
> But neither in a place in which it is (for there it is at rest) nor in a place

---

[336] See II 146.

[337] Cf. I 238.

[338] A Hippocratic axiom: see e.g. Hippocrates, *de flatibus* 1.

[339] Not the celebrated 'horned man' paradox of Eubulides (for which see e.g. Diogenes Laertius, II 111); rather, a fallacy which depends on ignoring the difference between 'Not-[P and Q]' and '[not-P and Q]'.

in which it is not (for how could it do anything in a place in which it simply is not?).

Therefore, it is not the case that anything moves.[340]

[243]

Either what is comes into being or what is not comes into being.

Now what is does not come into being (for it already is).

But neither does what is not (for what comes into being is acted on and what is not is not acted on).

Therefore, nothing comes into being.[341]

[244]

Snow is frozen water.

But water is black.

Therefore, snow is black.[342]

Having accumulated rubbish of this sort, he frowns and takes out his dialectic and solemnly tries to establish for us by deductive proofs that some things come into being, and that some things move, and that snow is white, and that we do not have horns – although if we set in opposition to these arguments what appears evidently, that is no doubt enough to shatter their positive affirmation with the equipollent disconfirmation given by what is apparent. Indeed, a certain philosopher,[343] when the argument against motion was propounded to him, said nothing and walked about. And ordinary men set out on journeys by land and by sea, and construct ships and houses, and produce children, without paying any attention to the arguments against motion and coming into being. [245] A witty anecdote is told about Herophilus the doctor. He was a contemporary of Diodorus, who vulgarized dialectic and used to run through sophistical arguments on many topics including motion. Now one day Diodorus dislocated his shoulder and went to Herophilus to be treated.

---

[340] From Diodorus Cronus: II 245 (cf. III 71; *M* X 87–9; *M* I 311); see SEDLEY [1977].

[341] A variant on a familiar Eleatic type of argument: see e.g. *M* VII 71, for a similar argument ascribed to Gorgias.

[342] Ascribed to Anaxagoras at I 33.

[343] A Cynic (cf. III 66; *M* X 68), identified as Diogenes (Diogenes Laertius VI 39) or as Antisthenes (Elias, *Commentary on Aristotle's Categories* 109.18–22).

Herophilus wittily said to him: 'Your shoulder was dislocated either in a place in which it was or in a place in which it wasn't. But neither in which it was nor in which it wasn't. Therefore it is not dislocated.' So the sophist begged him to leave such arguments alone and to apply the medical treatment suitable to his case.

[246] It is enough, I think, to live by experience and without opinions, in accordance with the common observations and pre-conceptions,[344] and to suspend judgement about what is said with dogmatic superfluity and far beyond the needs of ordinary life. Thus if dialectic cannot resolve those sophisms which might usefully be solved and if the resolution of those which no doubt one might grant that it does solve is useless, then dialectic is useless with regard to the solution of sophisms.

[247] Indeed, setting out from the very things the dialecticians say, one might briefly suggest that their artifices over sophisms are superfluous, thus. The dialecticians say that they have resorted to the expertise of dialectic not merely in order to know what is concluded from what, but principally to learn to distinguish truths and false-hoods by probative arguments[345] – thus they say that dialectic is the science of what is true and false and indifferent.[346] [248] Now since they themselves say that a true argument is one which concludes to a true conclusion from true assumptions,[347] as soon as an argument with a false conclusion is propounded we shall know that the argument is false and we shall not assent to it; for it is necessary that the argument itself either is not conclusive or has assumptions which are not true. [249] This is clear from the following considerations. Either the false conclusion in the argument follows the conjunction of the assumptions, or else it does not follow. But if it does not follow, then the argument will not be conclusive; for they say[348] that an argument is conclusive when its conclusion follows the conjunction of its assumptions. And if it does follow, then it is necessary that the conjunction of the assumptions be false, according to their own

---

[344] See I 23–4.
[345] Cf. Diogenes Laertius VII 45.
[346] See II 94.
[347] See II 139.
[348] See II 137.

technical treatments of the matter. For they say[349] that what is false follows what is false but not what is true. [250] And that an argument which is not conclusive or not true is, according to them, not probative either, is clear from what we have said earlier.[350]

Thus when an argument is propounded in which the conclusion is false, we know directly that the argument is not true and not conclusive[bf] from the fact that it has a false conclusion; and so we shall not assent to it, even if we do not know the cause of the error. For just as we do not assent to the truths of what conjurors do but know that they are deceiving us even if we do not know how they are deceiving us, so we do not go along with arguments which are false but seem to be plausible even if we do not know how they are fallacious.

[251] Or rather, since they say that sophisms lead not only to falsity but also to other absurdities,[351] we should proceed in a more general fashion, thus. The argument propounded leads us either to something unacceptable or to something which we should accept. If the second, we shall assent to it without absurdity. If to something unacceptable, we need not rashly assent to the absurdity because of its plausibility: rather, they must relinquish an argument which compels assent to absurdities – if, at any rate, they have chosen, as they profess, not to babble like children but to seek what is true. [252] If a road is leading us to a precipice, we do not drive ourselves over the precipice because there is a road leading to it; rather, we leave the road because of the precipice:[352] similarly, if there is an argument leading us to something agreed to be absurd, we do not assent to the absurdity because of the argument – rather, we abandon the argument because of the absurdity.

[253] Thus, when an argument is propounded to us in this way, we shall suspend judgement over each proposition; and then, when the whole argument has been propounded, we shall introduce what seems to us to be the case. And if Chrysippus and his fellow Dogmatists say that, when the sorites is being propounded, they

---

bf   Retaining οὐδέ with the mss: Mutschmann–Mau print ἤ οὐ.

349   See e.g. Diogenes Laertius VII 81 (cf. above, II 105).
350   See II 143.
351   See II 229.
352   The same simile was used by Chrysippus in connexion with the sorites: Cicero, *Luc* xxix 94.

ought to halt and suspend judgement while the argument is advancing in order not to fall into absurdity,[353] so much the more appropriate is it for us, who are sceptics, when we suspect an absurdity, not to be rash while the assumptions are being propounded but to suspend judgement about each of them until the whole argument is propounded.

[254] And whereas we set out without opinions from the observance of ordinary life[354] and thus avoid deceptive arguments, the Dogmatists will not be able to distinguish sophisms from arguments which seem to be correctly propounded, given that they are obliged to decide dogmatically both that the form of the argument is conclusive and that the assumptions are true (or that these things are not the case). [255] For we suggested earlier that they can neither apprehend conclusive arguments nor judge that anything is true, since they have neither an agreed standard nor a proof (as we suggested on the basis of what they themselves say). Thus, so far as those considerations go, the technical treatment of sophisms which the dialecticians talk so much about is redundant.

[256] We make similar remarks in connexion with the distinguishing of ambiguities. If an ambiguity is a phrase which signifies two or more things,[355] and if phrases signify by convention,[356] then those ambiguities which it is useful to resolve, i.e. those which involve some matter of experience, will be resolved by those who are trained in each expertise (since it is they who have experience of the conventional use – which they have created – of words and their significations). [257] The dialecticians will not resolve them. E.g. in the case of this ambiguity: At the abatement a varied diet and wine should be prescribed.[357]

Indeed, in ordinary life too we see even slaves distinguishing ambiguities where the distinction seems useful to them. For example, if someone who has servants of the same name were to order a slave to

---

[353] Cf. *M* VII 415–21; Cicero, *Luc* xxviii 92–xxix 94; on the sorites in general see below, III 80; BARNES [1982].

[354] See I 23–4.

[355] See Diogenes Laertius VII 62; for the place of the study of ambiguity in dialectic see Diogenes Laertius VII 44; Galen, *On Sophisms* 4, XIV 595 ff. K.

[356] See II 214.

[357] See II 238.

have Manes, say, summoned (suppose this to be the name common to the servants), the slave will ask which one. And if a man has several different wines and were to say to his slave 'Pour me some wine to drink', in the same way the slave will ask which one. [258] In this way experience of what is useful in each case leads to the distinction.

But as for those ambiguities which do not involve any of the areas of ordinary experience but are found among dogmatic notions and are no doubt useless with regard to a life without opinions, here dialecticians, who have a special attitude to them, will be compelled to suspend judgement in the same way[358] by the sceptical attacks, inasmuch as the ambiguities are no doubt linked to objects which are unclear and inapprehensible or even non-existent. [259] (We shall discuss these matters again later.[359]) And if a Dogmatist attempts to argue against any of our remarks, he will support the sceptical argument, himself confirming suspension of judgement about the matters under investigation which are attacked from both sides and involved in an undecidable dispute.

With these remarks on ambiguity we bring to an end the second Book of the *Outlines*.

---

[358] I.e. in the same way as they are in the case of sophisms (II 254–5).
[359] No other discussion is found in Sextus' surviving works.

BOOK III

These are the Contents of the Third Book of the *Outlines of Scepticism*:

[1] As for the logical part of what they call philosophy, then, so much, in an outline,[1] should be enough.

i The part concerned with physics

Our essay will keep the same character as we approach the part concerned with physics: we shall not argue against each of the things they say on this[a] – rather, we shall try to shake the more general of them in which the others are encompassed.[2] Let us begin with the account of first principles.

ii Active principles

Since it is agreed by most thinkers that of the principles some are material and others active,[3] we shall begin our account with the active principles; for they say that these are in fact principles in a stricter sense than the material principles are.

iii God

[2] Since the majority have asserted that god is a most active cause, let us first consider god, remarking by way of preface that, following ordinary life without opinions,[4] we say that there are gods and we are pious towards the gods and say that they are provident: it is against the rashness of the Dogmatists that we make the following points.[5]

We ought to form a conception of the substance[6] of the things we conceive, e.g. whether they are bodies or incorporeal. Also of their form – no-one could conceive of a horse unless he had previously

---

[a] Reading κατὰ ⟨τοῦτον⟩ τὸν τόπον (Mutschmann): Mutschmann–Mau print κατὰ τόπον.

[1] See I 4, note.
[2] Cf. II 84.
[3] See *M* IX 4–12: the classification is Stoic in origin (e.g. Diogenes Laertius VII 134; Seneca, *ep* lxv 2); but later it was widely accepted – and read back into earlier thinkers.
[4] See I 23–4.
[5] Cf. *M* IX 49.
[6] Here, as often, Sextus uses the word 'substance' (οὐσία) to refer to the matter or ὕλη of a thing: the usage was Stoic – see e.g. Mnesarchus, apud Stobaeus, *ecl* I 179. 6–17.

learned the form of a horse. Further, what is conceived of ought to be conceived of somewhere.

[3] Now, since some of the Dogmatists say that god is a body, others that he is incorporeal, some that he is anthropomorphic, others not, some in space, others not – and of those who say that he is in space, some say that he is within the universe, others that he is outside it[7] – how shall we be able to acquire a conception of god if we possess neither an agreed substance for him nor a form nor a place in which he is? Let them first agree and form a consensus that god is of such-and-such a kind; and only then, having given us an outline account, let them require us to form a concept of god. As long as they remain in undecidable dispute, we have no agreement from them as to what we should think. [4] But, they say, conceive of something indestructible and blessed, and hold that to be god.[8] This is silly: just as, if you do not know Dio, you cannot think of his attributes as attributes of Dio, so, since we do not know the substance of god, we shall not be able to learn and to conceive of his attributes.[9] [5] Moreover, let them tell us what it is to be blessed – whether it is to act in accordance with virtue and to provide for the things subordinated to you, or rather to be inactive and take no trouble to yourself and cause none to others.[10] They have had an undecidable dispute about this too,[11] thus making blessedness – and therefore god – inconceivable by us.

[6] Even granting that god is indeed conceivable, it is necessary to suspend judgement about whether gods exist or not, so far as the Dogmatists are concerned. For it is not clear that gods exist: if the gods made an impression on us in themselves, the Dogmatists would be in agreement as to what they are and of what form and where; but the undecidable dispute has made it seem to us that the gods are unclear and in need of proof.

[7] Now anyone who tries to prove that there are gods, does so

---

[7] See III 218.

[8] According to Epicurus, this is the common conception of God: *ad Men* 123 (cf. below, III 219). For the Stoic view see Diogenes Laertius VII 147.

[9] Cf. III 173–4 (but the argument goes back to Plato).

[10] Sextus here sketches first the Stoic and then the Epicurean picture of the gods: see e.g. Diogenes Laertius VII 147, and below, III 219.

[11] See III 219.

either by way of something clear or else by way of something unclear. Certainly not by way of something clear; for if what proves that there are gods were clear, then since what is proved is thought of in relation to what proves and is therefore also apprehended together with it, as we have established,[12] it will also be clear that there are gods, this being apprehended together with what proves it, which itself is clear. But it is not clear, as we have suggested;[13] therefore it is not proved by way of something clear. [8] Nor yet by way of something unclear. For the unclear item which is to prove that there are gods is in need of proof: if it is said to be proved by way of something clear, it will no longer be unclear but clear. Therefore the unclear item which is to prove that there are gods is not proved by way of something clear. Nor yet by way of something unclear: anyone who says this will fall into an infinite regress,[14] since we shall always demand a proof of the unclear item brought forward to prove the point at issue.

The existence of gods, therefore, cannot be proved from anything else. [9] But if it is neither clear in itself nor proved by something else, then it will be inapprehensible whether or not there are gods.

Again, there is this to be said. Anyone who says that there are gods says either that they provide for the things in the universe or that they do not – and that if they provide, then either for all things or for some. But if they provided for all things, there would be nothing bad and evil in the universe; but they say that everything is full of evil.[15] Therefore the gods will not be said to provide for everything. [10] But if they provide for some things, why do they provide for these and not for those? Either they both want to and can provide for all, or they want to but cannot, or they can but do not want to, or they neither want to nor can. If they both wanted to and could, then they would provide for all; but they do not provide for all, for the reason I have just given; therefore it is not the case that they both want to and can provide for all. If they want to but cannot, they are weaker than the cause in virtue of which they cannot provide for the things for

[12] See II 117 (and note II 169).
[13] Above, III 6.
[14] See I 166.
[15] The argument is Epicurean in origin (cf. I 155; III 219); but 'they' in 'they say' probably refers to people in general.

which they do not provide; [11] but it is contrary to the concept of god that a god should be weaker than anything. If they can provide for all but do not want to, they will be thought to be malign. If they neither want to nor can, they are both malign and weak – and only the impious would say this about the gods.

The gods, therefore, do not provide for the things in the universe. But if they have providence for nothing and have no function and no effect, we will not be able to say how it is apprehended that there are gods, since it is neither apparent in itself nor apprehended by way of any effects. For this reason too, then, it is inapprehensible whether there are gods.

[12] From this we deduce that those who firmly state that there are gods are no doubt bound to be impious: if they say that the gods provide for everything, they will say that they are a cause of evil; and if they say that they provide for some things or even for none at all, they will be bound to say either that the gods are malign or that they are weak – and anyone who says this is clearly impious.

iv Causes[16]

[13] Lest the Dogmatists should try to slander *us* because they are at a loss to produce substantial counter arguments, we shall raise more general puzzles about active causes, having first tried to focus on the concept of a cause.

So far as what the Dogmatists say goes, no-one could even conceive of a cause, since, in addition to offering disputed and contradictory concepts of cause, they have also actually made the subsistence of causes undiscoverable because of their dispute about them. [14] Some say that causes are bodies, others that they are incorporeal.[17] A cause would seem in general, according to them,[18] to be that because of which, by being active, the effect comes about – as e.g. the sun or the heat of the sun is cause of the wax melting or of the melting of the wax. (On this point too they have been in dispute, some saying that causes are causes of nouns – e.g. of the melting – others that they are

---

[16] On this and the following chapter see BARNES [1990a], pp. 2668–89.

[17] See *M* IX 211–12; [Galen], *hist phil* XIX 244–5 K.

[18] See e.g. Seneca, *ep* lxv 11.

causes of predicates – e.g. of melting.[19]) Hence, as I have said, in general a cause will be that because of which, by being active, the effect comes about.

[15][20] Of these causes, the majority hold that some are comprehensive, some co-operative, and some auxiliary. They are comprehensive[21] if when they are present the effect is present and when they are removed it is removed and when they are diminished it is diminished (they say that in this way the placing of a noose is a cause of strangulation); they are co-operative if they supply a force equal to another co-operative cause towards the existence of the effect[22] (they say that in this way each of the oxen drawing the plough is a cause of the drawing of the plough); and they are auxiliary if they supply a force which is slight and which contributes to the easy existence of the effect (e.g. when two men are lifting a weight with difficulty and a third comes along and helps to lighten it). [16] Some, however, have said that there are also present causes of future effects, i.e. preparatory causes,[23] as intense exposure to the sun is a cause of fever. But others have rejected these causes, since causes, being relative to something, i.e. to an effect, cannot precede that thing as causes.[24]

We raise the following puzzles about causes.

v Is anything a cause of anything?

[17][25] It is plausible that there are causes – how could things increase or decrease or be generated or be destroyed or in general change, or how could there be any natural or psychological effect, or how could the universe as a whole make its orderly progress, or how could anything else happen if not in virtue of some cause? Even if none of

[19] Cf. Clement, *strom* VIII ix 26.3–4.
[20] The distinctions among causes made here, along with other distinctions, are found in many texts (see e.g. Cicero, *fat* xviii 41; Clement, *strom* VIII ix 33.1–9; [Galen], *def med* XIX 392 K); but their interpretation is difficult in the extreme. See e.g. FREDE [1980].
[21] On 'comprehensive' or 'containing' causes, αἴτια συνεκτικά, see Galen's essay *On Containing Causes*.
[22] Cf. III 173.
[23] On 'preparatory' causes, αἴτια προκαταρκτικά, see Galen's essay *On Procatarctic Causes*.
[24] See II 126.
[25] With III 17–19 compare *M* IX 200–4.

these things is real in its nature, we shall say that it is certainly because of some cause that they appear to us to be such as they are not. [18] Moreover, everything would come from everything, as chance had it, were there no causes – e.g. horses, say, will be born from flies, and elephants from ants;[26] and in Thebes in Egypt there would be heavy rains and snow, whereas the northern regions would have no rain, if there were no causes because of which the southern regions are stormy and those towards the east dry. [19] And anyone who says that nothing is a cause is turned about;[27] for if he states that he says this simply and without any cause, he will be unconvincing, and if because of some cause, then while wishing to deny causes he posits them by offering[b] a cause because of which there are no causes.

For these reasons, then, it is plausible that there are causes. [20] That it is also plausible to say that nothing is a cause of anything will be evident when we have set out for the present a few of the many arguments[28] which suggest this.

Thus, it is impossible to conceive of a cause before apprehending its effect as an effect of it; for we recognize that it is a cause of its effect only when we apprehend the latter as an effect. [21] But we cannot apprehend the effect of a cause as its effect if we have not apprehended the cause of the effect as its cause; for we think that we know that it is its effect only when we have apprehended its cause as a cause of it. [22] Thus if, in order to conceive of a cause, we must already have recognized its effect, and in order to know its effect, as I have said, we must already know the cause, the reciprocal mode of puzzlement[29] shows that both are inconceivable: the cause cannot be conceived of as a cause nor the effect as an effect; for each of them needs to be made convincing by the other, and we shall not know from which to begin to form the concept. Hence we shall not be able to assert that anything is a cause of anything.

[23] To concede that it is possible to conceive of causes, they will be deemed to be inapprehensible because of the dispute. For some say

---

[b] Reading ἀποδιδούς (Kayser) for ἀποδιδόσθω (the MS reading which Mutschmann–Mau print behind an obelus).

[26] Cf. e.g. Lucretius I 159–73.

[27] See I 122.

[28] See I 58, note.

[29] See I 169.

that some things are causes of others, some say that they are not, and some have suspended judgement.[30] Anyone, therefore,[c] who says that some things are causes of others either states that he says this simply and impelled by no reasonable cause or else will say that he came to give assent to this because of certain causes. If simply, then he will not be more convincing than someone who says simply that nothing is a cause of anything; and if he states causes because of which he deems that some things are causes of others, then he will be attempting to establish the matter under investigation by way of the matter under investigation – for we are investigating whether anything is a cause of anything, and he says, as though there were causes, that there is a cause of there being causes. [24] Again, since we are investigating the reality of causes, he will have to provide a cause for the cause of there being causes – and another for that, and so on *ad infinitum*.[31] But it is impossible to provide infinitely many causes. Therefore it is impossible to assert firmly that anything is a cause of anything.

[25] Furthermore, a cause produces its effect either when it already is and subsists as a cause or when it is not a cause. Certainly not when it is not; but if when it is, then it must have subsisted earlier and first become a cause, then in this way introducing the effect which is said to be effected by it when it is already a cause. But since causes are relative to something, i.e. relative to their effects, it is plain that they cannot subsist before them as causes.[32] Therefore a cause cannot effect that of which it is a cause when it is a cause. [26] But since it does not effect anything either when it is not a cause or when it is, it does not effect anything at all. Hence it will not be a cause; for a cause cannot be thought of as a cause without effecting something.[33]

Hence some also make the following point.[34] A cause must either co-subsist with its effect or pre-subsist it or exist after its effect has come about. Now to say that a cause is brought into subsistence after

---

[c] Reading ἄρα for γάρ. (The sentence is not preserved in the Greek MSS; and the Latin translation, from which Mutschmann–Mau have reconstructed their text, reads *igitur* at the place in question.)

[30] Cf. *M* IX 195, whence it emerges that causes were rejected by 'the sophists who have rejected change and locomotion'.

[31] See I 166.

[32] See above, III 16.

[33] For parallel considerations see II 123 and note.

[34] Cf. *M* IX 232–6.

the coming about of its effect is surely ridiculous. Nor can it pre-exist it; for it is said to be thought of relative to it, [27] and they themselves say that relatives, insofar as they are relatives, co-exist and are thought of together with one another.[35] Nor can it co-subsist with it; for if it is to effect it, and if what comes into being must come into being by the agency of something which already exists, then a cause must first become a cause and then in this way produce its effect. Thus, if a cause neither pre-subsists its effect nor co-subsists with it, and the effect does not come about before it, presumably it has no share in subsistence at all.

[28] (It is no doubt plain that for these reasons too the concept of a cause is again turned about.[36] For if a cause, being relative, cannot be conceived of before its effect, while in order to be thought of as a cause of its effect it must be conceived of before its effect, and if it is impossible for something to be conceived of before that before which it cannot be conceived of,[37] then it is impossible for causes to be conceived of.)

[29] From these considerations we deduce, finally, that if the arguments in virtue of which we have suggested that one should say that there are causes are plausible, and if those which purport to establish that it is not right to assert that anything is a cause are also plausible, and if it is not possible to prefer one set to the other, since we possess no agreed[d] signs or standards or proofs, as we have established earlier,[38] it is necessary to suspend judgement also about the subsistence of causes, saying that – so far as what the Dogmatists say goes – there no more are than are not causes.

vi Material principles

[30][39] What we have said about active causes will be enough for the present; but we must also speak briefly about what are called material principles. That these are inapprehensible is easy to see from the

---

d   Reading ὁμολογουμένην for ὁμολογουμένως (MSS, Mutschmann–Mau).

35   See II 177, 126.
36   See I 122.
37   Cf. II 120.
38   Above II 104–33 (signs), 18–79 (standards), 144–92 (proofs).
39   With III 30–2 compare M IX 359–64 (and X 310–18).

dispute which has gone on about them among the Dogmatists. Pherecydes of Syros said that the principle of everything was earth, Thales of Miletus said water, Anaximander (his pupil) the infinite, Anaximenes and Diogenes of Apollonia air, Hippasus of Metapontum fire, Xenophanes of Colophon earth and water, Oenopides of Chios fire and air, Hippo of Rhegium fire and water, Onomacritus (in the Orphic verses) fire and water and earth, [31] Empedocles and the Stoics fire, air, water and earth (as for the mythical qualityless matter of some of them,[40] which even they themselves do not affirm that they apprehend, why even mention it?), Aristotle the Peripatetic fire, air, water, earth and the body which moves in a circle,[41] [32] Democritus and Epicurus atoms, Anaxagoras of Clazomenae uniform stuffs, Diodorus (surnamed Cronus) minimal and partless bodies, Heraclides of Pontus and Asclepiades of Bithynia seamless masses, Pythagoras numbers, the mathematicians the limits of bodies, Strato the natural scientist qualities.

[33] So large – and even larger – being the dispute which has taken place among them about material principles, we shall assent either to all the positions I have described (and to the others too) or to some of them. It is not possible to assent to all: we shall surely not be able to assent both to Asclepiades, who says that the elements are frangible and possess qualities, and to Democritus, who asserts that they are atomic and qualityless, and to Anaxagoras, who allows his uniform stuffs every perceptible quality. [34] But if we prefer one position to the others, we shall prefer it either simply and without proof or with proof. Now we shall not assent[c] without proof. If with proof, the proof must be true. But it will not be granted to be true unless it has been judged by a true standard, and a standard is shown to be true by way of a proof which has been judged. [35] If, then, in order for the proof which prefers a particular position to be shown to be true, its standard must have been proved, and in order for the standard to be proved its proof must already have been judged, the reciprocal mode

---

[c] Reading συγκαταθησόμεθα (Bekker) for συνθησόμεθα (MSS, Mutschmann–Mau).

[40] See e.g. M x 312; Diogenes Laertius VII 134 (and VII 136–7 for the four Stoic elements).

[41] I.e. the fifth element or 'quintessence' out of which the heavenly spheres are constructed: see. e.g. M x 316.

turns up[42] and will not allow the argument to advance, since a proof always requires a proved standard and a standard a judged proof. [36] And if anyone should wish to judge each standard by a standard and to prove each proof by a proof, he will be thrown back *ad infinitum*.[43]

If, then, we can assent neither to all the positions about elements nor to any one of them, it is right to suspend judgement about them.

[37] It is no doubt possible to suggest by these considerations alone the inapprehensibility of the elements and the material principles; but in order to be able to refute the Dogmatists more comprehensively, let us spend a reasonable amount of time on the topic. Since there are many – indeed, pretty well infinitely many – opinions about the elements, as we have suggested,[44] we shall here refrain, given the distinctive character of our essay,[45] from discussing each opinion one by one; rather, we shall argue implicitly against all of them. For whatever position may be taken on the elements, they will be reduced either to bodies or to incorporeal items; and so we think it enough to suggest that bodies are inapprehensible and incorporeal items are inapprehensible – by this it will be plain that the elements too are inapprehensible.[46]

vii Are bodies apprehensible?

[38][47] Some say that a body is that which can act and be acted upon.[48] But so far as this concept goes, bodies are inapprehensible. For causes are inapprehensible, as we have suggested;[49] and if we cannot say whether there are any causes, we cannot say either whether anything is acted upon – for what is acted upon is certainly acted upon by a cause. But if both causes and what is acted upon are inapprehensible, for this reason bodies too will be inapprehensible.

[39] Others say that a body is that which is three-dimensional and

---

[42] See I 169.
[43] See I 166.
[44] At III 30–3.
[45] See I 4, note.
[46] Cf. *M* IX 365.
[47] With III 38–40 compare *M* IX 366–8.
[48] The view is ascribed to Pythagoras at *M* IX 366; see also Plato, *Sophist* 247DE.
[49] See III 17–29.

has resistance.[50] A point, they say, is that which has no parts, a line is a length without breadth, a plane is a length with breadth; and when a plane gains both depth and resistance, there is a body – which is our present subject – composed of length, breadth, depth and resistance.

[40] The argument against these people too is easy. They will say either that a body is nothing apart from these items or that it is something else apart from the combinations of the items we have listed. Now without length and breadth and depth and resistance, nothing will be a body; but if a body is these items, then anyone who shows that they are unreal will do away with bodies too (for wholes are done away with together with all their parts[51]). It is possible to refute these items in a variety of ways; but here it will be enough to say that if there are limits, they are either lines or planes or bodies. [41] Now if anyone should say that there are surfaces or lines, then[f] they will be said either to be able to subsist in their own right or else to be observed only in connexion with so-called bodies. But to dream of a line or a surface existing in its own right is no doubt silly. And if it is said that each of these items is observed only in connexion with bodies and does not subsist by itself, then first it will be directly granted that bodies have not come into being from them (for they ought, I think, first to have possessed subsistence by themselves and then to have combined together and made bodies); [42] and secondly they do not even subsist in so-called bodies. This can be suggested by several arguments, but here it will be enough to state the puzzles deriving from touch.

If[52] bodies which are set side by side touch one another, they contact each other at their limits, i.e. at their surfaces. Now the surfaces will not be unified through and through with one another in virtue of touching, since then touching would be fusion and separation a tearing apart – and this is not observed to be so. [43] But if the surface touches the surface of the body set alongside it with some of

---

f Deleting καὶ τῶν προειρημένων ἕκαστον.

50 See II 30; III 126, 152; *M* I 21 (where the view is ascribed to Epicurus: see *M* XI 226); [Galen], *Are Qualities Incorporeal?* XIX 493 K. (The conception discussed at the parallel passage in *M* and ascribed to 'the geometers' is different: a body is defined simply as anything extended in three dimensions.) See MUELLER [1982].

51 See III 99.

52 With the following argument compare *M* IX 415–17; *M* III 62–4.

its parts while with others it is unified with the body of which it is a limit, then it will not be without depth, since its parts are thought of as differing in respect of depth, some of them touching what is set alongside it and others unifying it with the body of which it is a limit. Depthless length and breadth, then, cannot be observed in connexion with bodies – nor, therefore, can surfaces.

Similarly, if two surfaces are supposed to be set side by side with one another at the limits where their edges are, along what is called their length (i.e. line to line), then these lines at which the surfaces are said to touch one another will not be unified with one another (then they would be fused); and if each of them touches the line set alongside it with some of its breadthwise parts while with others it is unified with the surface of which it is a limit, then it will not be without breadth – and hence will not be a line.

But if there are neither lines nor surfaces in bodies, there will not be length or breadth or depth in bodies either.

[44] If anyone says that limits are bodies, our answer to him will be brief.[53] If length is a body, then it will have to be divided into the three dimensions; and each dimension, being a body, will itself in turn be divided into three dimensions – and those likewise into others, and so *ad infinitum*. Thus the body, being divided into infinitely many parts, becomes infinite in size, which is absurd. The dimensions in question, then, are not bodies either. But if they are neither bodies nor lines nor surfaces, they will not be deemed to exist.

[45][54] Resistance, too, is inapprehensible. If it is apprehended it will be apprehended by touch. Thus, if we show that touch is inapprehensible, it will be plain that resistance cannot be apprehended. That touch is inapprehensible we deduce in the following way. Things which touch one another do so either with their parts or whole with whole. Certainly not whole with whole; for then they will be united and will not touch one another. Nor parts with parts; for their parts are parts relative to the wholes but wholes relative to their own parts. Now these parts, which are parts of different things, will not touch whole with whole for the reason just given; [46] nor yet

---

[53] Cf. *M* IX 434–5.
[54] With III 45–6 compare *M* IX 259–62: the argument was originally used by the Stoics against the Epicureans (see Plutarch, *comm not* 1080E; below, III 128).

parts with parts – for *their* parts, being wholes in relation to their own parts, will not touch either whole with whole or parts with parts. But if we apprehend touch neither as occurring by way of wholes nor by way of parts, then touch will be inapprehensible – and for this reason so will resistance.

Hence bodies too – for if bodies are nothing apart from the three dimensions and resistance, and we have shown that each of these is inapprehensible, then bodies too will be inapprehensible. In this way, then, so far as the concept of body goes, it is inapprehensible whether there are any bodies.

[47][55] We should also make the following remark about the matter. Of the things which exist, they say, some are objects of perception and others objects of thought, some being apprehended by the intellect and others by the senses;[56] and the senses are simply affected,[57] while the intellect proceeds from the apprehension of objects of perception to the apprehension of objects of thought.[58] Now if there are bodies, they are either objects of perception or objects of thought. They are not objects of perception; for they are thought to be apprehended in virtue of a conglomeration of length and depth and breadth and resistance and colour and various other items together with which they are observed. But they say that the senses are simply affected.[g] [48] If bodies are said to be objects of thought, there must certainly exist in the nature of things some object of perception from which the thought of bodies, which are objects of thought, will be derived. But nothing exists apart from bodies and what is incorporeal; and what is incorporeal is directly an object of thought, while bodies – as we have suggested – are not objects of perception. Thus, since there exists in the nature of things no object of perception from which the thought

g Mutschmann–Mau mark a lacuna after these words, supposing lost a sentence which said: 'So that we shall not be able to co-remember all of them'.

55 With III 47–8 compare *M* IX 436–9 (and for the pattern of argument cf. below, III 108).

56 The distinction, ascribed specifically to the Peripatetics at *M* VII 216–17, became a commonplace.

57 Cf. III 108: the senses are simply affected in the sense that they are affected only by simple items – e.g. by a hue or a pitch. This view of sense perception was presumably taken by the sceptics to be implicit in every dogmatic theory of perception.

58 This 'empiricist' supposition was accepted by all ancient philosophers except the Platonists; see e.g. III 50; *M* VIII 56–60.

of a body will be derived, bodies will not be objects of thought either. But if they are neither objects of perception nor objects of thought, then so far as the argument goes we must say that bodies do not exist at all.[h]

[49] For these reasons, then, setting the arguments against bodies in opposition to the fact that bodies seem to appear real, we conclude to suspension of judgement about bodies.[59]

From the inapprehensibility of bodies it may be concluded that what is incorporeal is inapprehensible. For negatives are thought of as negatives of positive states – e.g. blindness of sight, deafness of hearing, and so on.[60] Hence, in order to apprehend a negative we must first have apprehended the positive of which the negative is said to be a negative. For someone who had no concept of sight could not say that so-and-so does not possess sight – and that is what being blind is. [50] Thus if what is incorporeal is a negation of body, and if when positives are not apprehended it is impossible for their negatives to be apprehended, and if it has been shown that bodies are inapprehensible, then what is incorporeal will also be inapprehensible.

Again, it is either an object of perception or an object of thought. If it is an object of perception, it is inapprehensible because of the differences among animals and humans and the senses and circumstances and because of the admixtures and the other items I discussed earlier in my remarks on the Ten Modes.[61] If it is an object of thought, then since we do not directly grant that objects of perception are apprehended and we think that it is starting from such apprehension that we light on objects of thought,[62] then we shall not directly grant that objects of thought are apprehended – hence neither that which is incorporeal is apprehended.

[51] Anyone who says that he apprehends what is incorporeal will establish that he apprehends it either by perception or by argument. Certainly not by perception, since the senses are thought to grasp

---

[h] Reading μηδέ with the mss: Mutschmann–Mau emend to μηδέν.

[59] See II 133.
[60] Cf. Diogenes Laertius VII 53, for concepts formed in this way by negation.
[61] See I 36–163.
[62] See III 47.

objects of perception by pressure and impact[63] – this is so with e.g. sight (whether it comes about because of tension in the cone, or because of the emission and selection of images, or because of the effusion of rays or of colours[64]), and hearing (whether it is air being struck or whether parts of the sound travel to the ears[i] and strike the acoustic breath and thereby bring it about that the sound is grasped[65]); and again, smells strike the nose, and flavours the tongue, and similarly with what affects the touch. [52] But incorporeal items cannot exert pressure in these ways; so that they cannot be apprehended by perception.

Nor by argument either. If arguments are sayables and incorporeal, as the Stoics say,[66] then anyone who says that what is incorporeal is apprehended by argument takes for granted the matter under investigation. For while we are investigating whether anything incorporeal[j] can be apprehended, he simply assumes something incorporeal and wants apprehension of what is incorporeal to be produced by it. But the argument itself, since it is incorporeal, belongs to the group of items under investigation. [53] How, then, will anyone prove that this incorporeal item – I mean, his argument – is already apprehended? If by another incorporeal item, we shall demand a proof that this is apprehended, and so *ad infinitum*.[67] If by a body, we are also investigating whether bodies can be apprehended – by what, then, shall we show that the body adduced to prove that the incorporeal argument is apprehended is itself apprehended? If by a body, we are thrown back *ad infinitum*; if by something incorporeal, we fall into[k] the reciprocal mode.[68] Hence, as arguments, since they are incor-

---

[i] Reading πρός, with most MSS: Mutschmann–Mau prefer the variant περί.

[j] Reading τι ἀσώματον with most MSS: Mutschmann–Mau print τὸ ἀσώματόν τι.

[k] Reading ἐμπίπτομεν (Heintz): ἐκπίπτομεν MSS, Mutschmann–Mau.

[63] The terms are probably Stoic (see e.g. Alexander, *an mant* 130. 14–30, 132. 11–15, 30–33), but the view was a commonplace.

[64] The cone – i.e. the visual 'cone' with the eye as apex and the surface of the observed object as base – is Stoic (e.g. Diogenes Laertius VII 157); the images are Epicurean (e.g. *ad Hdt* 46–8); the rays come from Plato, *Tim* 45B.

[65] For beaten air see Diogenes Laertius VII 158; for the acoustic breath see Diogenes Laertius VII 52.

[66] See II 104, 107; on sayables see II 81.

[67] See I 166.

[68] See I 169.

poreal, thus remain inapprehensible, no-one will be able to say that incorporeal items are apprehended by argument.

[54] But if arguments are bodies, then since there has been a dispute as to whether bodies are apprehended or not (because of their so-called continuous flux, which means that they do not admit of the demonstrative 'this' and are deemed not even to exist – hence Plato calls bodies things which are coming into being but never exist[69]), I am at a loss as to how the dispute about bodies will be decided, seeing that it can be decided neither by a body nor by anything incorporeal because of the absurdities mentioned a little earlier.

Thus it is not possible to apprehend incorporeal items by argument. [55] But if they neither fall under perception nor are apprehended by argument, they will not be apprehended at all. If it is possible to make positive affirmations neither about the reality of bodies nor about what is incorporeal, we should suspend judgement about the elements too – and perhaps also about the items which come after the elements, if some of these are bodies and others incorporeal, and if puzzles have been raised about both. Thus, since both active and material principles are for these reasons subject to suspension of judgement, the account of the principles is at an impasse.

viii Blending

[56] But to pass over these difficulties too, how can they say that compounds come about from the primary elements if contact or touch and blending or mixing do not exist at all? That touch is nothing I suggested a little earlier when I was discussing the subsistence of bodies;[70] and that blending is also impossible, so far as what they say goes, I shall briefly show.

Many things are said about blending, and the disagreements among the Dogmatists on this topic of inquiry are pretty well

---

[69] See II 28; *M* VIII 7: Plato, *Theaet* 152D; *Tim* 27E (and 49D for the demonstrative 'this').
[70] See III 45–6.

interminable[71] – hence you might conclude at once from the undecidable dispute that the topic is inapprehensible. Refraining here from a counterargument against each of them, given the purpose of our essay,[72] we suppose that the following considerations will suffice for the present.

[57] Things which are blended are composed, they say, of substance[73] and qualities. Thus you will say either that their substances are mixed but not their qualities, or that their qualities are mixed together but not their substances, or that neither are mixed together with the others, or that both are unified with one another.[74]

If neither substances nor qualities are mixed together with one another, blending will be inconceivable; for how will we get a single perception from the things which are blended if they are mixed with one another in none of these ways? [58] If qualities should be said simply to lie alongside one another while substances are mixed, here too what is said will be absurd; for we do not grasp the qualities in the blends as separate – rather, we perceive them as one quality effected by the things blended. If anyone were to say that qualities are mixed but not substances, then he would claim the impossible; for the subsistence of qualities depends on substances, so that it would be ridiculous to say that qualities are separated from substances and somehow mix with one another *on their own*,[1] while the substances are left behind separate and qualityless.

[59] It remains to say that both the qualities and the substances of the blended items run through one another and, by being mixed, effect the blending. And this is more absurd than the previous views. For a blending of this sort is impossible. If, for example, a cup of hemlock juice were mixed with ten cups of water, the hemlock would be said to be blended together with all the water – thus if you take

---

[1]   Retaining καί with the mss: Mutschmann–Mau, following the Latin translation, omit.

[71]   The topic of blending or κρᾶσις, which *M* ignores, was central to Stoic physics: different Stoics took different views, and their theories were attacked by the Peripatetics. The chief text is Alexander, *On Mixture*; see TODD [1976]; SORABJI [1988].

[72]   See I 4.

[73]   I.e. matter: III 2.

[74]   The first option was taken by the Peripatetics, the fourth by the Stoics: see e.g. Galen, *Commentary on Hippocrates' On the Nature of Man* XV 32 K.

even the smallest part of the mixture, you will find that it has been filled with the power of the hemlock. [60]⁷⁵ But if the hemlock is mixed up with every part of the water and extends as a whole over the whole of it inasmuch as both their qualities and their substances pass through one another in order for the blending to come about, and if items which extend over one another in every part occupy an equal space,⁷⁶ so that they are actually equal to one another, then the cup of hemlock will be equal to the ten cups of water – and the mixture ought to be twenty cups or only two, so far as the present hypothesis about the mode of blending goes. And if a cup of water were again added to the twenty cups (so far as this version of the hypothesis goes), then the measure ought to be forty cups or again only two, since it is possible to think of the cup as twenty cups (as many as those over which it extends) and the twenty cups as one (with which they are made equal). [61] By adding one cup at a time in this way, and arguing in the same fashion, it is possible that the twenty cups of the mixture we see ought to be 200,000 and more, so far as the hypothesis about the mode of blending goes, and that the same cups should be just two; and this is the height of incongruity. Thus this hypothesis about blending is also absurd.

[62] If blending can come about neither when substances alone are mixed with one another nor qualities alone nor both nor neither, and if it is not possible to conceive of any option apart from these, then blending – and in general mixing⁷⁷ – is inconceivable. Hence, if the so-called elements can produce the compounds neither by being set alongside one another in contact nor by being blended together or mixed, then the natural science of the Dogmatists, so far as this account too goes, is inconceivable.⁷⁸

---

⁷⁵ With III 60–1 compare Alexander, *an mant* 140. 10–23.

⁷⁶ See III 96.

⁷⁷ The terms 'mixing' (μίξις) and 'blending' are used interchangeably in III 56–61; in Stoic theory, however, they were distinguished (see e.g. Arius ap. Stobaeus, *ecl* I 154.8–155.11), and perhaps Sextus is here alluding to this fact.

⁷⁸ Cf. III 63, 114.

ix Motion

[63] In addition to what we have already said, we must spend some time on the account of the kinds of motion; for here too[m] the natural science of the Dogmatists will be deemed to be impossible.[79] It is certainly in virtue of some motion in the elements and the active principle that the compounds ought to come about. Thus, if we suggest that no form of motion is agreed upon, it will be plain that, even if everything we have already discussed should be granted by way of hypothesis, the Dogmatists have elaborated their physical theory in vain.

x Local motion

[64] Those who are thought to have treated motion pretty fully[80] say that there are six kinds – change of place, natural change, increase, decrease, generation, destruction. We shall spend time on each of these kinds of motion individually, beginning with change of place.

This,[81] according to the Dogmatists, is motion in virtue of which the moving object goes from place to place,[n] either as a whole or in respect of a part[82] – as a whole when, e.g., people go for a walk, in respect of a part when, e.g., a sphere moves around its centre (the whole sphere remains in the same place but its parts change their places).

[65][83] The most fundamental positions on motion have, I think, been three in number. Common sense and some of the philosophers suppose that there is such a thing as motion; Parmenides and Melissus and some others think that there is not; and the Sceptics have said that there no more is than is not – so far as appearances go there seems to be motion, so far as philosophical argument goes it is unreal. We shall set out the counterarguments of those who suppose that there is such

[m] Reading καὶ γὰρ καὶ οὕτως: καὶ ὡς MSS, Mutschmann–Mau.
[n] Retaining περιέρχεται with the MSS: Mutschmann–Mau print μετέρχεται.

[79] Cf. III 6.
[80] Sextus has Aristotle in mind: see M x 37, referring to *Categories* 15a13–33.
[81] With this paragraph compare M x 41 (cf. 52).
[82] The definition is Chrysippean: e.g. Arius ap. Stobaeus, *ecl* I 165. 15–17.
[83] Cf. M x 45–9.

a thing as motion and of those who assert that motion is nothing, and, if we find the dispute equipollent, we shall be compelled to say that, so far as what is said goes, there no more is than is not such a thing as motion.[84]

[66][85] Let us begin with those who say that motion is real.

They rely mainly on evident impression: if there is no such thing as motion, they say, how does the sun travel from its rising to its setting, and how does it produce the seasons of the year, which come about because it is near to us or far from us? How do ships which have put out from harbour come in to other far distant ports? In what way does someone who denies motion leave his house and return to it again? These considerations, they say, are perfectly uncontestable. (This is why one of the Cynics,[86] when the argument against motion was propounded, gave no answer but stood up and walked away, establishing by his action and evidently that motion is real.)

This, then, is how these people attempt to discountenance those who take the contrary position. [67]° Those who deny the reality of motion attempt to do so by arguments of the following sort.

If anything is moved, it is moved either by itself or by something else. If by something else, then since what produces motion acts and what acts is moved, that item too will need something else to move it, and the second a third, and so *ad infinitum*, so that the motion comes to have no beginning – which is absurd. Not everything which is moved, therefore, is moved by something else.[87]

Nor by itself. What is said to be moved by itself [68] will be moved either without any cause or in virtue of some cause. But they say that nothing happens without any cause.[88] And if it is moved in virtue of some cause, the cause in virtue of which it is moved will be productive of motion in it – hence we are thrown back into an infinite regress by

---

° In this section the MSS offer a peculiarly corrupt text: we translate Mutschmann–Mau, who accept the major alterations proposed by Heintz.

84 Cf. II 133 (for 'no more' see I 188–91).
85 Cf. *M* x 66–8.
86 See II 244.
87 For this argument see *M* x 76; and note IX 75–76, where a very similar argument is ascribed to the Stoics; cf. Aristotle, *Phys* 254b7–258b9.
88 A Stoic doctrine (e.g. Cicero, *fat* x 20; [Plutarch], *On Fate* 574D; Alexander, *fat* XXII), usually taken to be denied by the Epicureans (e.g. Cicero, *fat* x 22) and accepted by everyone else (cf. below, III 103).

the argument stated a moment ago. Moreover,[89] since everything which produces motion does so either by pushing or by pulling or by lifting or by depressing, whatever moves itself will have to do so in one of these ways. [69] If it moves itself by pushing, it will be behind itself; if by pulling, in front of itself; if by lifting, below; if by depressing, above. But it is impossible for anything to be above or in front of or below or behind itself. It is therefore impossible for anything to be moved by itself.

But if nothing is moved either by itself or by something else, then nothing is moved at all.

([70] If anyone should seek refuge in impulse or choice,[90] we should remind him of the dispute over what is up to us,[91] which remains undecidable since we have not up to now discovered a standard of truth.)

[71] Again, the following point should also be made. If something is moved, then it is moved either in a place in which it is or in a place in which it is not. But neither in a place in which it is (it is at rest in it, since it is in it), nor a place in which it is not (a thing can neither act nor be acted upon where it is not). Therefore nothing moves.[92]

This argument comes from Diodorus Cronus; it has met with many counterarguments, the more striking of which, following the style of our essay,[93] we shall set out, together with what appears to us to be the decision upon them.

[72][94] Some say that a thing can move in the place in which it is – thus spheres which revolve around their centres move while remaining in the same place.[95] Against this we must transfer the argument to each of the parts of the sphere, and, suggesting that so far as the argument goes a thing is not moved in respect of its parts either, conclude that nothing is moved in the place in which it is.

[89] Cf. *M* x 83–4.
[90] I.e. if anyone should suggest that self-movers do not need to push or pull themselves.
[91] A celebrated philosophical dispute in the ancient world, known to us from numerous texts (e.g. Cicero, *fat*; Alexander, *fat*) and otherwise ignored by Sextus.
[92] Cf. II 242; *M* x 87–90; *M* I 311; Diogenes Laertius IX 99; see SEDLEY [1977].
[93] See I 4, note.
[94] Cf. *M* x 93, 103–4.
[95] See III 64.

[73][96] We shall deal in the same way with those who say that what is moved occupies two places, the one in which it is and the one into which it is travelling. We shall ask them *when* what is moved is travelling from the place in which it is into the other place – when it is in the first place or when it is in the second? When it is in the first place it is not going into the second: it is still in the first. And when it is not in that place it is not going away from it. [74] In addition, they are taking for granted the matter under investigation.[p] For surely you will not allow that something is travelling into a place if you do not grant that it is moving at all.

[75][97] Some people make the following point. We speak of place in two senses – broadly, e.g. the house is my place, and accurately, e.g. (for the sake of argument) the air enclosing the surface of my body.[98] Now a thing which is moved is said to be moved in a place not in the accurate but in the broad sense. Against this it is possible to subdivide place in the broad sense and say that the body said to be moved is properly speaking in one part of it, viz. in its place in the accurate sense, and is not in the others, viz. in the remaining parts of its place in the broad sense. Then we conclude that a thing can move neither in a place in which it is nor in a place in which it is not, and deduce that a thing cannot move even in what is called its place in the broad and[q] loose sense; for this is constituted from the part in which it is accurately speaking and the part in which it is not accurately speaking; and it has been shown that a thing can be moved in neither of these.

[76] The following argument should also be propounded. If something moves, either it moves over the first part first or else it moves over a divisible interval all at once. But a thing can move neither over the first part first nor over a divisible interval all at once, as we shall show. Therefore nothing moves.

That [99] it is not possible for something to move over the first part

p After this sentence the MSS – and Mutschmann–Mau – offer: 'for it cannot act in a place in which it is not'. Following Kayser and Heintz, we regard the sentence as an intrusive marginal gloss (cf. II 242).

q Adding καί before καταχρηστικῶς (Heintz).

96 Cf. *M* X, 94, 106–7.

97 Cf. *M* X 95, 108–10.

98 See III 119, 131 (where the account of 'accurate' place is ascribed to the Peripatetics: see Aristotle, *Phys* 209a31–b2); see BURNYEAT [1984].

99 Cf. *M* X 139–41.

first is clear directly. If bodies and the places and times in which they are said to move are divided *ad infinitum*, then motion will not occur, since it is impossible to find among infinitely many parts a first part from which the thing said to move will start[r] to move. [77][100] But if the items I listed end in something partless, and if each moving thing traverses the first partless portion of its place in the first partless portion of its time, then everything which moves – e.g. a very fast horse and a tortoise – has the same speed; and this is more absurd than the former conclusion. Motion, therefore, does not take place over the first part first.

Nor over a divisible interval all at once. [78][101] For if, as they say, what is apparent should be taken as evidence for what is unclear,[102] then since in order for anyone to complete an interval of a furlong he must first complete the first part of the furlong and secondly the second part and so on, everything which moves should move over the first part first. If what moves is said to cross all at once all the parts of the place in which it moves, it will be in all these places at the same time; and if one part of the place through which it is moving were cold and the other hot, or one part (say) black and the other white (in such a way that they could actually colour what occupied them), then the moving object would at the same time be both hot and cold and both black and white – and that is absurd.

[79] Again, let them say *how much* place a moving object crosses all at once. If they say that it is indeterminate, they will admit that something can move across the whole earth all at once – and if they retreat from that, let them determine for us the size of the place. To attempt to determine the place with accuracy, so that a moving object cannot pass all at once through an interval which is even a hairsbreadth greater, no doubt not only is capricious[103] and rash – or even ridiculous – but it also falls into the impasse we found at the start:[104] everything will have the same speed, since each thing alike goes through the stages of its motion by determinate places. [80] If they say

---

[r] Reading πρώτως for πρώτῳ (mss, Mutschmann–Mau).

[100] Cf. *M* x 154.
[101] Cf. *M* x 123–7.
[102] See Anaxagoras' dictum: I 138.
[103] Cf. III 261.
[104] I.e. at III 77.

that moving objects move all at once over a place which is small but not accurately determined, we shall, in virtue of the sorites puzzle,[105] always be able to add a hairsbreadth of place to the size they hypothesize. If they stop at some point while we are propounding this argument, they will end up again with an accurate determination and the same monstrosity as before; and if they allow the increases we shall compel them to concede that something can move all at once across a distance the size of the whole earth.

Thus, items said to move do not do so over a divisible interval all at once. [81] If things move neither over a divisible place all at once nor over the first part first, then nothing moves.

Those who deny local motion make these and yet further points. For our part, being unable – so far as the opposition between the appearances and the arguments goes – to overthrow either these arguments or the appearances, following which they urge that motion subsists, we suspend judgement as to whether there is or is not such a thing as motion.[106]

xi Increase and decrease

[82] Following the same line of reasoning we also suspend judgement about increase and decrease.[107] Evident impression urges their subsistence, and the arguments seem to overthrow it.

Consider: what is increasing should gain in size as something which exists and subsists, so that if, when an addition has been made to one thing, you should say that another thing has increased, you would be wrong. Now since substances[108] never stand still but are always flowing,[109] one supplanting another, what is said to have increased does not possess its former substance together with another substance added to it – rather, it has a wholly different substance. [83] Thus just as, for the sake of argument, if there is a three-foot length of wood and

---

[105] See II 253.
[106] Cf. *M* x 168.
[107] See III 64.
[108] See III 2.
[109] A commonplace (see e.g. III 115, 145), ascribed in particular to the Platonists (e.g. Apuleius, *dog Plat* I vi 194) and the Stoics (e.g. Plutarch, *comm not* 1083A–1084A); see also I 217.

someone brings along another ten-foot length and says that the three-foot length has increased, he is wrong – since the second length is wholly different from the first – so in the case of everything which is said to increase, if what is said to be added is added to it while its former matter is flowing away and new matter entering, you will not call this an increase but rather a complete alteration.[110]

[84] The same argument applies to decrease – how could what does not subsist at all be said to decrease?

Moreover, if decrease comes about by subtraction and increase by addition, and if there is no such thing as subtraction or addition, then there is no such thing as decrease or increase.

xii Subtraction and addition

[85] That there is no such thing as subtraction they deduce from the following considerations. If one thing is subtracted from another, either the equal is subtracted from the equal or the greater from the less or the less from the greater. But subtraction comes about in none of these ways, as we shall establish. Therefore subtraction is impossible. That subtraction comes about in none of these ways is clear from the following considerations.

What[111] is subtracted must, before the subtraction, be contained in that from which it is subtracted. [86] But the equal is not included in the equal, e.g. six in six: what includes something must be greater than what is included, and that from which something is subtracted must be greater than what is subtracted, in order that something should be left behind after the subtraction – this is how subtraction seems to differ from total annihilation. Nor is the greater included in the smaller, e.g. six in five – that is incongruous. [87] And for the following reason the less is not included in the greater. If five is included in six as the less in the greater, four will be included in five, three in four, two in three, and one in two. Thus six will contain five, four, three, two and one, which when put together make fifteen – so

---

110 This is a version of the celebrated 'growing argument', invented by Epicharmus and discussed by the Stoics and Academics: see esp. Plutarch, *comm not* 1083A–1084A; and see SEDLEY [1982].

111 With the argument from here to III 88 compare *M* IX 297–8 + 301 + 303–7.

we conclude that this number is included in six, once it is granted that the less is included in the greater. And[112] similarly, in the five which is included in the six … the number thirty-five is included – and infinitely many numbers as we go downwards. But it is absurd to say that infinitely many numbers are contained in the number six. Therefore it is also absurd to say that the less is contained in the greater. [88] Thus, if what is subtracted must be included in that from which it is to be subtracted, and if the equal is not included in the equal nor the greater in the smaller nor the smaller in the greater, then nothing is subtracted from anything.

Again,[113] if one thing is subtracted from another, either a whole is subtracted from a whole or a part from a part or a whole from a part or a part from a whole. [89] Now, to say that a whole is subtracted either from a part or from a whole is clearly incongruous. So it remains to say that parts are subtracted either from wholes or from parts – and this is absurd. For instance – to rest the argument, for the sake of clarity, on numbers – take ten and let one be said to be subtracted from it. This one can be subtracted neither from the whole ten nor from the part of the ten which remains, i.e. nine, as I shall establish. Thus it is not subtracted at all.

[90] If the one is subtracted from the whole ten, then, since ten is neither something apart from ten ones nor yet one of these ones, but rather the combination of all the ones, the one ought to be subtracted from each one in order to be subtracted from the whole ten. But from a one, at any rate, nothing can be subtracted – ones are indivisible. So for this reason the one will not be subtracted from the ten in this way. [91] Even if we grant that the one is subtracted from each of the ones, it will then have ten parts – and having ten parts it will be ten. But since we have left over the ten other parts from which the ten parts of the so-called one have been subtracted, the ten will be twenty. But it is

---

[112] The MSS text is unsound, and Mutschmann–Mau print a lacuna. From the parallel at M IX 304–6 it is clear how the argument originally went. 'First, we show that $6 = 5 + 4 + 3 + 2 + 1$ (i.e. $6 = 15$). Similarly, $5 = 4 + 3 + 2 + 1$ and so on. But since 5 is included in 6, $4 + 3 + 2 + 1$ is included in 6; and $6 = 5 + 4 + 3 + 2 + 1 + 4 + 3 + 2 + 1 + 3 + 2 + 1 + 2 + 1 + 1 = 35$. Next we 'go downwards' from 35: by the same argument we first show that $35 = 34 + 33 + \ldots + 1 \ldots$ And so on *ad infinitum*.'

[113] With the argument from here to III 93 compare M IX 308–17 (and M I 162–4; IV 24–6); see BARNES [1988c].

absurd to say that one is ten and that ten is twenty and that what according to them is indivisible is divided. It is absurd, therefore, to say that the one is subtracted from the whole ten.

[92] Nor is the one subtracted from the remaining nine. For that from which something is subtracted does not remain intact; but nine remains intact after the subtraction of this one. Again, nine is nothing apart from nine ones: hence if the one is said to be subtracted from the whole nine, nine will be subtracted; and if from a part of nine, then if from eight the same absurdities will follow, and if from the last one they will say that ones are divisible – and that is absurd. [93] Thus the one is not subtracted from the nine.

But if it is subtracted neither from the whole ten nor from a part of it, a part cannot be subtracted either from a whole or from a part. Thus, if a whole cannot be subtracted from a whole nor a part from a whole nor a whole from a part nor a part from a part, nothing can be subtracted from anything.

[94][114] Addition too has been supposed by them to be something impossible. What is added, they say, is added either to itself or to what was there beforehand or to the compound of both. But none of these options is sound. So nothing is added to anything. For example, take an amount measuring four cups and add a cup. To what, I ask, is it added? It cannot be added to itself, since what is added is different from that to which it is added and nothing is different from itself. [95] Nor to the compound of both – of the four cups and the cup – for how could anything be added to what does not yet exist? Again, if the added cup is mixed with the four cups and the cup, the amount from the four cups and the cup and the added cup will be six cups. [96] But if the cup is added to the four cups alone, then, since what extends over anything is equal to what it extends over,[115] the cup which extends over the amount of four cups will double the four cupsful so that the whole amount comes to eight cups – and this is not observed to be so.

Thus, if what is said to be added is added neither to itself nor to what was there beforehand nor to the compound of both, and if there is no option apart from these, then nothing is added to anything.

[114] With III 94–6 compare *M* IX 321–5 (and *M* I 166–8; IV 31–3).
[115] See III 60.

xiii Transposition

[97][116] Along with the subsistence of addition and subtraction and local motion, transposition too is cancelled for it is a matter of being subtracted from one thing and added to another by way of loco-motion.

xiv Whole and part

[98][117] And so are wholes and parts. For a whole is thought to come about by the combination and addition of its parts and to cease to be a whole by the subtraction of one or more of them.

Again, if anything is a whole, it is either something different apart from its parts or else is its parts themselves. [99][118] Now a whole appears to be nothing different from its parts; at any rate, if the parts are destroyed nothing is left behind[119] which would encourage us to reckon the whole to be something different apart from them. But if the whole is the parts themselves, then a whole will be merely a name and an empty noun, and it will have no subsistence of its own – just as a separation is not anything apart from the things separated, or a timbering apart from the timbers. Therefore there are no wholes.

[100] Nor are there parts. For if there are parts, they are either parts of the whole or parts of one another or each is a part of itself. Not of the whole, since there is nothing apart from the parts – and again, in this case the parts will be parts of themselves, since each of the parts is said to help fill the whole.[120] Nor of one another, since a part is thought to be contained in that of which it is a part, and it is absurd to say that a hand, say, is included in a foot. [101] Nor yet will each be a part of itself; for by dint of being included, a thing will then be both greater and less than itself.

Thus, if what are said to be parts are parts neither of the whole nor of themselves nor of one another, they are parts of nothing; and if they

---

116 Cf. *M* IX 328.
117 With III 98–101 compare II 215–18; see BARNES [1988c].
118 Cf. *M* IX 339, 343; *M* I 134–5.
119 See III 40.
120 See e.g. *M* IX 337, 348; *M* I 139; and below, III 172.

are parts of nothing they are not parts at all[121] – for items relative to one another are destroyed together.[122]

So much[s] for these matters, by way of digression, since we mentioned wholes and parts.[123]

xv Natural change

[102] Some say that so-called natural change[124] does not subsist. They use arguments of the following sort.

If anything changes, what changes is either a body or incorporeal; but each of these has led to an impasse:[125] therefore the account of change will also reach an impasse.

[103] If anything changes, it changes in virtue of certain actions of a cause and by being acted upon.[126] . . .[t] For the subsistence of causes is overthrown,[127] and what is acted upon is turned about together with causes, not having anything by which it is acted upon.[128] Therefore nothing changes.

[104][129] If anything changes, what exists changes or what does not exist changes. Now what does not exist is non-subsistent and can neither be acted upon nor act;[130] hence it does not admit change either. If what exists changes, it changes either insofar as it is existent

---

s Reading οὕτως for ἄλλως (MSS, Mutschmann–Mau).
t There is a lacuna in the MSS: the text must have said something like 'But this is impossible'.

121 See II 123, note.
122 See II 126.
123 The chapter is a digression inasmuch as it interrupts the programme laid down at III 64. The last clause is obscure: 'since we mentioned the matter at III 98 we found ourselves digressing into it'; or 'since we discussed the matter at II 215–18 we need say no more about it here'?
124 'Natural change' (see III 64), which is called 'change' *simpliciter* at M X 37 (what does the qualification 'natural' mean?), is change *of quality* (see the example at III 107; and note esp. M X 38–40). At M X 42–4, Sextus argues – after Epicurus – that change of quality requires local motion and hence does not need a separate refutation; at M X 324, change of quality is assimilated to transposition (cf. M IX 277–8, 328).
125 See III 38–55.
126 See III 68.
127 See III 17–29.
128 Cf. III 106; M IX 267.
129 Cf. M IX 276.
130 See III 112–13.

or insofar as it is not existent. [105] It does not change insofar as it is not existent; for it is *not* not existent. But if it changes insofar as it is existent, it will be[u] something different from being existent, i.e. it will be non-existent. But it is absurd to say that what is existent comes to be non-existent. Therefore what exists does not change either. But if neither what exists nor what does not exist changes, and if there is no option apart from these, it remains to say that nothing changes.

[106] Again, some offer the following remarks. What changes must change in some time. But nothing changes either in the past or in the future or yet in the present, as we shall show. Therefore nothing changes. Nothing changes in past or future time; for neither of these is present, and it is impossible for anything to act or be acted upon in a time which is not existent and present. [107] Nor yet in the present. Present time is, no doubt, actually unreal; but to pass over that point for the moment,[131] it is partless. But it is impossible to think that in a partless time iron, say, changes from hard to soft or that any other change occurs; for changes appear to need duration.[132] Thus if nothing changes either in past time or in the future or in the present, it must be said that nothing changes at all.

[108] Moreover, if there are changes, either ...[v] senses are simply affected[133] whereas change seems to need the co-consciousness[134] of that from which it changes and that into which it is said to be changing. And if they are objects of thought, then since among past philosophers there has been an undecidable dispute about the reality of objects of thought, as we have already often suggested,[135] we shall not be able to say anything about the reality of change either.

---

u   Reading ἔσται (with the early editors) for ἔστι (MSS, Mutschmann–Mau).
v   A line or two has dropped out of the text. Sextus must have written something like this: '... either ⟨they are objects of perception or they are objects of thought. But they are not objects of perception; for the⟩ senses ...'.

131   See III 144–6.
132   Cf. *M* IX 271–3.
133   See III 47.
134   συμμνημόνευσις: see *M* IX 353–6; X 64; BARNES [1988c].
135   See e.g. I 170; II 57.

xvi Generation and destruction

[109][136] Generation and destruction are turned about together with addition and subtraction and natural change; for apart from these nothing could come into being or be destroyed.[137] For instance, it is when ten is destroyed, they say, that nine is generated, by the subtraction of a one; and ten is generated when nine is destroyed, by the addition of a one; and rust when bronze is destroyed, by natural change. Hence, if these sorts of motion are rejected,[138] it is no doubt necessary for generation and destruction to be rejected too.

[110] Nonetheless, some[139] make the following point too. If Socrates was born, then Socrates was generated either when Socrates did not exist or when Socrates already existed. But if he is said to have been generated when he already existed, he will have been generated twice; and if when he did not exist, then at the same time Socrates both existed and did not exist – he existed insofar as he had been generated and he did not exist by hypothesis. [111] And if Socrates died, he died either when he was alive or when he was dead. He did not die when he was alive – for then the same man would have been both living and dead. Nor when he was dead; for then he would have been dead twice. Therefore Socrates did not die.

It is possible to apply this argument to anything said to be generated or destroyed, and so to reject generation and destruction.

[112] Some people propound the following argument as well.[140] If anything is generated, either what exists is generated or what does not exist is generated. But what does not exist is not generated; for nothing holds of what does not exist, and so being generated does not hold of it. Nor what exists. If what exists is generated, it is generated either insofar as it is existent or insofar as it is not existent. Now it is not generated insofar as it is not existent; but if it is generated insofar as it is existent, then since they say that what is generated comes to be

---

136 Cf. *M* x 323–4.
137 See e.g. Arius ap. Stobaeus, *ecl* I 177.21–179.5, on Posidonius' account of generation.
138 See III 85–96, 102–8.
139 Sextus is probably thinking of Diodorus Cronus: see *M* x 347; *M* I 310–12; cf. *M* IX 269.
140 Cf. III 104–5 (and *M* x 326–7; Diogenes Laertius IX 100).

different from what it was, what is generated will be different from what exists, i.e. it will be non-existent. Therefore what is generated will be non-existent – and that is incongruous. [113] Thus, if neither what is existent nor what is non-existent is generated, nothing is generated.

For the same reasons[141] nothing is destroyed. If anything is destroyed, either what is existent or what is non-existent is destroyed. Now what is non-existent is not destroyed; for what is destroyed must be acted upon in some way. Nor what is existent. For it is destroyed either while remaining in the state of being existent or while not so remaining. If while remaining in the state of being existent, the same thing will at the same time be both existent and non-existent; [114] for since it is destroyed not insofar as it is non-existent but insofar as it is existent, then insofar as it is said to have been destroyed it will be different from what is existent and for that reason non-existent, and insofar as it is said to have been destroyed while remaining in the state of existing it will be existent. But it is absurd to say that the same thing is both existent and non-existent. Therefore what exists is not destroyed while remaining in the state of existing. But if what exists is not destroyed while remaining in the state of existing but first comes round to a state of not existing and then is destroyed, it is no longer what exists but what does not exist which is destroyed. And we have suggested that this is impossible. Thus, if neither what is existent nor what is not existent is destroyed, and if there is no option apart from these, then nothing is destroyed.

This will be enough, in an outline,[142] about the kinds of motion; and it follows that the natural science of the Dogmatists is unreal and inconceivable.[143]

xvii Rest

[115] Next, some have also puzzled about rest in nature, saying that what moves does not rest but that all bodies move continuously according to the supposition of the Dogmatists who say that

---

[141] Cf. *M* x 344–5.
[142] See I 4, note.
[143] See III 62.

substances are in flux[144] and are always producing effluxions and additions – so that Plato says that bodies are not even existent but rather calls them coming into being[145] and Heraclitus compares the mobility of our matter to the swift flowing of a river.[146] Therefore no body rests.

[116] What is said to rest is thought to be contained by the things about it, and what is contained is acted upon. But nothing is acted upon, since nothing is a cause, as we have suggested.[147] Therefore nothing rests.

Some have also propounded the following argument. What rests is acted upon; and what is acted upon moves: therefore what is said to rest moves. But if it moves it does not rest.

[117] From the following consideration it is plain that what is incorporeal cannot rest either. If what rests is acted upon, and being acted upon is peculiar to bodies, if it occurs at all, and not to what is incorporeal,[148] then nothing incorporeal can either be acted upon or rest. Therefore nothing rests.

[118] So much for rest. Since each of the items we have just discussed cannot be conceived of without place and time, we should turn our inquiry to them. For if they are shown to be non-subsistent, the former items will each be non-subsistent for this reason too. Let us begin with place.

xviii Place

[119] We speak of places in two senses,[149] strictly and loosely – in the loose sense there are places broadly speaking, e.g. the city is my place; in the strict sense, there are places which enclose something accurately, e.g. the air by which I am surrounded.[w] Here we are investigating place in the accurate sense.[150]

---

w Adding τι, ὡς ἐμὲ ὁ ἀήρ after κατέχων (Heintz) and deleting the second πρὸς ἀκρίβειαν (Kayser).

[144] See III 82.

[145] See III 54.

[146] See frag. 12 Diels–Kranz; BARNES [1987], pp. 116–17.

[147] See III 17–29 (and 103).

[148] See III 129; M VIII 263.

[149] See III 75; M X 95.

[150] So too at M X 15: Sextus presumably allows that things have places in the loose sense, a sense accepted by common sense and not invented by the Dogmatists.

Some[151] have posited it, some have rejected it, and others have suspended judgement about it. [120] Those who say that it is real take refuge in evident impressions. Who, they ask, would say that there is no such thing as place when he sees the parts of place – right and left, up and down, in front and behind – when he is in different places at different times, when he observes that where my teacher used to talk there I now talk, and when he apprehends that the place of things light by nature is different from the place of things heavy by nature;[152] [121] and again when he hears the ancients saying 'For indeed first came chaos into being'[153] (place, they say, is chaos from the fact that it makes room for[154] the things which come into being in it). And if there is such a thing as body, they say, there is also such a thing as place; for without place there would be no bodies.[155] And if there are things by which and things from which, there are also things in which – and they are places. But the first in each case: therefore the second in both cases.[156]

[122][157] Those who reject place do not allow that the parts of place exist: place is nothing apart from its parts, and anyone who tries to conclude that there is such a thing as place by assuming its parts as existing wants to establish the matter under investigation by way of itself. Similarly, those who say that something is coming to be or has come to be in some place are talking idly, since place is simply not granted. (And they also take as given the reality of bodies, which is not directly granted.) Again, that from which and that by which are shown to be unreal in the same way as place is. [123] Nor is Hesiod a respectable judge of philosophical matters.[158] And knocking down in

---

[151] With the argument from here to III 121 compare *M* x 7–11 (and also Aristotle, *Phys* 208b1–209a2).

[152] A view common to the Stoics (e.g. Stobaeus, *ecl* I 14.4) and the Peripatetics (e.g. Aristotle, *Phys* 208b1–209a2) – on Sextus' use of Aristotle in this section see ANNAS [1992c].

[153] Hesiod, *Theogony* 118 (the verse which allegedly drove Epicurus to philosophy: *M* x 18–19; and it was interpreted by Zeno: [Valerius Probus], *Commentary on Virgil's Eclogues* 344 Hagen).

[154] χωρητικόν: perhaps a fanciful etymology for χάος – see *M* x 11.

[155] See e.g. Epicurus, *ad Hdt* 39.

[156] For this Stoic use of 'the first' and 'the second' see II 142.

[157] With III 122–3 compare *M* x 13–19.

[158] On the Stoic habit of citing poets as witnesses to philosophical views see esp. Galen, *PHP* III iv 15–16 (= v 314–15 K); see TIELEMAN [1992], pp. 204–27.

this way the points brought forward to establish the existence of place, they then establish with a considerable variety of arguments that it is unreal, making use of what are thought to be the weightier positions of the Dogmatists about place – those of the Stoics and the Peripatetics – in the following fashion.

[124][159] The Stoics call void that which can be occupied by an entity but is not so occupied, or an interval devoid of bodies, or an interval unoccupied by body; they call place an interval occupied by an entity and equal to that which occupies it (here calling bodies entities[160]); and space an interval partly occupied by bodies and partly unoccupied (some[161] say that space is the place of a large body, the difference between place and space being a matter of size).

[125] Since they say that place is an interval occupied by a body, in what sense – we ask them – do they mean that it is an interval? Is it the length of the body or its breadth or its depth only, or is it all three dimensions? If one dimension, then a place will not be equal to the object whose place it is; and in addition, what includes something will be part of what is included – and that is wholly incongruous.[162] [126] If all three dimensions, then since in what is called a place there is found neither void nor any other body having dimensions but only the body said to be in the place, which[x] is composed of the dimensions (it is length and breadth and depth and resistance,[163] which is said to be an attribute of these dimensions), the body will itself be its own place, and the same thing will include and be included – which is absurd. Therefore there are no dimensions when a place is present, and for this reason there is no such thing as a place.

[127] The following argument is also propounded. When anything is said to be in a place, the dimensions are not observed to be doubled – rather, there is one length and one breadth and one depth. Then are these the dimensions of the body alone or of the place alone or of

---

[x]   Reading ὅ (Pappenheim) for οὐ (the MSS reading, which Mutschmann–Mau delete).

[159] Cf. *M* X 3–4; Stobaeus, *ecl* I 20. I.
[160] I.e. incorporeals do not exist (see e.g. Plutarch, *comm not* 1074D) but are merely things (see II 86).
[161] Among them Chrysippus: Arius ap. Stobaeus, *ecl* I xviii 4d, 161, 8–26.
[162] See III 86.
[163] See III 39.

both? If of the place alone, the body will not have any length or breadth or depth of its own, so that the body will not actually be a body – which is absurd. [128] If of both, then, since a void has no subsistence apart from its dimensions, if the dimensions of the void are present in the body and compose the body itself, then what composes a void will also compose a body. For, as we have suggested earlier,[164] we cannot affirm anything about the reality of resistance; and if the dimensions are the only things which are apparent in what are called bodies, and they are the dimensions of a void and are the same as the void, then a body will be a void – which is absurd. And if they are the dimensions of the body alone, there will be no dimensions of place, and hence no place either. So if dimensions of place are found in none of these ways, there is no such thing as a place.

[129][165] In addition, it is argued that when a body enters a void and a place comes into being, the void either remains or withdraws or is destroyed. But if it remains, the same thing will be both full and void. If it withdraws by way of local motion or is destroyed by changing, then the void will be a body; for these properties are peculiar to bodies.[166] But it is absurd to say that the same thing is void and full, or that a void is a body. Therefore it is absurd to say that a void can be occupied by a body and become a place.

[130] For this reason, void too is found to be non-subsistent, since it is not possible for it to be occupied by a body and become a place, and yet it was said to be that which can be occupied by a body.[167]

Space too is overturned at the same time. If space is a large place, then it is overturned together with place; and if space is an interval partly occupied by a body and partly void, then it is rejected along with body and void.

[131] These considerations – and yet more – are advanced against the position of the Stoics on place. The Peripatetics say that a place is the limit of what includes insofar as it includes, so that my place is the surface of the air enclosing my body.[168]

---

[164] See III 45–6.
[165] Cf. *M* x 21–3 (the form of the argument goes back to Plato, *Phaedo* 102D–103C).
[166] See III 117.
[167] See III 124.
[168] See III 75; cf. *M* x 30; Aristotle, *Phys* 212a20–1. (By 'the surface of the air' Sextus means the *inner* surface.)

But if this is what place is, then the same thing will both exist and not exist. When a body is about to come into being at a certain place, then insofar as nothing can come into being in what does not exist, the place must pre-exist in order that in this way the body may come into being in it; and for this reason the place will exist before the body which is in the place comes into being in it. But insofar as a place is effected when the surface of what includes encloses what is included, a place cannot subsist before the body comes to be in it; and for this reason it will not then exist. But it is absurd to say that the same thing both exists and does not exist. Therefore a place is not the limit of what includes insofar as it includes.

[132] In addition, if there are such things as places, they are either generated or ungenerated.[169] Places are not ungenerated; for they are effected, they say, as they enclose the body in them. Nor are they generated; for if a place is generated, it comes into being either when the body is in it (and it comes into being at the point where what is in it is already said to be) or else when the body is not in it. [133] But neither when it is in it (for the place of the body in it already exists), nor when it is not in it (since, as they say, what includes encloses what is included and a place thereby comes into being, whereas nothing can enclose what is not in it). But if places come into being neither when a body is in them nor when it is not, and if no option apart from these can be conceived of, then places are not generated either. And if they are neither generated nor ungenerated they do not exist.

[134][170] More generally, the following points can also be made. If there is such a thing as a place, it is either a body or incorporeal. But each of these is at an impasse, as we have suggested.[171] Place too, then, is at an impasse. A place is thought of in relation to the body whose place it is. But the account of the reality of bodies is at an impasse. So too, therefore, is the account of place. The place of anything is not eternal. But if it is said to come into being, it is found to be non-subsistent since generation is not real.[172]

[135] It is possible to make many other points too; but, in order not

---

[169] Cf. III 147–8, on time.
[170] Cf. *M* x 34.
[171] See III 38–48, 49–54.
[172] See III 109–14.

to lengthen our account,[173] we should infer that the Sceptics are confounded by the arguments and discountenanced by the evident impressions; hence we subscribe to neither side, so far as what is said by the Dogmatists goes, but suspend judgement about place.[174]

xix Time

[136] We are affected in the same way when we investigate time: so far as the appearances go, there seems to be such a thing as time; but so far as what is said about it goes, it appears non-subsistent.

Some[175] say that time is an interval of the motion of the whole (by the whole I mean the universe); some[176] that it is the motion itself of the universe; Aristotle[177] (or, as some say, Plato) that it is the number of what is before and after in motion; Strato[178] (or as some say Aristotle[179]) that it is a measure of motion and rest; [137] Epicurus[180] (according to Demetrius of Laconia) that it is an accident of accidents, belonging to days and nights, and seasons, and feelings and non-feelings, and motions and rests. [138] As to its substance, some have said that it is a body (e.g. Aenesidemus,[181] who says that it does not differ at all from what exists and from the primary body), others[182] that it is incorporeal.

Now either all these positions are true, or all are false, or some are true and some false. But they cannot all be true (most of them conflict), nor will the Dogmatists grant that they are all false. [139] Or again, if it is granted that it is false that time is a body and false that it is incorporeal, the unreality of time will be immediately granted. For there cannot be anything else apart from these. Nor is it possible to apprehend which are true and which false, both because of the

---

173 See I 4, note.
174 See II 133.
175 The Stoics: see *M* x 170; Diogenes Laertius VII 141; Arius ap. Stobaeus, *ecl* I 106 5–11.
176 Plato: see *M* x 228 (cf. x 170); Plato, *Tim* 47D (cf. Aristotle, *Phys* 218a33–b1).
177 See *M* x 176; *Phys* 220a24–5.
178 See *M* x 177.
179 And note e.g. *Phys* 220b32–221a1.
180 See *M* x 219.
181 See *M* x 216 (and above, I 210, note, for the Dogmatic aspect of Aenesidemus' thought).
182 The Stoics: see *M* x 218.

equipollent dispute and because of the impasse with respect to standards and proofs.[183] So that for these reasons we shall not be able to affirm anything about time. [140] Again, since time is thought not to subsist without motion (or rest too), then, since motion is rejected (and similarly rest too),[184] time is rejected.

Nonetheless,[185] some people also make the following points against time. If there is such a thing as time, either it is limited or it is infinite.[186] [141] If it is limited, it began at some time and will cease at some time; and for this reason there was a time when there was no time (before it began), and there will be a time when there is no time (after it has ceased) – and this is absurd. Hence time is not limited. [142] If it is infinite, then since part of it is said to be past, part present, and part future, the future and the past either exist or do not exist. If they do not exist, then since the present alone is left and this is minuscule, time will be limited and the puzzles we set down a moment ago will follow. But if the past exists and the future exists, each of them will be present – and it is absurd to say that past time and future time are present. Thus time is not infinite either. But if it is neither infinite nor finite, time does not exist at all.

[143][187] In addition, if time exists it is either divisible or indivisible. Now it is not indivisible: it is divided into the present, the past and the future, as they themselves say. Nor is it divisible. For everything divisible is measured by one of its parts, the measuring part being set against each part of what is measured, as when we measure a foot by an inch. But time cannot be measured by any of its parts. If the present – for the sake of argument – measures the past, it will be set against the past and for this reason it will be past; and similarly in the case of the future it will be future. If the future measures the others it will be present and past; and the past, similarly, will be future and present. And this is incongruous. Thus, time is not divisible either. But if it is neither indivisible nor divisible, it does not exist.

---

[183] See II 18–79, 144–92.

[184] See III 64–81, 115–17.

[185] With the argument from here to III 142 compare M x 189–91 (and M VI 62).

[186] Finite according to e.g. Plato (*Tim* 37D–38B), infinite according to e.g. the Stoics (e.g. Arius ap. Stobaeus, *ecl* I 106 11–13).

[187] Cf. M x 193–6 (and M VI 64–5).

[144][188] Time is said to be tripartite – one part being past, one present, one future. Of these, the past and the future do not exist;[189] for if past and future time exist now, each of them will be present. Nor does the present. If present time exists, it is either indivisible or divisible. It is not indivisible; for things which change are said to change in the present, and nothing changes in a partless time – e.g. iron becoming soft, and the rest.[190] So present time is not indivisible. [145] Nor is it divisible. It could not be divided into presents; for because of the rapid flux of things in the universe[191] present time is said to pass with inconceivable speed[y] into past time. Nor into past and future;[192] for then it will be unreal, one part of it no longer existing and the other not yet existing. [146] (Hence the present cannot be an end of the past and a beginning of the future,[193] since then it will both exist and not exist – it will exist as present and it will not exist since its parts do not exist.[194]) Thus it is not divisible either. But if the present is neither indivisible nor divisible, it does not exist. And if the present and the past and the future do not exist, there is no such thing as time – for what consists of unreal parts is unreal.[195]

[147][196] The following argument too is produced against time. If time exists, it is either generated and destructible or ungenerated and indestructible.[197] It is not ungenerated and indestructible, since part of it is said to be past and no longer to exist and part to be future and not yet to exist. [148] Nor is it generated and destructible. For what comes into being must come into being from something existent and what is destroyed must be destroyed into something existent,

---

y   Retaining ἀπερινοήτως with the mss: Mutschmann–Mau print ἀνεπι-
νοήτως (Kayser).

188 With III 144–6 compare *M* x 197–200 (and *M* vi 66–7).
189 According to Chrysippus, past and future do not exist (ὑπάρχειν) but they subsist (ὑφίστανται): Plutarch, *comm not* 1081F; Arius ap. Stobaeus, *ecl* I 106. 18–23; see SCHOFIELD [1988].
190 See III :06–7.
191 See III 82.
192 As Chrysippus held: Plutarch, *comm not* 1081F.
193 So e.g. Aristotle, *Phys* 222a10–12; Archedemus (see Plutarch, *comm not* 1081E).
194 Cf. *M* x 200–2.
195 Cf. *M* x 192; *M* vi 63.
196 With III 147–8 compare *M* x 203–5.
197 Cf. III 132–3, on place.

according to the principles of the Dogmatists themselves.[198] If it is destroyed into the past, it is destroyed into something non-existent; and if it comes into being from the future, it comes into being from something non-existent (for neither of these exists). But it is absurd to say that something comes into being from something non-existent or is destroyed into something non-existent. Therefore time is not generated and destructible. And if it is neither ungenerated and indestructible nor generated and destructible, it does not exist at all.

[149][199] In addition, since everything which comes into being is thought to come into being in time, if time comes into being it comes into being in time. Now either it comes into being in itself or else in a different time. If in itself, the same thing will both exist and not exist: since that in which something comes into being ought to pre-exist that which comes into being in it, time, coming into being in itself, does not yet exist insofar as[z] it is coming into being and already exists insofar as[aa] it is coming into being in itself. Hence it does not come into being in itself. [150] Nor in a different time. If the present comes into being in the future, the present will be future; and if in the past, past. (And the same should be said about the other times.) Hence one time does not come into being in a different time. But if it comes into being neither in itself nor in a different time, it does not come into being at all. It was shown that it is not ungenerated either. Thus, being neither generated nor ungenerated, it does not exist at all. For everything which exists ought to be either generated or ungenerated.

xx Number

[151] Since time is thought not to be observed without number,[200] it will not be absurd briefly[201] to discuss number too. So far as ordinary custom goes, we speak, without holding opinions, of numbering

---

z   Reading (Heintz): εἰ MSS, Mutschmann–Mau.

aa   Reading (Heintz): εἰ MSS, Mutschmann–Mau.

198   The rejection of creation *ex nihilo* and destruction *in nihilum* was an axiom of the early philosophers, according to Aristotle (*Metaphys* 983b 7–18); and few later thinkers questioned the axiom.

199   With III 149–50 compare *M* x 207–11.

200   Cf. *M* x 248; VII 104 (see Aristotle's definition cited above, III 136).

201   See I 163.

things and we accept that there are such things as numbers.[202] But the superfluities of the Dogmatists have provoked an argument against number too.

[152][203] For instance, Pythagoras' followers say that numbers are the elements of the universe.[204] They say that apparent items are composed of something and that the elements must be simple – therefore the elements are unclear items.[205] Some unclear items are bodies (e.g. atoms[ab] and masses[206]) and some are incorporeal (e.g. shapes and forms and numbers). Of these, bodies are composite, being composed of length and breadth and depth and resistance or weight.[207] Therefore the elements are not only unclear but also incorporeal. [153] Each incorporeal item is observed to have a number – it is either one or two or more. From all this they conclude that the elements of the things which exist are the unclear and incorporeal numbers which are observed in everything.[208] But not all numbers – only the one and the indefinite two, which comes from the one by addition and by participation in which particular twos become twos.[209] [154] It is from these, they say, that the other numbers which are observed in numbered objects are generated[210] and that the universe is constructed. For points are analogous to ones, lines to twos (lines are observed between two points), surfaces to threes (they say that a surface is the breadthways flux of a line towards another point lying to its side), and bodies to fours (a body is the raising of a surface to some superjacent point).[211] [155] In this way they romance about[212] bodies and the whole universe, which they say is governed by harmonic ratios – the fourth, which is one-and-a-third to one (as 8 to

---

[ab] Reading αἱ ἄτομοι (Pappenheim) for οἱ ἄτμοι (MSS, Mutschmann–Mau).

[202] See I 23.
[203] With III 152–5 compare M x 248–83.
[204] What follows is a version of Platonico-Pythagorean metaphysics: see e.g. M VII 94–109; M IV 3–10.
[205] Cf. M x 250–1.
[206] See III 32.
[207] Cf. M x 257 (and see above, III 39).
[208] Cf. M x 258.
[209] Cf. M x 261–2.
[210] Cf. M x 277 (and M IV 4).
[211] Cf. M x 278–80 (and VII 99–100; M IV 4–5).
[212] See II 222.

6), the fifth, which is one-and-a-half to one (as 9 to 6), and the octave, which is two to one (as 12 to 6).[213]

[156] This, then, is what they dream up; and they try to establish that numbers are something different apart from numbered objects, arguing[214] that if an animal (say) is, by its own definition, one thing, then a plant, since it is not an animal, will not be one thing. But a plant too is one thing. Therefore an animal is one thing, not insofar as it is an animal, but in virtue of something else, outside it and observed in it, in which each animal participates and because of which it comes to be one thing. Again, if numbered objects are numbers, then since[ac] men and cows (say) and horses are numbered, numbers will be men and cows and horses – and white and black and bearded, if the objects measured should happen to be so. [157] But this is absurd. Therefore numbers are not the objects numbered but possess a subsistence of their own apart from them in virtue of which they are observed in the numbered objects and are elements.

Once they had concluded in this way that numbered objects are not numbers, the puzzles against numbers entered the scene. It is argued that if numbers exist they are either the numbered objects themselves or something different, outside and apart from them. But numbers are neither the numbered objects themselves, as the Pythagoreans have proved, nor something different apart from them, as we shall suggest. Therefore numbers are nothing.

[158][215] We shall establish that numbers are nothing outside and apart from the numbered objects, basing our argument on the one for the sake of lucid exposition. If, then, the one is something in its own right, by participation in which each of the things participating in it becomes one, then this one is either one or as many as are the things participating in it. If it is one, does each of the things said to participate in it participate in it as a whole or in a part of it?[216] If one man, say, possesses all the one, there will no longer be a one in which one horse or one dog or any of the other things we call one will

---

ac   Omitting οἱ before ἀριθμητοί (Kayser).

213 Cf. *M* x 283 (and VII 95–7; *M* IV 6–7).

214 With the argument here compare *M* x 285–6 and *M* IV 11–13 (where virtually the same argument is ascribed to Plato).

215 With III 158–61 compare *M* x 293–8 (and *M* IV 18–20).

216 Cf. II 220–1 (ultimately from Plato, *Parm* 131A–132B).

participate – [159] just as, if we suppose many naked men and a single cloak which one of them wears, the rest will remain naked and without a cloak. But if each participates in a part of it, then first the one will have parts – indeed it will have *infinitely* many parts into which it can be divided; and this is absurd.[217] And secondly, just as a part of ten – two, say – is not ten, so a part of a one will not be a one; and for this reason nothing will participate in the one. Hence there is not just one one in which particular things are said to participate. [160] But if the ones by participation in which each of the particulars is said to be one are equal in number to those numbered objects which are said to be one, then the ones participated in will be infinite. Moreover, these ones either participate in a superordinate one (or in ones equal in number to them) and for this reason are ones, or else they do not. But without any participation they are not ones – [161] for if *they* can be ones without participation, then any perceptible object will also be able to be one thing without participation in a one, and the one said to be observed in its own right is directly turned about.[218] But if they too are ones by participation, either they all participate in one one or each participates in its own. If all in one, each will be said to participate either in a part or in the whole – and the initial absurdities remain. [162] If each in its own, then a one must be observed in each of these ones too, and others in these, and so *ad infinitum*.

Thus, if we are to apprehend that there are certain ones in their own right, by participation in which everything which exists is one thing, then we must apprehend infinitely many times infinitely many ones as objects of thought; and if it is impossible to apprehend infinitely many times infinitely many ones as objects of thought, then it is impossible to assert that there are any ones of this sort or that everything which exists is one by participating in its own one.[ad] [163] It is absurd, therefore, to say that there are as many ones as there are things participating in them. But if the ones so called in their own right are neither one in number nor as many as the things which participate in them, then ones in their own right do not exist at all. Similarly, none of the other numbers will exist in its own right; for we can apply to

---

[ad] Omitting γινόμενον ἕν (MSS, Mutschmann–Mau).

[217] See III 90.
[218] See I 122.

each of the numbers the argument here propounded by way of example in the case of the one. But if numbers neither exist in their own right, as we have suggested, nor are the numbered things themselves, as Pythagoras' followers have established, and if there is no option apart from these, then we should say that numbers do not exist.

[164]²¹⁹ And how can those who believe that numbers are something outside and apart from the numbered objects say that twos are generated from ones? When we put a one together with another one, either something is added to the ones from outside or something is subtracted from them or nothing is either added or subtracted. If nothing is either added or subtracted, there will not be a two. For when the ones were separate from one another there was no two observed in them by virtue of their own definition; nor has anything now come to them from outside, [165] or been subtracted either, according to the hypothesis. Hence, putting a one together with a one will not make a two if nothing is either subtracted or added from outside. But if something is subtracted, not only will there not be a two but the ones will actually be decreased. And if the two is added to them from outside in order that a two may come into being from the ones, then what are thought to be two will be four; for we had one one and another one, and if a two were added to them from outside we would get four.

[166] The same argument applies to the other numbers too, which are said to be produced by combination.²²⁰ Thus if the so-called composite numbers are not generated from the superordinate numbers either by subtraction or by addition or without subtraction or addition, then there is no such thing as the generation of the numbers said to exist on their own and apart from the numbered objects. And that the composite numbers are not in fact ungenerated they themselves make plain when they say that they are compounded and generated from the superordinate numbers, i.e. from the one and the indefinite two. Thus numbers do not subsist on their own.

[167] But if numbers neither are observed on their own nor have

---

²¹⁹ With III 164–5 compare *M* x 302–4; *M* IV 21–2. In both these texts the puzzle is ascribed to Plato's book *On the Soul*: see *Phaedo* 96E.
²²⁰ See III 154.

their subsistence in the numbered objects, then there are no such things as numbers, so far as the superfluities peddled by the Dogmatists go.[221]

So much, in an outline,[222] will suffice for the part of philosophy they call physics.

xxi The ethical part of philosophy[223]

[168][224] There remains the ethical part of philosophy, which is thought to deal with the distinction among fine, bad and indifferent things.[225] In order to give a summary account[226] of this part too, let us investigate the reality of good, bad and indifferent things, first setting out the concept of each.

xxii Good, bad and indifferent things

[169][227] The Stoics say that what is good is benefit or not other than benefit.[228] By benefit they mean virtue and virtuous action; by not other than benefit, virtuous people and friends. Virtue, being the ruling part[229] in a certain condition, and virtuous action, being activity in accordance with virtue, are immediately benefits, while virtuous men and friends are not other than benefit. [170] Benefit, then, is a part of the good man, since it is his ruling part. Now wholes, they say, are neither the same as their parts (a man is not his hand) nor something else over and above their parts (they do not subsist without the parts). Hence, they say, wholes are not other than their parts.[230] So, since the virtuous are wholes with respect to their ruling part (which they called a benefit), they say that they are not other than benefit.

---

221 See III 151.
222 See I 4, note.
223 Cf. *M* XI 20–3.
224 Cf. *M* XI 1–2.
225 And, of course, with very much more than this: see e.g. Diogenes Laertius VII 84; Arius ap. Stobaeus, *ecl* II 39.20–45.10.
226 See I 4, note.
227 With III 169–71 compare *M* XI 22–7 (and see Diogenes Laertius VII 94; Arius ap. Stobaeus, *ecl* II 69.17–70.7).
228 On the Stoic account of 'good' see e.g. TSEKOURAKIS [1974].
229 See I 128, note.
230 See BARNES [1988c].

Hence they say that 'good' has three senses.[231] [171] In one sense, they say, that by which something can be benefited is good – this is the principal good, and is virtue. In another sense, that in virtue of which something comes to be benefited is good – e.g. virtue and actions in accordance with virtue. In the third sense, that which can benefit is good – this too is virtue and action in accordance with virtue, but also virtuous people and friends and gods and virtuous spirits.[232] Hence the second signification of 'good' contains the first and the third contains the second and the first.[233] [172] Others say that good is what is chosen for its own sake,[234] yet others that it is what contributes to happiness or helps to fill it.[235] (Happiness, so the Stoics say, is a prosperous flow of life.[236])

This is the kind of thing said about the concept of the good. [173][237] But if you say that what benefits or what is chosen for its own sake or what co-operates[238] towards happiness is good, you do not establish what the good is – rather, you state one of its attributes. But this is idle.[239] For these items are either attributes of the good alone or else of other things too. If of other things too, then since they are common items they are not distinguishing characteristics of the good. If of the good alone, it is not possible for us to think of the good on this basis; [174] for just as someone with no conception of a horse does not know what neighing is, and cannot in this way come to a concept of a horse without first coming into contact with a neighing horse, so someone who is investigating what good is because he does not know the good cannot recognize what is peculiar to it and belongs to it alone and in this way come to think of the good itself. First he must learn the nature of the good itself and then understand that it benefits and is chosen for its own sake and produces happiness.

---

[231] See Arius ap. Stobaeus, *ecl* II 69.17–70.7.
[232] For Stoic spirits see e.g. Diogenes Laertius VII 151 (cf. e.g. Apuleius, *dog Plat* I xi 206, on Platonic spirits).
[233] Cf. *M* XI 30.
[234] See Arius ap. Stobaeus, *ecl* II 72.14–18.
[235] I.e. 'or is a part of happiness': see III 100 for parts 'helping to fill' wholes. – See Diogenes Laertius VII 97; Arius ap. Stobaeus, *ecl* II 71.15–72.13.
[236] See e.g. Diogenes Laertius VII 87; Arius ap. Stobaeus, *ecl* II 77.20–1.
[237] With III 173–4 compare *M* XI 38–9.
[238] Cf. III 15.
[239] See the parallel line of argument at III 4.

[175]²⁴⁰ In their practice the Dogmatists make it clear that these attributes are insufficient to manifest the concept and nature of the good. Everyone no doubt concedes that the good benefits, that it is chosen (which is why the good has been said to be the as it were agreeable²⁴¹), and that it produces happiness. But when they are asked what it is which has these attributes, they fall into a war without truce, some saying that it is virtue, others pleasure, others absence of pain, others something else. Yet if it were shown by the above definitions what the good itself is, they would not dissent from one another as though its nature were unknown.

[176]²⁴² Such, then, are the differences over the concept of the good among the Dogmatists who are thought to be most reliable. They differ similarly about the bad, some saying that what is bad is harm, or not other than harm; some that it is what is avoided for its own sake; others, what produces unhappiness. But with these terms they state not the substance of the bad but, no doubt, some of its attributes, and thus they fall into the same impasse as before.²⁴³

[177]²⁴⁴ 'Indifferent', they say, has three senses. In one sense it is that relative to which there is neither impulse nor repulsion – e.g. that the stars, or the hairs on your head, are even in number.²⁴⁵ In another sense it is that relative to which there is an impulse or repulsion, but not for this rather than for that – e.g. when you must choose one of two indistinguishable pennies:²⁴⁶ there is an impulse to choose one of them, but not to choose this rather than that. In a third sense they say that the indifferent is what contributes neither to happiness nor to unhappiness – e.g. health, wealth – for they say that something is indifferent if it can be used sometimes well and sometimes badly,²⁴⁷ a point to which they say they give particular treatment in their

---

²⁴⁰ Cf. *M* XI 35–7.
²⁴¹ Cf. *M* XI 40.
²⁴² A fanciful derivation of ἀγαθόν ('good') from ἀγαστόν ('agreeable'): see III 184; Plato, *Cratylus* 412C, 422A.
²⁴³ See III 173–4.
²⁴⁴ Cf. *M* XI 59–61; see also Diogenes Laertius VII 104; Arius ap. Stobaeus, *ecl* II 79.1–17 (who, however, omits the second of Sextus' three senses).
²⁴⁵ See II 90.
²⁴⁶ The example comes from Chrysippus: Plutarch, *Stoic rep* 1045E.
²⁴⁷ Cf. Plutarch, *Stoic rep* 1048C.

ethics.[248] [178] What we should think about this concept is clear from what we have said about good and bad.

It is plain, then, that they have not put us on to the conception of any of these things – a not unlikely result, since they are stumbling about among objects which perhaps have no subsistence. For that nothing is by nature good or bad or indifferent some deduce as follows.

xxiii Is anything by nature good, bad or indifferent?

[179][249] Fire, which heats by nature, appears heating to everyone; and snow, which chills by nature, appears chilling to everyone: indeed, everything which affects us by nature affects in the same way everyone who is in what they call a natural state.[250] But none of the so-called good things affects everyone as good, as we shall suggest. Nothing, therefore, is by nature good.

That none of the things said to be good affects everybody in the same way is, they say, clear. [180][251] Let us pass over ordinary people – of whom some deem bodily well-being good, others sex, others overeating, others drunkenness, others gambling, others still worse things. Among the philosophers themselves some say (e.g. the Peripatetics[252]) that there are three kinds of goods – some concern the soul (e.g. the virtues), some the body, (e.g. health and the like), and others are external (e.g. friends, wealth and the like). [181] The Stoics also say that there is a triple division of goods[253] – some concern the soul (e.g. the virtues), some are external (e.g. virtuous people and friends), and others neither concern the soul nor are external (e.g. the virtuous in relation to themselves). The things

---

[248] See ANNAS [1993d]. The point derives ultimately from Plato, *Euthydemus* 278E–282D; *Meno* 87C–89A.

[249] Cf. *M* XI 69 (and Diogenes Laertius IX 101).

[250] See III 182, 190, 196, 220, 222, 226; *M* VIII 37, 198; *M* I 147; see also *M* VIII 215, citing Aenesidemus (cf. *M* VIII 187–8, 239–40); above, I 177, note; and also e.g. Aristotle, *EN* 1134b25–6.

[251] With III 180–1 compare *M* XI 43–7.

[252] See e.g. Aristotle, *EN* 1098b12; *Politics* 1323a24. The division became a commonplace in Hellenistic philosophy.

[253] See e.g. Diogenes Laertius VII 95; Arius, apud Stobaeus, *ecl* II 70.8–20.

concerning the body, however, which the Peripatetics say are good they say are not good.[254]

Some have embraced pleasure as a good, while others say that it is downright bad[255] – so that one philosopher exclaimed: 'I would rather go mad than feel pleasure.'[256]

[182][257] If, then, things which affect us by nature affect everyone in the same way,[258] while we are not all affected in the same way in the case of so-called goods, then nothing is by nature good. It is impossible to be convinced either by all the positions set out above (because of the conflict) or by any one of them. For anyone who says that we should find this position convincing but not that one has opposing him the arguments of those who take different views and becomes a part of the dispute.[259] And so he will himself need to be judged along with the rest rather than being a judge of others. Since, then, there is no agreed standard or proof (because of the undecidable dispute about them[260]), he will end up in suspension of judgement and hence be able to make no affirmation as to what is by nature good.

[183][261] Again, some people say that good is either choosing in itself or the things which we choose.

Choosing, however, is not good in virtue of its own definition. Otherwise we would not be eager to get the things we choose lest we leave the state of still choosing them. For example, if it were pursuing drink which were good, we would not be eager to get a drink; for when we had enjoyed the drink we would cease from the pursuit. Similarly with hunger, sexual desire and the rest. Choosing, therefore, is not chosen for its own sake – if indeed it is not actually disturbing; for if you are hungry, you are eager to take food in order to get rid of the disturbance of being hungry; and similarly if you feel sexual desire or thirst.

[254] See Cicero, *fin* III x 34, xiii 44–5; ANNAS [1993a], ch. 19.
[255] Cf. Diogenes Laertius IX 101.
[256] Antisthenes: Diogenes Laertius VI 3.
[257] Cf. *M* XI 71–8.
[258] See III 179.
[259] See I 59.
[260] See II 18–79, 144–92.
[261] With III 183–6 compare *M* XI 80–9.

[184] But the good is not the object of choice either. For this is either external to us or in us. If it is external to us, then either it produces in us a civilized[262] motion and a welcome condition and an agreeable[263] feeling, or it does not put us in any condition at all. If it is not agreeable to us, it will not be good, nor induce us to choose it, nor in general will it be an object of choice. But if the external item produces in us a gratifying condition and a welcome feeling, then the external item will not be chosen for its own sake but for the sake of the condition it produces in us. [185] Hence what is chosen for its own sake cannot be external.

Nor can it be in us. It will be said to be either in the body alone or in the soul alone or in both. If it is in the body alone, it will escape our knowledge: knowledge is said to belong to the soul, while they say that the body, so far as it itself is concerned, is irrational. If it is said to extend as far as the soul,[264] it will seem to be chosen in virtue of the soul's grasping it and having an agreeable feeling – for according to them what is judged to be an object of choice is judged by the intellect and not by the irrational body.

[186] It remains to say that the good is in the soul alone. But this too is impossible, given what the Dogmatists say. The soul is perhaps unreal; and even if it is real, so far as what they say goes it is not apprehended, as we deduced in our account of the standard of truth.[265] But how could anyone be so bold as to say that something comes about in what he does not apprehend? [187] To pass over this too, how can they say that the good comes about in the soul? Epicurus, for instance, locates the aim in pleasure and says that the soul is composed of atoms (since everything is). But it is impossible to say how pleasure – and assent, or a judgement that this is an object of choice and good while that is to be avoided and bad – could come about in a heap of atoms. [188][ae] The Stoics, again, say that goods in

---

[262] ἀστεῖος: on the odd Stoic use of this word see SCHOFIELD [1991], Appendix G.
[263] See III 175.
[264] I.e. to be in the soul as well as in the body.
[265] See II 31–3.
[ae] Between III 187 and 188 the MSS have a new chapter heading ('xxiv What is the so-called expertise in living?'). The heading is malapropos; but it has not been simply misplaced, since there is a heading before III 239, the point at which the subject next changes.

the soul are certain kinds of expertise, namely the virtues.[266] They say that an expertise is a compound of apprehensions which have been exercised together,[267] and that apprehensions come about in the ruling part. But how there might come about in the ruling part (which according to them is breath) a deposit or accumulation of enough apprehensions for an expertise to develop it is impossible to conceive; for each succeeding imprinting erases the previous one, since breath is fluid and is said to be affected as a whole by each imprinting.[268] [189] To say that Plato's romancing[269] – I mean the blending of the indivisible and the divisible substances and of the other and the same – to say that this, or that numbers,[270] can be receptive of the good is merely to babble. Hence the good cannot be in the soul either.

[190] But if choosing is not itself good, and if there is nothing chosen for its own sake either externally or in the body or in the soul, as we have deduced, then nothing at all is by nature good.

For[271] these reasons nothing is by nature bad either. Things which some think bad others pursue as goods – for example, indulgence, injustice, avarice, lack of self-control and the like. Hence, if things which are so and so by nature naturally affect everyone in the same way,[272] while so-called bad things do not affect everyone in the same way, nothing is by nature bad.

[191][273] Similarly, nothing is by nature indifferent, because of the dispute over indifferent things. The Stoics, for example, say that among indifferents some are preferred, others dispreferred, others neither preferred nor dispreferred.[274] Preferred are things which have

---

266 See e.g. Diogenes Laertius VII 90; Arius, apud Stobaeus, *ecl* II 58.9–11, for the thesis that (some of) the virtues are expertises or τέχναι. (For the same view in Platonism see Apuleius, *dog Plat* II ix 234.) On the thesis see ANNAS [1993a], chh. 2, 19.
267 See II 70, note.
268 See II 70, note.
269 In his account of the soul at *Tim* 35AD.
270 An allusion to the Pythagorean view of the soul? or to Xenocrates' definition of the soul as a self-moving number?
271 With this paragraph compare *M* XI 90–5.
272 See III 179.
273 Cf. *M* XI 62–3.
274 See e.g. Diogenes Laertius VII 105–6; Arius, apud Stobaeus, *ecl* II 80.14–81.18, 83.10–85.11; cf. TSEKOURAKIS [1974].

an adequate value, such as health and wealth. Dispreferred are things which have an inadequate value, such as poverty and disease. Neither preferred nor dispreferred are such things as stretching out or crooking your finger. [192][275] But some[276] say that nothing indifferent is by nature either preferred or dispreferred: each indifferent thing appears sometimes preferred, sometimes dispreferred, depending on the circumstances. For instance, they say, if a tyrant were to plot against the rich while the poor were left in peace, everyone would choose to be poor rather than rich, so that wealth would become dispreferred. [193] Hence, since each so-called indifferent is said by some to be good and by others to be bad, while if it were by nature indifferent everyone would deem it indifferent in the same way,[277] nothing is by nature indifferent.

In this way,[278] if anyone says that courage is by nature to be chosen because lions are naturally daring and thought to show courage (and bulls too, if you like, and some humans, and cockerels), then we say that, so far as this goes, cowardice is also one of the things which are by nature to be chosen, since deer and hares and many other animals are naturally impelled to it. And most humans are observed to be cowardly – only rarely has someone sacrificed his life for his country . . .[af] the majority turn away from anything like this.

[194][279] This is how the Epicureans think to show that pleasure is by nature to be chosen:[280] animals, they say, are impelled as soon as they are born and while they are still uncorrupted towards pleasure and away from pain. [195] Against them we can say that what produces bad cannot by nature be good. But pleasure produces bad things, since to every pleasure is affixed pain, which according to them is bad. For instance, the drunkard and the gourmand take pleasure in filling themselves with wine and food, and the lustful in immoderate sex; but these things produce poverty and diseases which

---

[af] Here the MSS present a clause which is manifestly corrupt: Mutschmann–Mau obelize it, and no satisfactory emendation has yet been found.

[275] Cf. *M* XI 65–6.
[276] E.g. Ariston of Chios: *M* IX 64; Cicero, *Luc* XLII 130.
[277] See III 179.
[278] With this paragraph compare *M* XI 99–101.
[279] With III 194–6 compare *M* XI 96–8 (the parallel is not exact).
[280] Cf. e.g. Cicero, *fin* I ix 30; see BRUNSCHWIG [1986].

are, they say, painful and bad. Pleasure, therefore, is not by nature good. [196] Similarly, what produces good is not by nature bad, and pains effect pleasures: we acquire knowledge by exertion, and this is the way you come to possess wealth and the woman you desire. And pains secure health. Exertion, therefore, is not by nature bad. Indeed, if pleasure were by nature good and exertion bad, everyone would be disposed towards them in the same way, as we have said;[281] but we see many philosophers[282] choosing exertion and endurance and despising pleasure.

[197] Those who say that the life of virtue is by nature good are turned about[283] in the same way – by the fact that some sages choose a life including pleasure, so that the dispute among them overthrows the claim that anything is thus-and-so by nature. [198] In addition, it is no doubt not out of place to dwell briefly in a more specific way on the suppositions made about what is shameful and not shameful, unlawful and not so, about laws and customs, piety towards the gods, reverence towards the departed, and the like. In this way we shall discover much anomaly in what ought to be done and not done.

[199][284] Among us, for instance, homosexual sex is shameful – or rather, has actually been deemed illegal – but among the Germani, they say, it is not shameful and is quite normal. It is said that among the Thebans in the old days it was not thought shameful, and that Meriones the Cretan was so called to hint at this Cretan custom.[285] And some refer to this the ardent friendship of Achilles for Patroclus. [200] What wonder, when Cynic philosophers[286] and the followers of Zeno of Citium and Cleanthes and Chrysippus[287] say that it is indifferent?

Having sex with a woman in public, though shameful among us, is deemed not shameful among some Indians – at any rate, they have sex

---

281 See III 179.
282 E.g. Antisthenes: Diogenes Laertius VI 11.
283 See I 122.
284 Cf. I 152. Note that 'among us' here corresponds to 'in Rome' at I 152: should we infer that Sextus wrote in Rome?
285 'Meriones' from μηρός, 'thigh': cf. III 245.
286 See e.g. Diogenes Laertius VI 72.
287 See III 206, note.

indifferently in public[288] – and we hear the same about the philosopher Crates.[289] [201] Among us it is shameful and a matter of reproach for women to prostitute themselves; but with many Egyptians it is glorious – at any rate, they say that the women who have been with the most men wear amulets or ornaments, tokens of the esteem they enjoy; and among some of them the girls collect their dowry before marriage from prostitution and then marry. We see the Stoics too saying that there is nothing out of place in cohabiting with a prostitute or living off a prostitute's earnings.[290]

[202] Further, among us tattooing is thought to be shameful and a dishonour, but many Egyptians and Sarmatians tattoo their babies.[291] [203] Among us it is shameful for men to wear ear-rings,[292] but among some foreigners, such as the Syrians, this is a token of noble birth – and some of them extend this token of noble birth by piercing their children's nostrils and hanging silver or gold rings from them, something no-one among us would do. [204] In the same way no male here would wear a brightly-coloured full-length dress, although among the Persians this, which among us is shameful, is thought highly becoming.[293] When at the court of Dionysius, tyrant of Sicily, a dress of this kind was offered to the philosophers Plato and Aristippus, Plato returned it, saying

> I was born a man
> and never could dress up in women's clothes.[294]

But Aristippus accepted it, remarking

> Even in the Bacchic rites
> she who is pure will not be made corrupt.[295]

Thus this was thought not shameful by one of these wise men and shameful by the other.[296]

[205] Among us it is unlawful to marry your own mother or sister;

---

[288] See I 148.
[289] See I 153.
[290] See III 206, note.
[291] See I 148.
[292] But Plato did: *M* I 258.
[293] See I 148.
[294] Euripides, *Bacchae* 836–7.
[295] Euripides, *Bacchae* 316–17.
[296] See Diogenes Laertius II 78 (cf. above, I 155).

but the Persians – especially those of them thought to practise wisdom, the Magi – marry their mothers, Egyptians take their sisters in marriage,[297] and, as the poet says

> Zeus addressed Hera, his sister and wife.[298]

Again, Zeno of Citium says that there is nothing out of place in rubbing your mother's private parts with your own – just as nobody would say that it was bad to rub any other part of her body with your hand; and Chrysippus in his *Republic* expresses the belief that fathers should have children by their daughters, mothers by their sons, and brothers by their sisters.[299] Plato asserted even more generally that women should be held in common.[300]

[206] Zeno does not rule out masturbation, which among us is condemned;[301] and we hear of others, too, who engage in this bad practice as though it were something good.

[207] Again, tasting human flesh is among us unlawful; but it is indifferent among entire foreign nations.[302] And why speak of foreigners when even Tydeus is said to have eaten his enemy's brains, and when the Stoics say that there is nothing out of place in eating human flesh, others' or your own?[303] [208] Among most of us it is unlawful to defile the altar of a god with human blood; but Spartans are flogged mercilessly at the altar of Artemis Orthosia so that the blood may flow freely on the altar of the goddess. Further, some make human sacrifice to Cronus, just as the Scythians sacrifice strangers to Artemis; but we think that holy places are polluted by the killing of a human being.[304]

[209] Adulterers are, among us, punished by law; but among some people it is indifferent whether you have sex with other men's

---

[297] Cf. I 152.

[298] Homer, *Iliad* xvii 356.

[299] See III 206, note.

[300] *Republic* 423E.

[301] With the view ascribed here to Zeno compare I 160; III 200, 201, 207, 245–9; *M* XI 190–4. Similar passages from other authors are collected in VON ARNIM [1903–5] I 247–69; III 743–56. These things have upset modern scholars, and they offended some of the ancients (see Diogenes Laertius VII 32–4, 187–8: cf. SCHOFIELD [1991], ch. 1).

[302] Cf. III 225.

[303] See III 206, note; cf. III 248.

[304] Cf. I 149; III 221.

wives;[305] and some philosophers say that it is indifferent whether you have sex with another's wife.

[210] Among us the law orders that fathers should get proper care from their sons; but the Scythians cut the throats of everyone over sixty.[306] What wonder when Cronus cut off his father's genitals with a sickle, and Zeus hurled Cronus down to Tartarus, and Athena tried to put her father in chains with the help of Hera and Poseidon? Again, Cronus decided to destroy his own children, [211] and Solon laid down for the Athenians the law of immunity, according to which he permitted every man to kill his own child. But among us the laws forbid killing children.[307] The Roman lawgivers order sons to be their fathers' subjects and slaves, and the fathers – not the sons – to control the sons' property until the sons obtain their freedom, just like bought slaves. But among others this has been rejected as tyrannical.

[212][308] There is a law punishing manslaughter; but gladiators who kill often obtain honour. Again, the laws forbid the striking of free men; but athletes who strike free men, often actually killing them, are thought worthy of honours and prizes. [213] The law among us orders each man to have only one wife; but among the Thracians and the Gaetuli (a nation in Libya) each man has several. [214] Among us piracy is illegal and unjust; but among many foreigners it is not out of place. They say that the Cilicians deemed it actually to be glorious, so that they thought people killed during pirate raids worthy of honour.[309] And in Homer Nestor, after welcoming Telemachus and his friends, says to them,

> Or are you wandering without aim like pirates?[310]

– but if piracy had been something out of place he would not have[ag] welcomed them as he did because of his suspicion that this was what they were. [215] Again, among us stealing is unjust and illegal; but people who call Hermes a most thieving god bring it about that this is

[ag] Adding ἤν after ἄν (Bury).

[305] Cf. I 152.
[306] Cf. III 228.
[307] Cf. I 154.
[308] Cf. I 156.
[309] Cf. Diogenes Laertius IX 83.
[310] Homer, *Odyssey* iii 72.

not considered unjust – for how could a god be bad? And some say that the Spartans used to punish people who had stolen not for having stolen but for having been caught.

[216] Again, cowards and men who throw away their shields are in many places punished by law; which is why the Spartan woman, when she gave her son his shield as he left for war, said: 'Either with it, or on it.' But Archilochus, as though boasting to us about having thrown away his shield and fled, says about himself in his poems:

> Some Saian gloats over the shield which by a bush
> I left behind unwillingly, unblemished armour:
> myself, I escaped death's end.[311]

[217] The Amazons used to lame the male children they bore, to make them unable to do anything manly, and they looked after warfare themselves; but among us the opposite has been deemed fine. The Mother of the Gods accepts effeminate men;[312] and the goddess would not have made this judgement if being unmanly were by nature bad. [218] Thus there is much anomaly about just and unjust things, and about how fine it is to be manly.

Matters of piety and service to the gods are also full of much dispute. Most people say that there are gods, but some say that there are not – such as Diagoras of Melos, and Theodorus, and Critias of Athens.[313] Of those who assert that there are gods,[314] some believe in the traditional gods, others in those invented in the Dogmatists' schools – as Aristotle said that god is incorporeal and the limit of the heavens,[315] the Stoics that he is breath pervading even loathsome things,[316] Epicurus that he is anthropomorphic,[317] Xenophanes that he is an unfeeling sphere.[318] [219] Some think that the gods provide

---

[311] frag. 5 West.
[312] Her priests were eunuchs.
[313] Cf. *M* IX 50–6, where Critias is cited at length.
[314] For this dispute see III 3.
[315] Perhaps based on *de caelo* 278b14.
[316] God pervades the whole universe (e.g. Diogenes Laertius VII 138–9); and therefore even the vilest of things, a consequence which was cited with tedious frequency by the Stoics' opponents (texts in VON ARNIM [1903–5] III 1037–48).
[317] Cf. *M* IX 25; see e.g. Epicurus, KΔ 1 scholium; Cicero, *nat deorum* I xviii 46–9.
[318] See I 225.

for us, others that they do not.[319] For what is blessed and indestructible, Epicurus says, takes no trouble itself and causes none for others.[320] Again, among ordinary people, some say that there is one god, others that there are many and of different forms, so that they even fall in with the suppositions of the Egyptians who consider the gods to be dog-faced and hawk-shaped and cows and crocodiles and just about anything else.

[220] Again, matters of sacrifice, and in general of the cult of the gods, contain much anomaly: things which are deemed holy in some rites are unholy in others. Yet if things were holy and unholy by nature, this would not have been so.[321] Nobody, for instance, would sacrifice a piglet to Sarapis – but they do to Heracles and to Asclepius. It is unlawful to sacrifice sheep to Isis – but sheep are a proper sacrifice to the so-called Mother of the Gods and to other gods. [221] Some[ah] make human sacrifice to Cronus,[322] which by most people is considered impious. In Alexandria they sacrifice cats to Horus and cockroaches to Thetis, which no-one among us would do. A horse is a proper sacrifice to Poseidon – but to Apollo, especially Apollo of Didyma, the animal is hateful. It is pious to sacrifice goats to Artemis – but not to Asclepius. [222] Although I could give a vast number of other similar cases,[323] I pass them over since I am aiming at brevity. However, if any sacrifice were by nature pious or impious, it would be deemed everywhere to be so.[324]

Similar examples can be found in that part of the cult of the gods which concerns human diet. [223] A Jew or an Egyptian priest would die rather than eat pork. Libyans think it utterly unlawful to eat sheep – some Scythians to eat doves, others to eat sacrificed animals. In some rites eating fish is the custom, in others it is impious. Some of the Egyptians who have been considered wise men consider it unholy to eat an animal's head – others the shoulder-blade, others the feet, others some other part. [224] None of the devotees of Zeus Casius at

---

[ah]   Adding τινὲς δέ (Mutschmann): Mutschmann–Mau mark a lacuna.

[319] See I 151, 155; III 9–12.
[320] See III 5; cf. e.g. Epicurus, ΚΔ 1.
[321] See III 179.
[322] Cf. III 208.
[323] See I 58.
[324] See III 179.

Pelusium would consume an onion, just as no priest of Libyan Aphrodite would taste garlic. In some rites people abstain from mint, in others from wild mint, in others from parsley. Some people say that they would rather eat their fathers' heads than beans.[325] Among others these things are indifferent.

[225] We think it unholy to taste the flesh of dogs; but it is told of some Thracians that they eat dogs. (No doubt this was usual among the Greeks too, which is why Diocles – taking his cue from Asclepiad practice – prescribes puppy-flesh for certain patients.) Again, as I have said,[326] some people actually eat human flesh as a matter of indifference, something which among us has been deemed unholy.

[226] And yet if matters of cult and what is unlawful were so by nature, they would have been practised in the same way everywhere.[327]

Similar things can be said about reverence towards the departed.[328] Some people completely wrap up their dead and cover them with earth, deeming it impious to display them to the sun; but the Egyptians, after removing their entrails, pickle them and keep them with them above ground. [227] The fish-eating Ethiopians throw their dead into lakes to be eaten by fish; the Hyrcanians leave them out as food for the dogs; and some Indians leave them for the vultures. They say that the Troglodytes take the dead man to a certain hill, tie his head to his feet, and pelt him with stones, laughing as they do so; and then, when the stones have made a pile over him, they go away. [228] Some foreigners sacrifice and eat people over sixty,[329] whereas they bury in the earth those who die young. Some people burn their dead; and among these some gather up the bones and care for them, while others leave them lying around without caring. They say that the Persians impale their dead and pickle them in nitre, afterwards wrapping them in bandages. We can see ourselves how much grief other people endure over their dead.

---

[325] A celebrated Pythagorean prohibition: see e.g. Empedocles, frag. 141 Diels–Kranz.

[326] See III 207.

[327] See III 179.

[328] Cf. Diogenes Laertius IX 84.

[329] See III 210.

[229] Death itself some consider dreadful and to be avoided, others not so. Euripides, for instance, says

> Who knows if life is not the same as dying,
> and dying down below considered life?[330]

And Epicurus says:

> Death is nothing to us; for what has been dissolved has no perception,
> and what has no perception is nothing to us.[331]

They say that, since we are a compound of soul and body and death is the dissolution of soul and body, then when we are death is not (for we are not in a state of dissolution), and when death is we are not (for we are not inasmuch as the compound of soul and body is no longer). [230] Heraclitus says that both living and dying are in all living and in all dying: while we live our souls are dead and buried in us, and when we die our souls revive.[332]

Some people suppose that it is actually better for us to be dead than to be alive. Euripides, for instance, says

> For we should come together to lament
> the new-born and the evils he must face.
> The dead, now freed from evils, should with joy
> and thankful words be led out from the house.[333]

[231] The same supposition lies behind the following lines:

> Best is for mortals never to have been born
> at all, nor seen the rays of the bright sun;
> or else, once born, to pass through Hades' gates
> at breakneck speed and lie well wrapped in earth.[334]

We know the story of Cleobis and Biton, which Herodotus tells in his account of the priestess of Argos.[335] [232] It is also related that some Thracians sit round newly born babies and lament for them.

---

[330] frag. 638 Nanck.
[331] ΚΔ 2; cf. e.g. *ad Men* 124–5.
[332] See frag. 88 Diels–Kranz.
[333] frag. 449 Nanck.
[334] Theognis, 425–8.
[335] Herodotus I 31: after they had publicly honoured her, the priestess asked Hera to grant her sons Cleobis and Biton the gods' greatest favour: that night they died in their sleep.

Not even death, then, can be deemed something by nature dreadful, just as life cannot be deemed something naturally fine. None of these things is thus and so by nature: all are matters of convention and relative.

[233] The same mode of attack can be carried over to all the other cases, which we have not set out here because of the brevity of our account.[336] And even if in some cases we cannot immediately state an anomaly, we should say that possibly there is dispute about these matters too among nations unknown to us.[337] [234] Just as, if we had not, for example, known about the Egyptian custom of marrying their sisters,[338] we should have affirmed, wrongly, that it is agreed by all that you must not marry your sister, so it is right not to affirm that there is no dispute about these matters in which no anomalies make an impression on us, since it is possible, as I said, that among some nations of people not known to us there is a dispute about them.

[235][339] The Sceptics, then, seeing such anomaly in objects, suspend judgement as to whether anything is by nature good or bad, or generally to be done, here too refraining from dogmatic rashness; and they follow the observance of everyday life without holding opinions. They therefore remain without feeling in matters of opinion and with moderation of feeling in matters forced upon them: [236] being human, they are affected by way of their senses;[ai] but, not having the additional opinion that the way they are affected is by nature bad, their feelings are moderate. For having such an additional opinion about something is worse than actually feeling it: sometimes patients undergoing surgery or something of the kind bear it, while the onlookers faint because of their opinion that what is happening is bad.

[237][340] Those who hypothesize that something is good or bad, or generally to be done or not done, are troubled in a variety of ways. In the presence of what they deem to be natural evils they think that they are persecuted; and when they are in possession of apparent goods,

---

ai   Reading αἰσθητικῶς (Heintz): αἰσθητικός mss, Mutschmann–Mau.

336 See I 163.
337 See I 34, note.
338 See III 205.
339 With III 235–6 compare I 29–30; M XI 141–60. See ANNAS [1993a], ch. 8.
340 Cf. I 27; M XI 145–6. See STRIKER [1990a]; ANNAS [1993a], ch. 17.

then because of their pride and their fear of losing them, they worry lest they may again fall among what they deem to be natural evils, and thus they experience no ordinary troubles. [238] (As for those who say that good things cannot be lost, we shall bring them to suspension of judgement as a result of the impasse arising from dispute.[341])

Hence we deduce that, if what produces bad is bad and to be avoided, and if confidence that these things are by nature good and those bad produces troubles, then to hypothesize and be convinced that anything is bad or good in its nature is a bad thing and to be avoided.

This is enough for the present about the good, the bad, and the indifferent.

xxv Is there an expertise in living?

[239][342] It is clear from what we have said that there can be no expertise in living either. If there is such an expertise, it has to do with the study of good, bad and indifferent things. So since these are unreal, expertise in living is unreal.

Again, since the Dogmatists do not agree in laying down a single expertise in living, but rather some hypothesize one and some another, they land in dispute and in the argument from dispute which we have propounded in what we said about the good.[343] [240][344] But even if by hypothesis they were all to speak of a single expertise in living – such as the celebrated intelligence which is dreamed up by the Stoics and thought more striking than the others[345] – even so, just as many absurdities will follow.

Since intelligence is a virtue, and only the Sage[346] has virtue, the

---

341 The Stoics (but not Chrysippus) held that virtue, the only good thing, could not be lost: e.g. Diogenes Laertius VII 127; *contra* the Peripatetics: e.g. Simplicius, *in Cat* 402.19–20.

342 Cf. *M* XI 168–80.

343 See III 180–2.

344 Cf. *M* XI 180–1.

345 Intelligence, φρόνησις, was one of the primary Stoic virtues, and as such a τέχνη or expertise (see III 188): see III 270–2; Diogenes Laertius VII 92; Arius, apud Stobaeus, *ecl* II 59.4–7. It was identified as the expertise in living (see e.g. Cicero, *fin* V vi 16: *ars vivendi*): see ANNAS [1993a], chh. 2, 19. The Platonists claimed rather that justice was the art of living: Apuleius, *dog Plat* II ix 234.

346 See I 91, note.

Stoics – not being Sages[347] – will not possess the expertise in living.

[241][348] In general, there will be no expertise in living so far as what they say goes, since there can be no such thing as an expertise according to them. At any rate, they say that an expertise is a compound of apprehensions;[349] and that apprehension is assent to an apprehensive appearance.[350] But apprehensive appearances are undiscoverable.[351] Not every appearance is apprehensive, and it is impossible to recognize which appearances are apprehensive. We cannot simply use any appearance to judge which appearances are apprehensive and which not, and since we require an apprehensive appearance in order to recognize what sort of appearance is apprehensive, we are thrown back into an infinite regress,[352] demanding another apprehensive appearance to recognize the appearance taken to be apprehensive. [242] Moreover,[353] the Stoics proceed unsoundly in their elucidation of the concept of an apprehensive appearance: in saying that an apprehensive appearance is one which comes from something real, and also saying that a real object is one capable of producing an apprehensive appearance,[354] they fall into the reciprocal mode of puzzlement.[355]

If, then, for there to be an expertise in living there must first be expertises, and if for expertises to subsist apprehensions must first subsist, and if for apprehensions to subsist assent to an apprehensive appearance must have been apprehended, and if apprehensive appearances are undiscoverable, then expertise in living is undiscoverable.

[243] There is the following argument too.[356] Every expertise is thought to be apprehended from the products delivered specifically by it. But there is no product specific to expertise in living – whatever anyone might say to be its product will be found common to ordinary

---

[347] There were no, or very few, Sages: III 250; M IX 133.
[348] Cf. M XI 182.
[349] See II 70, note.
[350] See II 4, note.
[351] With the following argument compare M VII 427–9.
[352] See I 166.
[353] With the following argument compare M XI 183.
[354] Cf. M VII 246.
[355] See I 169.
[356] Cf. M XI 188, 197–9.

people too (e.g. honouring your parents, returning loans, and all the rest). There is therefore no expertise in living.

Nor[357] shall we, as some say, recognize something as a product of intelligence from the fact that it appears to be done or produced by an intelligent person on the basis of an intelligent condition. [244] For an intelligent condition is itself inapprehensible, being apparent neither simply from itself and directly nor from its products, which are common to ordinary people too.

If[358] you say that we apprehend those who possess expertise in living by the consistency of their actions, then you over-estimate human nature and express a hope rather than a truth.

> for the minds of mortal men
> change with the days which the father of gods and men brings them.[359]

[245][360] It remains to say that expertise in living is apprehended from those of its products which they write up in their books. There are many of these, all similar to one another: I shall set out a few[361] by way of example.[362] For instance, in his *Discourses* Zeno, the founder of the school, says many similar things about the education of children, including this:

> Have sex with favourites no more and no less than with non-favourites; with girls no more and no less than with boys. Favourite or not, girl or boy, makes no difference: what befits and is fitting is the same.

[246] As for piety to one's parents, the same man says, on the subject of Jocasta and Oedipus, that there was nothing dreadful about his rubbing his mother:

> If she is ill and he benefits her by rubbing some other part of her body with his hands, there is nothing shameful in that; so if by rubbing another part he pleased her, by ending her grief, and produced children who were noble on their mother's side, was that shameful?

---

[357] With this paragraph compare *M* XI 200–6.
[358] With this paragraph compare *M* XI 206–8.
[359] Homer, *Odyssey* xviii 136–7.
[360] With III 245–69 compare *M* XI 189–94.
[361] See I 58.
[362] On these examples see III 206, note.

With this Chrysippus is in agreement; at any rate, in his *Republic* he says:

> I think that one should arrange these matters in the way which is in fact the custom – and no bad thing – among some peoples: let mothers have children by their sons, fathers by their daughters, brothers by their sisters.

[247] In the same treatise he often introduces cannibalism to us. At any rate he says:

> If from the living a part is cut off which is useful for food, do not bury it or otherwise throw it away, but consume it, so that from our parts another part may come.

[248] And in his book *On Duty* he speaks about the burial of parents in these very words:

> When parents pass away they should make use of the simplest burials, as though the body (like nails or teeth or hair) were nothing to us and we had no need to give it any particular care and attention. Hence when the flesh is useful they will make use of it as food, just as, if one of their own parts were useful – such as an amputated foot – it was incumbent upon them to use it and anything like it. When the flesh is useless they will bury it and leave it, or burn it and leave the ashes, or throw it far away and pay it no more attention than nails or hair.

[249] Most of what the philosophers say is like this – but they would never dare to put it into action unless they were fellow-citizens of the Cyclopes or the Laestrygonians. But if they never perform these actions, and if the actions which they do perform are common to ordinary people too, then there is no product specific to those people suspected of having expertise in living.

If, therefore, an expertise ought certainly to be apprehended from its specific products, and if no specific product is seen in the case of the so-called expertise in living, then it is not apprehended. And hence no-one can affirm of it that it is real.

xxvi Is expertise in living found among people?

[250] If expertise in living is found among people, it comes about in them either by nature or through learning and teaching.[363] If by

---

[363] For the Stoic view on this hoary question, Is virtue teachable?, see Diogenes Laertius VII 91.

nature, then expertise in living will come about in them either insofar as they are human or insofar as they are not human.[364] Not insofar as they are not human – for they are *not* not human. But if insofar as they are human, then intelligence will belong to all humans so that everybody will be intelligent and virtuous and wise. But they say that most men are bad.[365] [251] And so expertise in living will not belong to them insofar as they are human either. Nor, therefore, by nature.

Again, since they want an expertise to be a compound of apprehensions which have been exercised together,[366] they show that it is rather through experience and learning that the expertises, including the one under discussion, are acquired.

xxvii Can expertise in living be taught?

[252][367] But it is not acquired by teaching and learning either. In order for these to be real, three things must be agreed upon beforehand: a subject taught, teachers and learners, a method of learning. But none of these is real. Teaching therefore is not real either.

xxviii Is anything taught?

[253][368] Thus what is taught is either true or false. If it is false, it cannot be taught; for they say that what is false is not real, and there can be no teaching of things which have no reality. Nor if it is said to be true; for we have suggested in our remarks on standards that what is true is unreal.[369] So if neither what is false nor what is true is taught, and if there is nothing teachable apart from them (for if they cannot be taught, no-one will say that he teaches only the puzzles[370]), then nothing is taught.

[254] The item taught is either apparent or unclear. If apparent it will not need teaching, since what is apparent appears to everyone in

---

364 For this sort of argument see III 156.
365 Indeed, that all are: *M* VII 432 (see above, III 240).
366 See II 70, note.
367 Cf. *M* XI 218; *M* I 9.
368 Cf. *M* XI 232; *M* I 29.
369 See II 85–94.
370 I.e. that all he does is school his pupils in logical conundrums. But the expression is odd and the text may be corrupt.

the same way.[371] But if unclear, then, since unclear things are inapprehensible because of the undecidable dispute over them, as we have often suggested, then it will not be teachable. How could anyone teach or learn what he does not apprehend? But if neither the apparent nor the unclear is taught, then nothing is taught.

[255][372] Again, what is taught is either a body or incorporeal. But each of these is either apparent or not made clear, and so cannot be taught according to the argument I have just given. Nothing, therefore, is taught.

[256][373] In addition, either what exists is taught or what does not exist is taught. Now, what does not exist is not taught; for if what does not exist is taught, then, since teaching is thought to be of what is true, what does not exist will be true. But being true, it will be real; for they say that what is true is what has reality and is the opposite of something.[374] But it is absurd to say that what does not exist is real. What does not exist, therefore, is not taught. [257] Nor is what does exist. If what exists is taught, it is taught either insofar as it exists or in virtue of something else. If it is taught insofar as it exists, then nothing existent will be non-teachable; and for this reason nothing will be teachable either – for teaching ought to start from certain items which are agreed upon and non-teachable. What exists, therefore, is not teachable insofar as it exists. [258] Nor is it teachable in virtue of something else. For what exists does not have anything else which is not existent as an attribute. So if what exists is not taught insofar as it exists, it will not be taught in virtue of something else either; for whatever attribute it has will be existent. Again, whether what exists (which they will say is taught) is apparent or unclear, it will fall into the earlier impasses[375] and so be non-teachable. But if neither what exists nor what does not exist is taught, then there is nothing that is taught.

---

[371] See II 8.
[372] A greatly expanded version of this paragraph at *M* XI 224–31; *M* I 19–29.
[373] With III 256–8 compare *M* XI 219–20 and 222–3; Diogenes Laertius IX 100.
[374] For this Stoic account of truth see *M* VIII 10; XI 220.
[375] See III 254.

xxix Are there any teachers and learners?

[259]^{376} And at the same time, teachers and learners are turned about. But they lead to no fewer impasses on their own.

Either the expert teaches the expert or the non-expert the non-expert or the non-expert the expert or the expert the non-expert. Now the expert does not teach the expert: insofar as each is an expert neither of them needs to learn. Nor does the non-expert teach the non-expert – any more than the blind can lead the blind. Nor does the non-expert teach the expert – that would be ridiculous. [260] It remains to say that the expert teaches the non-expert. But this too is impossible.

It is said that generally it is impossible for there to be experts. Nobody is observed to be an expert naturally and from birth, nor does anyone become expert from having been non-expert. For either one theorem and one apprehension can make the non-expert expert or else it cannot be done at all.^{377} [261] But if one apprehension renders the non-expert expert, then first we can say that expertise is not a compound of apprehensions;^{378} for someone who knew nothing at all would be said to be an expert if he had been taught even one theorem of the expertise. Further, suppose that someone has acquired some theorems of an expertise but, lacking one, is still for that reason non-expert, and suppose that he then acquires that one theorem – anyone who says that such a man thereby becomes expert instead of non-expert is speaking capriciously.^{379} [262] For he cannot point to any particular person who is still non-expert but will become expert if he acquires some one theorem – no-one surely can so enumerate the theorems in each expertise that he can number off the theorems already known and say how many are missing from the complete number of theorems of the expertise. Recognition of a single

---

^{376} With III 259–60 compare M XI 234–6; M I 31–2 (and note the similar argument ascribed to Anacharsis at M VII 55).

^{377} You are an expert insofar as you have mastered a certain number of the theorems of an expertise. If you learn the expertise, you must learn the theorems one by one. Hence if learning makes you expert, the acquisition of one theorem must, at some point, do the trick.

^{378} See II 70.

^{379} See III 79.

theorem, then, does not make the non-expert expert. [263] But if this is true, then since no-one acquires all the theorems of any expertise at once, but rather one at a time if at all (granting this as a hypothesis), then someone who is said to acquire the theorems[aj] of an expertise one at a time will not become an expert; for we have suggested[380] that the recognition of a single theorem cannot make the non-expert expert. Thus no-one becomes expert from being non-expert.

Hence for these reasons it appears that experts do not subsist. Hence teachers do not subsist either.

[264][381] Again, someone who, being non-expert, is said to learn, cannot learn and apprehend the theorems of the expertise in which he is non-expert. Just as someone blind from birth will not, so long as he is blind, acquire a grasp of colours, or someone deaf from birth a grasp of sounds, so the non-expert will not apprehend the theorems of the expertise in which he is non-expert. For if he did, the same person would be expert and non-expert in the same matters – non-expert since that is what he is hypothesized to be, expert since he has an apprehension of the theorems of the expertise.

So the expert cannot teach the non-expert. [265] But if neither the expert teaches the expert nor the non-expert the non-expert nor the non-expert the expert nor the expert the non-expert, and if there is no option apart from these, then there are no teachers and no-one is taught.

xxx Is there a way of learning?

If there are neither learners nor teachers, a way of teaching is redundant.[382] [266][383] Nonetheless, it also reaches an impasse in the following way.[ak]

The way of teaching is either by evidence or by argument. But, as we shall establish, it is neither by evidence nor by argument. The way of learning, therefore, is not easily travelled.

[aj] Reading τὰ θεωρήματα (Heintz): θεώρημα mss, Mutschmann–Mau.
[ak] Omitting οὗτος which Mutschmann–Mau add before διὰ τούτων.

[380] See III 261.
[381] With III 264–5 compare M XI 237–8; M I 33–4.
[382] I.e., presumably, 'it is redundant to discuss the method of learning'.
[383] With III 266–8 compare M XI 239–43; M I 36–8.

Teaching is not done by evidence; for evidence is of what is shown to us; what is shown is apparent; what is apparent, insofar as it is apparent, can be grasped by everyone;[384] and what can be grasped by everyone in common is non-teachable. Nothing therefore is teachable by evidence. [267] Nothing is taught by argument either. For an argument either signifies something or signifies nothing. If it signifies nothing it will not be capable of teaching anything. If it signifies something, it signifies either by nature or by convention. It does not signify by nature because not everyone understands everyone else when they hear them – e.g. Greeks foreigners and foreigners Greeks.[385] [268] Suppose, then, that it signifies by convention: clearly if you have already apprehended the things to which the words are assigned, then when you grasp the things you are not being taught by the words something which you did not know – rather, you are recollecting and reviving what you already knew. But if you need to learn the things which you do not already know and if you have not got knowledge of the things to which the words are assigned, then you will not get a grasp of anything.[386] [269] Hence the method of learning cannot subsist.

Again, the teacher ought to instil in the learner an apprehension of the theorems of the expertise being taught, so that the learner will in this way apprehend the compound of these and become expert. But, as we have suggested above,[387] there is no such thing as apprehension. This method of teaching, then, cannot subsist either.

And if there is nothing taught, no teachers and learners, and no method of learning, then there is neither learning nor teaching.

[270][388] That was the more general attack on teaching and learning. We can raise the following puzzles specifically for the so-called expertise in living. We showed above,[389] for instance, that the subject taught (in this case, intelligence[390]) is not subsistent; and teachers and learners too are not subsistent. For either the intelligent will teach the

---

[384] See II 8.
[385] See II 214.
[386] With this argument compare II 2–3.
[387] See III 241.
[388] With III 270–2 compare M XI 243–7.
[389] See III 253–8.
[390] See III 240.

intelligent expertise in living, or the foolish will teach the foolish or the foolish the intelligent or the intelligent the foolish. But none of these teaches anything. The so-called expertise in living, therefore, is not taught. [271] It is no doubt superfluous to mention other arguments. But if the intelligent teach the foolish intelligence, and if intelligence is knowledge of what is good and bad and neither,[391] then the foolish, who lack intelligence, possess ignorance of what is good and bad and neither; and since they possess ignorance of these things, then while the intelligent are teaching them about what is good and bad and neither, they will certainly only hear what is said and not recognize it. For if they grasp it while being in a condition of folly, then folly will be capable of studying what is good and bad and neither. [272] But according to them,[392] folly is in no condition to study any of these things – otherwise the foolish would be intelligent. The foolish, therefore, do not grasp what the intelligent say or do in virtue of their intelligence. But, not grasping this, they will not be taught by them – especially since they can be taught neither by evidence nor by argument, as we have already said.[393]

So if the so-called expertise in living does not come about in anyone through learning and teaching or by nature, then this expertise which the philosophers talk so much about is undiscoverable.

[273] Even if, however, one were to grant, for extra good measure,[394] that the expertise in living they have dreamed up is found in someone, it will appear harmful and a cause of trouble to its possessors rather than beneficial.

xxxi Does expertise in living benefit its possessors?

Thus[395] – to give a few cases out of many[396] by way of example – expertise in living might be thought to benefit the Sage[397] by

---

[391] The Stoic definition: *M* XI 246; Diogenes Laertius VII 92.
[392] See e.g. Arius ap. Stobaeus, *ed* II 104.10–17.
[393] See III 216–18.
[394] See I 62.
[395] With the argument from here to III 277 compare *M* XI 210–15.
[396] See I 4, note.
[397] See I 91, note.

providing him with self-control[398] in his impulses towards the bad[al] and revulsion from the good.[am] [274] The self-controlled Sage, then, as they call him, is said to be self-controlled either insofar as he never has an impulse to the bad and a revulsion from the good or else insofar as he does have bad impulses and revulsions but overcomes them by reason.[399] [275] But he will not be self-controlled in virtue of not having bad judgements: he will not control what he does not have. You would not call a eunuch self-controlled about sex, or someone with bad digestion self-controlled about the pleasures of eating (they do not crave for such things at all and so cannot show self-control in rising above their cravings): in the same way you should not call a Sage self-controlled because he has in him by nature no feeling for him to control. [276] If they claim that he is self-controlled insofar as he has bad judgements and overcomes them by reason, then first, they grant that intelligence did not benefit him at the very time when he was in trouble and needed help; and secondly, he turns out to be even more unhappy than those who are called bad. For insofar as he is impelled towards something he is certainly troubled, and insofar as he overcomes it by reason he retains the evil inside himself and is for this reason more troubled than a bad man who no longer feels it; [277] for a bad man is troubled insofar as he is impelled, but he ceases to be troubled insofar as he obtains his desires.

The Sage, then, is not self-controlled so far as his intelligence goes. Or rather, if he is, then he is the unhappiest man alive, so that expertise in living has brought him not benefit but the greatest of troubles. (We have suggested above[400] that anyone who deems that he has an expertise in living and by its means has recognized what things are good in their nature and what bad is greatly troubled both in the presence of good things and in the presence of bad.)

[278] We should say, then, that if it is not agreed that things good, bad and indifferent subsist, and if expertise in living perhaps does not subsist and – if we grant its subsistence as a hypothesis – brings no

---

[al] Reading κακόν with most MSS: Mutschmann–Mau print καλόν.
[am] Reading ἀγαθοῦ (Heintz): κακοῦ MSS, Mutschmann–Mau.

[398] See the Stoic definition of self-control, ἐγκράτεια: M IX 153; Diogenes Laertius VII 92; Plutarch, *On Moral Virtue* 449C.
[399] For the line which the Stoics actually took see ANNAS [1993a], ch. 2.
[400] See III 237.

benefit to its possessors but on the contrary instils in them the greatest of troubles, then in vain do the Dogmatists preen themselves in the so-called ethical part of what they call philosophy.

[279] Having said this much on ethical matters, at appropriate length for an outline,[401] we here bring to an end the third book and the entire treatise of the *Outlines of Scepticism*.

We add this coda:

xxxii Why do Sceptics sometimes deliberately propound arguments of feeble plausibility?[402]

[280] Sceptics are philanthropic and wish to cure by argument, as far as they can, the conceit and rashness of the Dogmatists. Just as doctors for bodily afflictions have remedies which differ in potency, and apply severe remedies to patients who are severely afflicted and milder remedies to those mildly afflicted, so Sceptics propound arguments which differ in strength – [281] they employ weighty arguments, capable of vigorously rebutting the dogmatic affliction of conceit, against those who are distressed by a severe rashness, and they employ milder arguments against those who are afflicted by a conceit which is superficial and easily cured and which can be rebutted by a milder degree of plausibility.

This is why those with a Sceptical impulse do not hesitate sometimes to propound arguments which are sometimes weighty in their plausibility, and sometimes apparently rather weak. They do this deliberately, since often a weaker argument is sufficient for them to achieve their purpose.

---

[401] See I 4, note.
[402] On this chapter see NUSSBAUM [1986]; ANNAS [1993a], ch. 11.

Bibliography

The following list merely catalogues the works to which we have referred in our footnotes. For introductory reading on Sextus and ancient scepticism see e.g. the bibliography to ANNAS and BARNES [1985]; there is an exhaustive bibliography on Pyrrhonism in Lucina FERRARIA and Giuseppina SANTESE [1981]: 'Bibliografia sullo scetticismo antico (1880–1978)', in GIANNANTONI [1981] – continued by: Patrizia MISURI [1990]: 'Bibliografia sullo scetticismo antico 1979–1988', *Elenchos* II, 257–334. New work can be discovered from, say, the excellent bibliographical sections in the journal *Elenchos*.

ANNAS, Julia [1986]: 'Doing without objective values: ancient and modern strategies', in SCHOFIELD and STRIKER [1986]

[1988]: 'The heirs of Socrates', *Phronesis* 33, 100–12

[1990]: 'Stoic epistemology', in EVERSON [1990]

[1992a]: *Hellenistic Philosophy of Mind* (University of California Press, Berkeley/Los Angeles)

[1992b]: 'Plato the Sceptic', in *Methods of Interpreting Plato and his Dialogues*, Oxford Studies in Ancient Philosophy supplementary volume (ed. J. Klagge and N. Smith) (Oxford University Press, Oxford)

[1992c]: 'Sextus Empiricus and the Peripatetics', *Elenchos* 13, 201–31

[1993a]: *The Morality of Happiness* (Oxford University Press, New York)

[1993b]: 'Scepticism, old and new', in the Festschrift for Günther Patzig (ed. Michael Frede and Gisela Striker) (Oxford University Press, Oxford)

[1993c]: 'Scepticism about value', in Proceedings of the Riverside Conference on Scepticism

[1993d]: 'Virtue as the use of other goods', *Virtue, Love and Form: Essays in Memory of Gregory Vlastos, Apeiron* 1993, 53–66.

Bibliography

ANNAS, Julia and Jonathan BARNES [1985]: *The Modes of Scepticism* (Cambridge University Press, Cambridge)

BARNES, Jonathan [1980]: 'Proof destroyed', in SCHOFIELD, BURNYEAT and BARNES [1980]

[1982]: 'Logic, medicine and experience', in BARNES, BRUNSCHWIG, BURNYEAT and SCHOFIELD [1982]

[1987]: *Early Greek Philosophy* (Penguin Books, Harmondsworth)

[1988a]: 'La possibilità di una vita scettica', *Atti e Relazioni dell'Accademia Pugliese delle scienze* 45, 1–30

[1988b]: 'Scepticism and relativity', *Philosophical Studies* 32, 1–31

[1988c] 'Bits and pieces', in BARNES and MIGNUCCI [1988]

[1989]: 'Antiochus of Ascalon', in GRIFFIN and BARNES [1989]

[1990a]: 'Pyrrhonism, belief and causation: observations on the scepticism of Sextus Empiricus', *Aufstieg und Niedergang der römischen Welt* (ed. W. Haase and H. Temporini), II 36.4 (de Gruyter, Berlin/New York)

[1990b]: 'Scepticism and naturalism', *Annales Universitatis Scientiarum Budapestiensis, sect. philos. sociol.* 22/23, 7–19

[1990c]: 'La διαφωνία pyrrhonienne', in VOELKE [1990]

[1990d]: *The Toils of Scepticism* (Cambridge University Press, Cambridge)

[1992]: 'Diogenes Laertius IX 61–116: the philosophy of Pyrrhonism', *Aufstieg und Niedergang der römischen Welt* (ed. W. Haase and H. Temporini), II 36.6 (de Gruyter, Berlin/New York)

BARNES, Jonathan, Susanne BOBZIEN, Kevin FLANNERY and Katerina IERODIAKONOU [1991]: *Alexander of Aphrodisias: Commentary on Aristotle, Posterior Analytics 1.1–7* (Duckworth, London)

BARNES, Jonathan, Jacques BRUNSCHWIG, M. F. BURNYEAT and Malcolm SCHOFIELD (edd.) [1982]: *Science and Speculation* (Cambridge University Press, Cambridge)

BARNES, Jonathan, and Mario MIGNUCCI (edd.) [1988]: *Matter and Metaphysics* (Bibliopolis, Naples)

BETT, R. [1989]: 'Carneades' *pithanon*: a reappraisal of its role and status', *Oxford Studies in Ancient Philosophy* 7, 59–94

BRUNSCHWIG, Jacques [1978a]: 'Le modèle conjonctif', in BRUNSCHWIG [1978b], reprinted in English translation in BRUNSCHWIG [1994]

(ed.) [1978b]: *Les Stoïciens et leur logique* (Vrin, Paris)

[1980]: 'Proof defined', in SCHOFIELD, BURNYEAT and BARNES [1980]

[1986]: 'The cradle argument in Epicureanism and Stoicism', in SCHOFIELD and STRIKER [1986]

[1988a]: 'Sextus Empiricus on the *kritērion*: the Skeptic as conceptual legatee', in DILLON and LONG [1988], reprinted in BRUNSCHWIG [1994]

[1988b]: 'La théorie stoïcienne du genre suprême et l'ontologie platoni-
cienne', in BARNES and MIGNUCCI [1988], reprinted in English translation, BRUNSCHWIG [1994]

[1990]: 'La formule ὅσον ἐπὶ τῷ λόγῳ chez Sextus Empiricus', in VOELKE
[1990], reprinted in English translation in BRUNSCHWIG [1994]

[1994]: *Papers in Hellenistic Philosophy*, translated by Janet Lloyd (Cambridge University Press, Cambridge)

BURNYEAT, M. F. [1976]: 'Protagoras and self-refutation in later Greek
philosophy', *Philosophical Review* 85, 44–69

[1980a] 'Can the Sceptic live his Scepticism?', in SCHOFIELD, BURNYEAT
and BARNES [1980] (reprinted in BURNYEAT [1983])

[1980b]: 'Tranquillity without a stop: Timon frag. 68', *Classical Quarterly*
30, 86–93

[1982]: 'The origins of non-deductive inference', in BARNES, BRUNSCHWIG,
BURNYEAT and SCHOFIELD [1982]

(ed.) [1983]: *The Skeptical Tradition* (University of California Press,
Berkeley/Los Angeles)

[1984]: 'The Sceptic in his time and place', in RORTY, SCHNEEWIND and
SKINNER [1984]

COUISSIN, V. [1929]: 'L'origine et l'évolution de l' ἐποχή', *Revue des Etudes
Grecques* 42, 373–97 (English translation in BURNYEAT [1983])

DECLEVA CAIZZI, Fernanda [1988]: 'La "materia scorrente": sulle tracce di un
dibattito perduto', in BARNES and MIGNUCCI [1988]

DEICHGRÄBER, Karl [1965]: *Die griechische Empirikerschule* (Weidmann,
Berlin/Zurich) [first edition 1930]

DE LACY, P. [1958]: 'οὐ μᾶλλον and the antecedents of ancient scepticism',
Phronesis 3, 59–71

DILLON, J. M. and A. A. LONG (edd.) [1988]: *The Question of 'Eclecticism'*
(University of California Press, Berkeley/Los Angeles)

DÖRING, Klaus [1972]: *Die Megariker* (B. R. Gruner, Amsterdam)

DÖRING, Klaus and Theodor EBERT (edd.) [1993]: *Dialektiker und Stoiker*
(Stuttgart)

EBERT, Theodor [1987]: 'The origin of the Stoic theory of signs in Sextus
Empiricus', *Oxford Studies in Ancient Philosophy* 5, 83–126

[1991]: *Dialektiker und frühe Stoiker bei Sextus Empiricus*, Hypomnemata 95
(Vandenhoeck & Ruprecht, Göttingen)

EDELSTEIN, L. [1967]: 'Empiricism and Skepticism in the Teaching of the
Greek Empiricist School' (reprinted in EDELSTEIN [1967], pp. 195–204)

[1967]: *Ancient Medicine* (Johns Hopkins University Press, Baltimore)

EVERSON, Stephen (ed.) [1990]: *Epistemology*, Companions to Ancient
Thought 1 (Cambridge University Press, Cambridge)

FREDE, Michael [1974]: *Die stoische Logik* (Vandenhoeck & Ruprecht, Göttingen)

[1979]: 'Des Skeptikers Meinungen', *Neue Hefte für Philosophie* 15, 102–29 (reprinted in English translation in FREDE [1987])

[1980]: 'The original notion of cause', in SCHOFIELD, BURNYEAT and BARNES [1980] (reprinted in FREDE [1987])

[1982]: 'On the method of the so-called Methodical school of medicine', in BARNES, BRUNSCHWIG, BURNYEAT and SCHOFIELD [1982] (reprinted in FREDE [1987])

[1983]: 'Stoics and Skeptics on clear and distinct impressions', in BURNYEAT [1983] (reprinted in FREDE [1987])

[1985]: *Galen: Three Treatises on the Nature of Science* (Hackett, Indianapolis)

[1987]: *Essays in Ancient Philosophy* (Oxford University Press, Oxford)

[1988]: 'The Empiricist attitude towards reason and theory', in HANKINSON [1988]

GIANNANTONI, Gabriele (ed.) [1981]: *Lo scetticismo antico* (Bibliopolis, Naples)

[1990]: *Socraticorum Reliquiae* (Bibliopolis, Naples [first edition 1983/5])

GLIDDEN, David [1983]: 'Skeptic semiotics', *Phronesis* 28, 213–55

GLUCKER, John [1978]: *Antiochus and the Late Academy*, Hypomnemata 56 (Vandenhoek & Ruprecht, Göttingen)

GRAESER, Andreas [1978]: 'The Stoic theory of meaning', in RIST [1978]

GRIFFIN, Miriam and Jonathan BARNES (edd.) [1989]: *Philosophia Togata* (Clarendon Press, Oxford)

HADOT, Pierre [1979]: 'Les divisions des parties de la philosophie dans l'antiquité', *Museum Helveticum* 36, 201–23

HANKINSON, R. J. (ed.) [1988]: *Method, Medicine and Metaphysics* (Academic Press, Edmonton)

HEINTZ, Werner [1932]: *Studien zu Sextus Empiricus* (Niemeyer Verlag, Halle)

HUBY, P. M. and G. NEAL (edd.) [1989]: *The Criterion of Truth* (Liverpool University Press, Liverpool)

IERODIAKONOU, Katerina [1993]: 'The Stoic indemonstrables in the later tradition', in DÖRING and EBERT [1993]

JANÁČEK, [1970]: 'Skeptische Zweitropenlehre und Sextus Empiricus', *Eirene* 8, 47–55

LONG, A. A. [1971a]: 'Language and thought in Stoicism', in LONG [1971b]

(ed.) [1971b]: *Problems in Stoicism* (Athlone Press, London)

[1978a]: 'Sextus Empiricus on the criterion of truth', *Bulletin of the Institute of Classical Studies* 25, 35–49

[1978b]: 'The Stoic distinction between truth and the true', in BRUNSCHWIG [1978b]

Bibliography

[1978c]: 'Dialectic and the Stoic Sage', in RIST [1978]

MACONI, Henry [1988]: 'Nova philosophia non philosophandi', *Oxford Studies in Ancient Philosophy* 6, 231–54

METTE, H. J. [1984]: 'Zwei Akademiker heute: Krantor und Arkesilaos', *Lustrum* 26, 7–94

[1985]: 'Weitere Akademiker heute: von Lakydes bis zu Kleitomachos', *Lustrum* 27, 39–148

MUELLER, Ian [1982]: 'Geometry and Scepticism', in BARNES, BRUNSCHWIG, BURNYEAT and SCHOFIELD [1982]

MUTSCHMANN, H. and J. MAU [1958]: *Sextus Empiricus* I (Teubner, Leipzig)

NASTI DE VINCENTIS, M. [1984]: 'Stopper on Nasti's contention and Stoic logic', *Phronesis* 29, 313–24

NUSSBAUM, Martha [1986]: 'Therapeutic arguments', in SCHOFIELD and STRIKER [1986]

RIST, J. M. (ed.) [1978]: *The Stoics* (University of California Press, Berkeley/ Los Angeles)

RORTY, R., J. SCHNEEWIND and Q. SKINNER (edd.) [1984]: *Philosophy in History* (Cambridge University Press, Cambridge)

SCHOFIELD, Malcolm [1983]: 'The syllogisms of Zeno of Citium', *Phronesis* 28, 31–58

[1988]: 'The retrenchable present', in BARNES and MIGNUCCI [1988]

[1991]: *The Stoic Idea of the City* (Cambridge University Press, Cambridge)

SCHOFIELD, M., M. F. BURNYEAT and Jonathan BARNES (edd.) [1980]: *Doubt and Dogmatism* (Clarendon Press, Oxford)

SCHOFIELD, Malcolm and Gisela STRIKER (edd.) [1986]: *The Norms of Nature* (Cambridge University Press, Cambridge)

SEDLEY, D. N. [1977]: 'Diodorus Cronus and Hellenistic philosophy', *Proceedings of the Cambridge Philological Society* 23, 74–120

[1982]: 'The Stoic criterion of identity', *Phronesis* 27, 255–75

SORABJI, Richard [1988]: 'The Greek origins of the idea of chemical combination: can two bodies be in the same place?', *Proceedings of the Boston Area Colloquium in Ancient Philosophy* 4, 35–63

STOPPER, M. R. [1983]: 'Schizzi pirroniani', *Phronesis* 28, 265–97

STRIKER, Gisela [1974]: Κριτήριον τῆς Ἀληθείας (Vandenhoeck & Ruprecht, Göttingen)

[1981]: 'Über den Unterschied zwischen den Pyrrhoneern und den Akademikern', *Phronesis* 26, 153–69

[1990a]: 'Happiness as tranquillity', *Monist* 73, 97–110

[1990b]: 'The problem of the criterion', in EVERSON [1990]

Bibliography

TARRANT, Harold [1985]: *Scepticism or Platonism?* (Cambridge University Press, Cambridge)

TIELEMANN, T. [1992]: *Galen and Chrysippus: argument and refutation in the* de Placitis *Books II–III* (diss. Utrecht)

TODD, R. B. [1976]: *Alexander of Aphrodisias on Stoic Physics* (Brill, Leiden)

TSEKOURAKIS, D. [1974]: *Studies in the Terminology of Early Stoic Ethics*, Hermes Einzelschriften 32 (Franz Steiner, Wiesbaden)

TSOUNA MCKIRAHAN, V. [1992]: 'The Cyrenaic theory of knowledge', *Oxford Studies in Ancient Philosophy* 10, 161–92

VOELKE, A. J. (ed.) [1990]: *Le Scepticisme antique*, Cahiers de la revue de Théologie et de Philosophie 13 (Geneva)

VON ARNIM, Hans [1903–5]: *Stoicorum Veterum Fragmenta* (Teubner, Leipzig)

VON SAVIGNY, Eike [1975]: 'Inwieweit hat Sextus Empiricus Humes Argumente gegen die Induktion vorweggenommen?', *Archiv für Geschichte der Philosophie* 57, 269–85

WOODRUFF Paul [1986]: 'The sceptical side of Plato's method', *Revue Internationale de la Philosophie* 156/7, 22–37

Glossaries

━━━

The Glossaries cover some of the key words in Sextus' Sceptical vocabulary: they contain all the 'technical terms' of Scepticism, and a few other terms beside; but they do not contain every one of the technical terms from Dogmatic philosophy which appear in the *Outlines*. Many of the terms in the Sceptical vocabulary come in families of cognates: in general, we have listed only one word from each family – thus the glossary reports that 'apprehend' represents *katalambanein*, but leaves it to be inferred that 'apprehensive' represents the appropriate cognate of the Greek verb (in this case, *kataleptikos*). Finally, note that we have not been tyrannized by the translations here marked: the Greek–English equivalences hold for the most part but they do not all hold universally.

(i) English–Greek

absolutely [*see also*: simply]	ἁπλῶς [*haplōs*]
absurd [*see also*: out of place]	ἄτοπος [*atopos*]
account [*see also*: argument]	λόγος [*logos*]
affirm	διαβεβαιοῦσθαι [*diabebaiousthai*]
affirmation [*see also*: assertion]	ἀπόφασις [*apophasis*]
aim (n.)	τέλος [*telos*]
anomaly	ἀνωμαλία [*anōmalia*]
apparent	φαινόμενος [*phainomenos*]
appear	φαίνεσθαι [*phainesthai*]
apprehend	καταλαμβάνειν [*katalambanein*]
appropriate (adj.)	οἰκεῖος [*oikeios*]
argument [*see also*: account]	λόγος [*logos*]
assent (n.)	συγκατάθεσις [*sunkatathesis*]

assertion [see also: affirmation]   ἀπόφασις [apophasis]

assumption   λῆμμα [lēmma]

bad   φαῦλος [phaulos]

be   εἶναι [einai]

belief   δόγμα [dogma]

(hold) beliefs   δογματίζειν [dogmatizein]

believe [see also: think]   δοκεῖν [dokein]

benefit (n.)   ὠφέλεια [ōphelia]

causal explanation   αἰτιολογία [aitiologia]

cause   αἰτία, αἴτιον [aitia, aition]

change [see also: motion]   κίνησις [kinēsis]

circumstance   περίστασις [peristasis]

clear   πρόδηλος [prodēlos]

clever   συνετός [sunetos]

compound (n.)   σύστασις, σύστημα

    [see also: constitution]   [sustasis, sustēma]

concede   συγχωρεῖν [sunchōrein]

concept   ἔννοια, ἐπίνοια [ennoia, epinoia]

conception   ἐννόημα [ennoēma]

conclude   συνάγειν [sunagein]

conclusion   συμπέρασμα [sumperasma]

condition   διάθεσις [diathesis]

confirm   βεβαιοῦν [bebaioun]

conflict (n.)   μαχή [machē]

constitution [see also: compound]   σύστασις, σύστημα [sustasis, sustēma]

conviction   πίστις [pistis]

convincingness   πίστις [pistis]

custom   ἔθος [ethos]

decide   ἐπικρίνειν [epikrinein]

deduction   συλλογισμός [sullogismos]

definition   ὅρος [horos]

deny   ἀναιρεῖν [anairein]

determine   ὁρίζειν [horizein]

discover   εὑρίσκειν [heuriskein]

dispute (n.)   διαφωνία [diaphōnia]

Dogmatist   δογματικός [dogmatikos]

Glossary

element	στοιχεῖον [*stoicheion*]
equipollence	ἰσοσθένεια [*isostheneia*]
establish	κατασκευάζειν [*kataskeuazein*]
everyday observances	βιωτικὴ τήρησις [*biōtikē tērēsis*]
evident	ἐναργής [*enargēs*]
exist	ὑποκεῖσθαι [*hupokeisthai*]
expertise	τέχνη [*technē*]
external	ἐκτός [*ektos*]
feeling	πάθος [*pathos*]
fine (adj.)	καλός [*kalos*]
good	ἀγαθός [*agathos*]
impasse [*see also*: puzzle]	ἀπορία [*aporia*]
implicitly [*see also*: potentially]	δυνάμει [*dunamei*]
impress	ὑποπίπτειν [*hupopiptein*]
impulse	ὁρμή [*hormē*]
inapprehensible	ἀκατάληπτος [*akatalēptos*]
(be) incongruous	ἀπεμφαίνειν [*apemphainein*]
independently	ἀπολύτως [*apolutōs*]
indifferent	ἀδιάφορος [*adiaphoros*]
induction	ἐπαγωγή [*epagōgē*]
inquire [*see also*: investigate]	ζητεῖν [*zētein*]
intellect [*see also*: thought]	διάνοια [*dianoia*]
intelligence	φρόνησις [*phronēsis*]
intense [*see also*: vigorous]	σύντονος [*suntonos*]
investigate [*see also*: inquire]	ζητεῖν [*zētein*]
judge	κρίνειν [*krinein*]
(ordinary) life	βίος [*bios*]
mode [*see also*: way]	τρόπος [*tropos*]
motion [*see also*: change]	κίνησις [*kinēsis*]
nature	φύσις [*phusis*]
negation	ἀποφατικόν [*apophatikon*]
no doubt	ἴσως [*isōs*]
non-assertion	ἀφασία [*aphasia*]

Glossary

non-existent	ἀνυπόστατος [anupostatos]
object of perception [see also: sense-object]	αἰσθητόν [aisthēton]
object of thought	νοητόν [noēton]
observance	τήρησις [tērēsis]
observe	θεωρεῖν [theōrein]
opinion	δόξα [doxa]
ordinary life [see also: life]	βίος [bios]
out of place [see also: absurd]	ἄτοπος [atopos]
perfect (adj.)	τελεῖος [teleios]
perhaps	τάχα [tacha]
persuasion [see also: way of life]	ἀγωγή [agōgē]
plausible	πιθανός [pithanos]
posit (vb.)	τίθεσθαι [tithesthai]
potentially [see also: implicitly]	δυνάμει [dunamei]
preconception	πρόληψις [prolēpsis]
predicate (n.)	κατηγόρημα [katēgorēma]
prefer	προκρίνειν [prokrinein]
principle	ἀρχή [archē]
proof	ἀπόδειξις [apodeixis]
proposition	πρότασις [protasis]
purely	εἰλικρινῶς [eilikrinōs]
puzzle [see also: impasse]	ἀπορία [aporia]
rashness	προπετεία [propeteia]
(be) real	ὑπάρχειν [huparchein]
relative	πρός τι [pros ti]
report (vb.)	ἀπαγγέλλειν [apangellein]
sayable (n.)	λεκτόν [lekton]
Sceptic	σκεπτικός [skeptikos]
school (of philosophy)	αἴρεσις [hairesis]
science	ἐπιστήμη [epistēmē]
sense-object [see also: object of perception]	αἰσθητόν [aisthēton]
sign	σημεῖον [sēmeion]
signify	σημαίνειν [sēmainein]
simply [see also: absolutely]	ἁπλῶς [haplōs]

soul	ψυχή [*psuchē*]
standard	κριτήριον [*kritērion*]
statement	ἀξίωμα [*axiōma*]
strictly	κυρίως [*kuriōs*]
subsist	ὑφίστασθαι [*huphistasthai*]
substance	οὐσία [*ousia*]
suspension of judgement	ἐποχή [*epochē*]

think [*see also*: believe]	δοκεῖν [*dokein*]
thought [*see also*: intellect]	διάνοια [*dianoia*]
tranquillity	ἀταραξία [*ataraxia*]
trouble	ταραχή [*tarachē*]
turning about	περιτροπή [*peritropē*]

unclear	ἄδηλος [*adēlos*]
undecidable	ἀνεπίκριτος [*anepikritos*]
unreal	ἀνύπαρκτος [*anuparktos*]

value	ἀξία [*axia*]
vigorous [*see also*: intense]	σύντονος [*suntonos*]
virtuous	σπουδαῖος [*spoudaios*]

way [*see also*: mode]	τρόπος [*tropos*]
way of life [*see also*: persuasion]	ἀγωγή [*agōgē*]

(ii) Greek–English

ἀγαθός [*agathos*]	good
ἀγωγή [*agōgē*]	persuasion, way of life
ἄδηλος [*adēlos*]	unclear
ἀδιάφορος [*adiaphoros*]	indifferent
αἵρεσις [*hairesis*]	school (of philosophy)
αἰσθητόν [*aisthēton*]	object of perception, sense-object
αἰτία [*aitia*]	cause
αἰτιολογία [*aitiologia*]	causal explanation
αἴτιον [*aition*]	cause
ἀκατάληπτος [*akatalēptos*]	inapprehensible
ἀναιρεῖν [*anairein*]	deny
ἀνεπίκριτος [*anepikritos*]	undecidable
ἀνύπαρκτος [*anuparktos*]	unreal

Glossary

ἀνυπόστατος [*anupostatos*]	non-existent
ἀνωμαλία [*anōmalia*]	anomaly
ἀξία [*axia*]	value
ἀξίωμα [*axiōma*]	statement
ἀπαγγέλλειν [*apangellein*]	report
ἀπεμφαίνειν [*apemphainein*]	be incongruous
ἁπλῶς [*haplōs*]	absolutely, simply
ἀπόδειξις [*apodeixis*]	proof
ἀπολύτως [*apolutōs*]	independently
ἀπορία [*aporia*]	impasse, puzzle
ἀπόφασις [*apophasis*]	affirmation, assertion
ἀποφατικόν [*apophatikon*]	negation
ἀρχή [*archē*]	principle
ἀταραξία [*ataraxia*]	tranquillity
ἄτοπος [*atopos*]	absurd, out of place
ἀφασία [*aphasia*]	non-assertion
βεβαιοῦν [*bebaioun*]	confirm
βίος [*bios*]	life, ordinary life
βιωτικὴ τήρησις [*biōtikē tērēsis*]	everyday observance
διαβεβαιοῦσθαι [*diabebaiousthai*]	affirm
διάθεσις [*diathesis*]	condition
διάνοια [*dianoia*]	intellect, thought
διαφωνία [*diaphōnia*]	dispute
δόγμα [*dogma*]	belief
δογματίζειν [*dogmatizein*]	hold beliefs
δογματικός [*dogmatikos*]	Dogmatist
δοκεῖν [*dokein*]	believe, think
δόξα [*doxa*]	opinion
δυνάμει [*dunamei*]	implicitly, potentially
ἔθος [*ethos*]	custom
εἰλικρινῶς [*eilikrinōs*]	purely
εἶναι [*einai*]	be
ἐκτός [*ektos*]	external
ἐναργής [*enargēs*]	evident
ἐννόημα [*ennoēma*]	conception
ἔννοια [*ennoia*]	concept
ἐπαγωγή [*epagōgē*]	induction

Glossary

ἐπικρίνειν [*epikrinein*]	decide
ἐπίνοια [*epinoia*]	concept
ἐπιστήμη [*epistēmē*]	science
ἐποχή [*epochē*]	suspension of judgement
εὑρίσκειν [*heuriskein*]	discover
ζητεῖν [*zētein*]	inquire, investigate
θεωρεῖν [*theōrein*]	observe
ἰσοσθένεια [*isostheneia*]	equipollence
ἴσως [*isōs*]	no doubt
καλός [*kalos*]	fine
καταλαμβάνειν [*katalambanein*]	apprehend
κατασκευάζειν [*kataskeuazein*]	establish
κατηγόρημα [*katēgorēma*]	predicate
κίνησις [*kinēsis*]	change, motion
κρίνειν [*krinein*]	judge
κριτήριον [*kritērion*]	standard
κυρίως [*kuriōs*]	strictly
λεκτόν [*lekton*]	sayable
λῆμμα [*lēmma*]	assumption
λόγος [*logos*]	account, argument
μαχή [*machē*]	conflict
νοητόν [*noēton*]	object of thought
οἰκεῖος [*oikeios*]	appropriate
ὁρίζειν [*horizein*]	determine
ὁρμή [*hormē*]	impulse
ὅρος [*horos*]	definition
οὐσία [*ousia*]	substance
πάθος [*pathos*]	feeling
περίστασις [*peristasis*]	circumstance
περιτροπή [*peritropē*]	turning about
πιθανός [*pithanos*]	plausible

Glossary

πίστις [*pistis*]	convincingness, conviction
πρόδηλος [*prodēlos*]	clear
προκρίνειν [*prokrinein*]	prefer
πρόληψις [*prolēpsis*]	preconception
προπέτεια [*propeteia*]	rashness
πρός τι [*pros ti*]	relative
πρότασις [*protasis*]	proposition
σημαίνειν [*sēmainein*]	signify
σημεῖον [*sēmeion*]	sign
σκεπτικός [*skeptikos*]	Sceptic
σπουδαῖος [*spoudaios*]	virtuous
στοιχεῖον [*stoicheion*]	element
συγκατάθεσις [*sunkatathesis*]	assent
συγχωρεῖν [*sunchōrein*]	concede
συλλογισμός [*sullogismos*]	deduction
συμπέρασμα [*sumperasma*]	conclusion
συνάγειν [*sunagein*]	conclude
συνετός [*sunetos*]	clever
σύντονος [*suntonos*]	intense, vigorous
σύστασις [*sustasis*]	compound, constitution
σύστημα [*sustēma*]	compound, constitution
ταραχή [*tarachē*]	trouble
τάχα [*tacha*]	perhaps
τέλειος [*teleios*]	perfect
τέλος [*telos*]	aim
τέχνη [*technē*]	expertise
τίθεσθαι [*tithesthai*]	posit
τρόπος [*tropos*]	mode, way
ὑπάρχειν [*huparchein*]	be real
ὑποκεῖσθαι [*hupokeisthai*]	exist
ὑποπίπτειν [*hupopiptein*]	impress
ὑποτύπωσις [*hupotupōsis*]	outline
ὑφίστασθαι [*huphistasthai*]	subsist
φαίνεσθαι [*phainesthai*]	appear
φαινόμενος [*phainomenos*]	apparent
φαῦλος [*phaulos*]	bad

Glossary

φρόνησις [*phronēsis*]	intelligence
φύσις [*phusis*]	nature
ψυχή [*psuchē*]	soul
ὠφέλεια [*ōpheleia*]	benefit

(iii) Index of Greek terms

ἀκολουθεῖν 105 n.224, 108 n.232, 119 n.280

ἀναπόδεικτος 109 n.235

ἀνεπίκριτος 24 n.108

ἀπορεῖν 4 n.9

ἀταραξία 5 n.17

ἐποχή 49 n.197, 63 n.265

ἡγεμονικόν 33 n.136

ἰδιοσυγκρασία 22 n.98

κρᾶσις 160 n.77

μίξις 160 n.77

οἰκεῖος 19 n.84

περιτροπή 32 n.130

σκέπτεσθαι 4 n.8

τὰ κατά διαφοράν 36 n.142

τέχνη 85 n.98

ὑπάρχειν 182 n.189

ὑποτύπωσις 3 n.2

ὑφίσταναι 182 n.189

φρόνησις 105 n.345

Index of names

This list contains only (1) people referred to in Sextus' text, (2) major authors referred to frequently in the notes (e.g. Diogenes Laertius, Cicero), and (3) sources referred to in the notes which, while not major, are important for the history of scepticism (e.g. Numenius).

The information is brief and selective, limited to what is of interest in the context of reference in Sextus. A name capitalized in an entry has its own entry.

ACADEMICS. Philosophical school founded by PLATO, named after the Academy gymnasium. The name is generally used for followers of the SCEPTICAL ACADEMY, sometimes also called the Middle or New Academy, founded by ARCESILAUS. The SCEPTICAL ACADEMY petered out after PHILO of Larissa.

AENESIDEMUS of Cnossus. Philosopher who in the first century BC broke away from the ACADEMY, which was becoming more dogmatic, and founded a more radical sceptical movement invoking the name of PYRRHO. He also had a puzzling interest in HERACLITUS. Generally regarded as the inventor (or codifier) of the Ten Modes; his *Pyrrhonian Arguments*, summarized in PHOTIUS, are usually supposed to have been a major source for Sextus.

AGRIPPA. Pyrrhonist philosopher, otherwise unknown, probably end of first century BC, who invented the Five Modes. From the way that Sextus regards these as additional to the Ten Modes Agrippa is presumably later than AENESIDEMUS.

ANAXAGORAS of Clazomenae. Philosopher active in the mid-fifth century BC at Athens until driven out by intolerance. His interests were in natural science; his theories feature a difficult account of the composition of matter from 'homoeomeries' and a role for cosmic Mind which ARISTOTLE later found insufficiently teleological.

ANAXIMANDER of Miletus. Sixth-century BC philosopher, best known for his theory that the 'Infinite' (*apeiron*) is the principle of everything.

ANAXIMENES of Miletus. Younger colleague of ANAXIMANDER; his theory was that *aēr* (air or vapour) is the principle of everything.

ANDRON of Argos. Otherwise unknown.

ANTIOCHUS of Ascalon, *c.* 130/120–68 BC. Member of the late ACADEMY under PHILO of Larissa, with whom he had an acrimonious debate over epistemology. Some time after the end of the ACADEMY he founded his own school, regarded by some as a continuation of the ACADEMY. Antiochus put forward a dogmatic and syncretic system of philosophy, a mixture of Platonic, Stoic and Aristotelian ideas, which he presented as the 'original tradition' of the pre-SCEPTICAL ACADEMY.

ANTIPATER of Tarsus. Head of the Stoa in the second century BC, who wrote on many topics, including logic.

ANTISTHENES of Athens, *c.* 445–360 BC. Follower and pupil of SOCRATES, famous for his ascetic version of an independent Socratic life-style, and influential on the CYNICS for his rejection of convention.

APELLES of Colophon. Fourth-century BC painter.

ARCESILAUS of Pitane, *c.* 315–240 BC. Head of the ACADEMY, who turned it to thorough SCEPTICISM. His practice was to argue against the views of others, putting forward no positive doctrines himself, a practice modelled on SOCRATES in PLATO's early dialogues. However, Arcesilaus claimed that the result was suspension of judgement, a feature absent from Socratic practice and suggesting influence from PYRRHO.

ARCHILOCHUS of Paros. Seventh-century BC poet, notorious in antiquity for his first-personal poems, which were often read in a literal-minded way as accounts of Archilochus' own life, rather than as poetic creations.

ARISTIPPUS of Cyrene. Fourth-century BC pupil and follower of SOCRATES, who adopted a form of hedonism as a way of living an independent Socratic life-style. The doctrines of the CYRENAIC school of philosophy, which regarded him as their founder, probably go back to his grandson, also named Aristippus. The elder Aristippus figures in anecdote as the archetypal pleasure-seeker.

ARISTO of Chios. Pupil of ZENO. he had a large but short-lived influence. In many ways his version of STOICISM differed from that of ZENO and the latter's other pupils. Later, under the influence of CHRYSIPPUS, whose works became standard, Aristo's position came to be regarded as 'deviant' from an orthodox Stoic line, particularly with regard to his views on the role of rules in ethics.

ARISTOCLES of Messene. First- or second-century AD Peripatetic philosopher; wrote *On Philosophy* in ten books, from which we have extensive extracts in Eusebius.

ARISTOTLE of Stagira. 383–322 BC. Founder of the PERIPATETIC school, pupil of PLATO; unsurpassed for the breadth and depth of his studies in philosophy and science.

ASCLEPIADES of Bithynia. First-century BC doctor with philosophical interests; held a strange theory of matter as constituted by a kind of friable atoms.

ATHENAGORAS of Argos. Otherwise unknown.

CARNEADES of Cyrene. 214–129/128 BC. After ARCESILAUS, the most famous head of the SCEPTICAL ACADEMY. He put forward no positive positions of his own, but argued against the theories of others, sometimes against the argumentative structure of sets of theories.

CHARMIDAS or Charmadas. Member of the last generation of the SCEPTICAL ACADEMY. Little is known about him other than that he had an interest in rhetoric.

CHRYSERMUS. Otherwise unknown doctor, follower of HEROPHILUS.

CHRYSIPPUS of Soli. *c.* 280–207 BC. Third head of the STOIC school, and its most voluminous and influential writer, regarded as the school's second founder because of the definitive way in which he articulated many of its doctrines.

Marcus Tullius CICERO. 106–43 BC. Roman politician, well educated in philosophy, who at the end of his life wrote a series of philosophical works from an academic standpoint, giving arguments for and against philosophical positions. Because of this he is a valuable source for the arguments in many areas of ancient philosophy.

CILICIANS. Inhabitants of present-day South Turkey.

CLITOMACHUS (originally HASDRUBAL) of Carthage. Pupil of CARNEADES and member of the SCEPTICAL ACADEMY. Wrote down over 400 books of

Carneades' arguments, but emphasized that he had no idea what, if anything, Carneades believed.

CRATES of Thebes. *c.* 365–285 BC CYNIC philosopher famous for rejecting social conventions, and for his marriage with HIPPARCHIA, notorious for the fact that they copulated in public.

CRITIAS of Athens. *c.* 460–403 BC. PLATO's uncle; Athenian politician who became one of the Thirty Tyrants. A fragment from a play *Sisyphus* in which the speaker gives a naturalistic account of the origins of belief in gods is ascribed by scholars either to Critias or to EURIPIDES; Sextus assigns it to Critias.

CYNICISM. Philosophical movement deriving both from ANTISTHENES and from DIOGENES of Sinope. The Cynics were never an established school. They stressed the importance of returning to nature, but because of their lack of interest in theory they were vague as to what this meant; stories about them stress a somewhat theatrical rejection of social conventions, particularly about sex. 'Cynic' comes from the Greek for dog, this being a symbol of shamelessness.

CYRENAICISM. Philosophical movement deriving from ARISTIPPUS, though probably established as a school with definite doctrines only by his grandson. Its main positions were an extreme form of present-moment hedonism, and an extreme form of empiricist epistemology.

DEMETRIUS of Laconia. Second-century BC Epicurean, who wrote on time and other matters.

DEMOCRITUS of Abdera. Fifth-century BC philosopher, best known for his developed version of atomism. It is uncertain how some sceptical-sounding views on knowledge fit in with his metaphysics.

DEMOPHON. Alexander the Great's waiter.

DIAGORAS of Melos. Late fifth-century BC poet, notorious as an atheist, allegedly because the gods failed to punish a perjurer who won a case against him.

DICAEARCHUS of Messene. *c.* 326–296 BC. PERIPATETIC philosopher of wide interests, political, historical and geographical. Remembered also for denying the existence of the soul.

DIOCLES of Carystus. Fourth-century BC doctor with philosophical interests.

DIODORUS CRONUS. Third/second-century BC philosopher and logician.

Most famous for the 'Master Argument' and for arguments against the coherence of motion.

DIOGENES LAERTIUS. Probably third century AD, but date very uncertain. Author of a ten-book *Lives of the Philosophers*, containing chatty gossip, but also important information about several philosophical schools.

DIOGENES of Apollonia. Fifth-century BC philosopher; held a later version of ANAXIMENES' theory that air is the principle and basis of everything.

DIOGENES of Sinope. *c.* 400–325 BC. First avowedly CYNIC philosopher, famous for his convention-flouting behaviour, about which there are many stories.

DIONYSIUS I of Syracuse. *c.* 430–367 BC. Figures in anecdotes as stereotypical tyrant, especially in stories about PLATO and ARISTIPPUS.

EMPEDOCLES of Acragas. *c.* 493–*c.* 433 BC. Philosopher who wrote in verse; his religious concern with reincarnation stands in obscure relation to his theory of the four elements and the world's progressive constitution and dissolution.

EPICURUS of Athens. 341–270 BC. Founder of a school best known for hedonism and a form of atomism, often misunderstood by critics in antiquity.

EUDOXUS of Cnidus. *c.* 390–340 BC. Influential mathematician, astronomer and geographer.

EURIPIDES of Athens. *c.* 485–406 BC. Author of many verse tragedies, more popular after his death than in his lifetime.

GALEN of Pergamum. 129–*c.* 210 AD. Doctor, scholar, philosopher and pedant; wrote voluminously on many subjects.

GORGIAS of Leontini. *c.* 483–376 BC. Orator and sophist, known for elaborate rhetorical set-pieces, and also for an odd work arguing for paradoxical theses about existence.

HERACLIDES of Pontus. Fourth-century BC ACADEMIC philosopher, with wide philosophical and religious interests. He held a physical theory of friable particles, often compared to the theory of ASCLEPIADES.

HERACLITUS of Ephesus. Sixth-century BC philosopher, known for his obscurity and profundity. The STOICS and AENESIDEMUS were interested in his ideas, and claimed him as some kind of forebear.

HEROPHILUS of Chalcedon. Third-century BC doctor and anatomist with scientific and philosophical interests.

HESIOD. Early Greek poet, regarded as slightly younger than HOMER; author of didactic *Works and Days* and a *Theogony*.

HIPPARCHIA. Wife of CRATES, known as a CYNIC philosopher in her own right.

HIPPASUS of Metapontum. Early PYTHAGOREAN, probably fifth century BC, round whom later claims and legends gathered.

HIPPO of Rhegium. Fifth-century physical philosopher, who treated water or the element of moisture as the principle of everything.

HIPPOCRATES of Cos. Fifth-century BC doctor. The HIPPOCRATIC CORPUS is a large body of medical works attributed to Hippocrates, many of them deriving from his school (and some from other schools).

HOMER. Earliest Greek poet, date unknown, massively influential and well-known at all periods of Greek culture.

ITALIANS. Here: inhabitants of the Greek colonial cities of southern Italy, famous for their wealth and luxurious lifestyle.

LYSIS. Otherwise unknown, unless identical with a second-century BC Pythagorean, who taught at Thebes and wrote nothing.

MASSAGETAE. Inhabitants of present-day southern Russia between the Caspian and Aral seas.

MELISSUS of Samos. Fifth-century admiral and philosopher, follower of PARMENIDES, in support of whose conclusions he wrote prose works of which ARISTOTLE had a low opinion.

MENANDER of Athens. 342/341–293/289 BC. Popular author of 'New Comedy' dramas.

MENODOTUS of Nicomedia. Second-century AD doctor and medical writer of the empiricist school.

NUMENIUS of Apamea. Second-century AD Platonist philosopher, interested in harmonizing Platonic ideas with various forms of Eastern thought. Wrote a satirical account of the SCEPTICAL ACADEMY, designed to represent it as an unworthy falling-off from Plato.

OENOPIDES of Chios. Fifth-century BC mathematician and astronomer.

ONOMACRITUS. Sixth-century BC writer at the court of Pisistratus of Athens. Allegedly, he was the inventor of 'Orphic' verses ascribing a mystical cosmology to the legendary figure of Orpheus.

PARMENIDES of Elea. Sixth/fifth-century BC. Author of a philosophical poem establishing conclusions repugnant to common-sense, such as the impossibility of motion, plurality, etc.

PERIPATETICS. Philosophical school founded by ARISTOTLE. After Theophrastus, Aristotle's pupil, the school turned more to scientific research, especially under STRATO.

PHERECYDES of Syros. Sixth-century BC author of prose work regarded by ARISTOTLE as a mixture of myth and theology.

PHILO of Alexandria. c. 30 BC–45 AD. Jewish scholar, philosopher and copious author. In part of his commentary on the Pentateuch he gives, without naming them, a summary of the Ten Modes.

PHILO of Larissa. 160/159–c. 80 BC. Last head of the SCEPTICAL ACADEMY. Engaged in epistemological dispute with ANTIOCHUS, also in ethical argument.

PHILO of Megara. Third–second-century BC pupil of DIODORUS CRONUS; logician, known for his view on conditionals.

PHOTIUS. Ninth-century Patriarch of Constantinople, who produced summaries of many books he read, including one by AENESIDEMUS.

PINDAR of Thebes. Sixth/fifth century BC poet.

PLATO of Athens. c. 429–347 BC. Philosopher who wrote for publication in dialogue form. Later philosophers were divided over which, if any, of the ideas discussed in the dialogues were to be taken as Plato's own, and also over the question of whether philosophizing in the spirit of Plato involved adopting ideas from the dialogues, or criticizing the ideas of others as SOCRATES does in the early dialogues without putting forward ideas of one's own. The latter was the view of the SCEPTICAL ACADEMY.

PLUTARCH of Chaeronea. c. 50–120 AD. Platonist philosopher and essayist, useful as source for Hellenistic philosophy, though his treatment of philosophies other than Platonism is very hostile.

POLEMO of Athens. Head of the ACADEMY 314/313–270 BC, about whose doctrines we know little.

PROTAGORAS of Abdera. Fifth-century BC sophist, most famous for his relativism, about which we have very little direct evidence.

PSYLLAEANS. Tribe in Libya.

PYRRHO of Elis. *c.* 360–*c.* 270 BC. The founding figure of ancient SCEPTICISM; like SOCRATES, he wrote nothing, though his ideas were written down by his pupil TIMON. Little is known about him personally, other than that he travelled with Alexander the Great to India; conflicting legends gathered round his life. He served as a symbolic figurehead for AENESIDEMUS' later form of scepticism.

PYTHAGORAS of Samos. Sixth-century philosopher and mathematician. Founder of a movement which combined mystical and mathematical interests, and played a political role in the Greek cities of southern Italy. Later developments and accretions make it impossible to determine exactly what Pythagoras' own contribution was.

RUFINUS of Chalcis. Otherwise unknown.

SARMATIANS. Nomad tribe, related to the Scythians.

SCEPTICS. From the Greek *skeptesthai*, to inquire. Three main trends in Greek philosophy have been called sceptical: (i) the thought of PYRRHO, never formalized or institutionalized; (ii) the phase of the ACADEMY during which PLATO's school followed Pyrrho's example by arguing against others without putting forward dogmatic beliefs of their own; and (iii) the breakaway movement led by AENESIDEMUS at a time when the Academy was becoming less sceptical, a movement harking back to the earlier figure of Pyrrho. Because of Sextus' writings we have by far the most information about (iii).

SCYTHIANS. Inhabitants of present-day southern Russia: to the Greeks, the type of a nomadic people.

SOCRATES of Athens. 469–399 BC. Philosopher who wrote nothing; various pupils, including PLATO, wrote dialogues in which he figures. Served as figurehead for a number of extremely divergent philosophical schools; he seems to have been the best available symbol of a philosopher in general, regardless of the content of the theories in question.

SOLON of Athens. Sixth-century lawgiver and politician.

SOTERICHUS. Otherwise unknown surgeon.

Index of subjects

References give book-number and section-number (not page-number). An asterisk indicates that further passages are cited in a footnote to the section.

actual *vs.* potential II 27, 225–6
addition III 94–6, 109, 153, 164–6 [*see also*: subtraction]
admixture I 124–8, 136
affirmation, not a Sceptical practice I 4, 15, 18, 35, 195, 196, 197, 200, 206, 208, 233, 236; II 79; III 55 [*see also*: assent]
age I 105–6, 219
aim I 25–30, 215, 231, 232; III 187
all *vs.* some II 64–8, 76–8, 88–9, 91–3, 204; III 9–10, 33, 138, 182
alteration II 70; III 102–8, 129
ambiguity II 256–9
animals I 40–59, 69, 73–5, 136; II 26; generation of I 40–3; III 18
anomaly I 12, 29, 112, 114, 132, 163, 214; III 198, 218, 220, 233, 234, 235
anterior conditions I 111
appearance I 8–9, 22, 31–4, 61; II 8, 70–2, 219; III 254, 266; apprehensive I 68; II 4; III 241; *vs.* reasoning III 65, 81, 136; and Scepticism I 4, 13, 16–17, 19–20, 191; *vs.* thought I 9, 31–3; *vs.* unclear items I 185–6 [*see also*: nature, perception, unclear]
apples I 94–9
apprehension II 2–10, 15, 206–11; III 188, 241, 251, 268, 269 [*see also*: inapprehensibility]
appropriate I 65–6, 70–1, 238
argument I 36, 205; II 135, 141, 193–203; III 280–1; categorical II 163–6; conclusive II 137, 145, 167, 249–50, 255; inconclusive II 137, 145–66; parts of

connectedness II III [*see also*: conditionals]

consequence [= conclusion] I 202; II 136–8, 144, 146, 152, 171–6 [*see also*:
   argument]

contraries I 210–2; II 225–6, 239 [*see also*: opposition]

courage III 193, 216 [*see also*: virtue]

custom I 17, 23–4, 145–6, 148, 152–5, 231, 237; III 198, 199 [*see also*: law,
   ordinary life]

death III 110–11, 226–32, 248–9

decrease III 82–4 [*see also*: increase]

deduction, *see*: argument

deficiency II 146, 150, 155

definition II 205–12; III 156; exemplified II 24–8, 209, 211

destruction III 109–11, 113–14, 148 [*see also*: generation]

dialectic I 68, 234; II 94, 146, 151, 156, 166, 167, 229, 235, 236–47, 256–8

diet III 222–5

dimensions II 30; III 39–44, 125–9 [*see also*: body]

disconnectedness II 146, 152–3, 238

disjunction II 158, 162, 191, 201–2

dispute, explained I 165, 170, 172, 175–7; in general I 26, 88, 185; II 8, 37, 116,
   168, 181, 222, 259; III 108, 234, 238, 254; parts of I 59, 90, 98, 112; II 60, 67;
   III 182; about blending III 56; about bodies III 54; about causes III 13, 14,
   23; about conditionals II 110–13, 145; about definition II 212; about
   expertise in living III 239–40; about free will III 70; about gods III 3–5, 6,
   218–9; about good III 175, 180–2, 197, 239; about humans II 22; about
   indifferents III 191; about matter III 30–3; about motion III 65–6; about
   nature I 98; about parts of philosophy II 13; about perception II 49, 56;
   about place III 119–20; about proof II 134, 180–1, 182; III 182; about ruling
   part I 128; II 32, 57, 58; about sayables II 107; about signs II 121; about
   souls II 31–2; about standards I 178; II 18, 21, 43, 48; III 182; about time III
   136–8, 139; about truth II 85

divisible *vs.* indivisible III 143, 144–6

division II 213; of meanings II 214

doctors, *see*: medicine

dogs I 49, 63–75, 238; II 23

drunkenness I 109, 131; III 180

elements I 147, 151, 183; III 30–7, 55, 62, 63, 152

empiricism I 99, 128; II 63, 72; III 47–8, 50

Empiricism, medical I 236